THE
LONG RACE
TO GLORY

First published in 2013 by Andre Deutsch,
an imprint of Carlton Books Ltd

Carlton Books Ltd
20 Mortimer Street
London W1T 3JW

Text © Chris Sidwells
Design © Carlton Books Ltd

A CIP catalogue record for this book is available from
the British Library.

ISBN: 978-0-233-00404-4

Printed and bound by CPI Group (UK) Ltd,
Croydon, CR0 4YY

THE
LONG RACE
TO GLORY

How the British Came to Rule
the Cycling World

CHRIS SIDWELLS

ANDRE
DEUTSCH

CONTENTS

PROLOGUE

In 2012 a British cyclist won the Tour de France. Then a year later, another British rider followed suit. Two in a row, which is incredible because up until a few years ago a British Tour winner seemed, if not impossible, at least very unlikely. Then, slowly at first but accelerating rapidly, it began to look like the logical progression in a story that started in the 1990s – or rather the latest chapter of it did. The whole story is a lot longer, and that as much as the recent success is what this book is about.

What happened in 2012 changed Britain's attitude to cycling for ever. During three weeks in July, as Bradley Wiggins led and then convincingly won the Tour, people who had never been interested in cycling, or had watched it on television chiefly for the scenery, became passionate followers of the sport. When the Olympics began in London less than a week later, few events were as eagerly awaited as the road races through the Surrey hills, in which Lizzie Armitstead secured Team GB's first medal of the Games, and then the time trials, which saw Wiggins crowned again. It was no surprise when the quirky hero with the iconic sideburns was voted BBC Sports Personality of the Year.

Amid all the recent triumphs the Tour de France inevitably looms largest. Professional road racing is the pinnacle of cycling, and the Tour de France is at the top of that pinnacle. It towers above the other Grand Tours, of Italy and Spain, as well as the smaller stage races and the historic single-day Classics. It's the ultimate goal of all professional bike racers, who not only do all they can to get to the Tour; they try to bring with them everything they have. A former winner, Stephen Roche of Ireland, sums it up best when he says: "You never hear anyone say they are using the Tour to prepare for something else. It's everyone's objective, whether they are a team leader, a sprinter, or a domestique rider who's there to help his leader; they want to be the best they can be for the Tour."

And the race is huge. It's the biggest annual sporting event in the world, a massive, gaudy, mobile mix of athletic endeavour and crass commercialism that dominates July for cycling fans all over the world. And there are lots of them. Cycling is a growth sport, in the UK as elsewhere. Millions have taken to two wheels for exercise, transport and just because it's fun; and in turn they have learned to love the sport – especially its showpiece event.

As remarkable as Wiggins winning the Tour was that another British cyclist, Chris Froome, finished in second place. No British cyclist had ever done better than third, which was Wiggins in 2009 – he finished fourth but was given third after most of Lance Armstrong's record was wiped out of cycling. Before Wiggins, Robert Millar was fourth in 1984 and tenth in 1989 and Tom

Simpson was sixth in 1962. And that's it. No other British cyclist had ever finished in the Tour de France top ten since it started back in 1903. Then the top two spots on the podium are claimed in the same year. It was truly incredible.

It was also a reflection of the cycling revolution that has taken place in Britain – and on the widest scale. Because although the Tour de France is disproportionally important in the sport, competitive cycling is not just the Tour, nor just road cycling. Away from the road there's track cycling, mountain biking and BMX, all of which are part of the Olympic Games, and British Olympic cycling success is unprecedented today as well.

Out of 12 events in track cycling at the London Olympics, British cyclists won seven gold medals, one silver medal and one bronze. And that was after a rule change was introduced stipulating that in track cycling, unlike most sports, no matter how good a country's second ranked athlete was in any event, only one from each country could compete. That made it impossible for Britain's cyclists to take both gold and silver, as they did in some track cycling events in Beijing.

Great Britain won eight gold, four silver and three bronze medals at the Beijing Olympics, where Chris Hoy won three golds and earned himself a knighthood. That set a precedent. Bradley Wiggins became Sir Bradley Wiggins after his historic Tour de France victory and Olympic gold in 2012, and Sarah Storey was made Dame Sarah Storey after becoming the most successful athlete in Paralympic history.

At the London Games Sir Chris Hoy also became Britain's greatest Olympian with a career total of six gold medals and one silver medal, surpassing Steve Redgrave's five golds and one bronze. Wiggins is third in the all-time Olympic medal rankings with four golds, one silver and two bronze. Jason Kenny is another cyclist in the top ten. There are no women cyclists in there yet, but for a good reason.

Women's cycling has been treated badly by the Olympics. In fact there was no women's Olympic cycling until the 1984 Games, and then there was only one event. More were added over the years, but only very slowly, and it took until 2012 for women to have medal parity in cycling with men. Hundreds of women were deprived of a shot at Olympic glory that was taken for granted in other sports.

The story of how Britain became the world's top cycle racing nation is an amazing one, made more amazing by the fact that it happened so quickly. There have always been talented British cyclists, some of whom have been world champions and won big races, especially on the track, where UK riders won a steady stream of world and Olympic medals, and their story will be told in this book. It's only in the last ten to 15 years, however, that champions have rolled out of Manchester, the home of British Cycling, the sport's governing body in the UK, as if it was some kind of champion production line. And the march looks set to continue.

This book tells how it happened. How cycling took hold of the country at the same time as a group of dedicated people came together, led by a man who had a unique combination: both vision and the ability to carry out a plan and make that vision become reality. He is Sir David Brailsford, the third knight in this story. He's the head of the performance side of British Cycling.

Brailsford has a way of getting what he wants that borders on the uncanny, but it's actually achieved by purity of thought. He sees only what's there. He understands what is needed to achieve something, knows how to get the best from the best people to help him achieve it, and has a deft hand in creating an environment that lets them do it. And he has passion, lots of passion.

That's why British cyclists are at the top of the sport now. It's not because some super breed of athletes suddenly took up cycling. Britain has had some great champions, riders who are comparable to Wiggins and Hoy, Victoria Pendleton, Nicole Cooke and Dame Sarah Storey – and arguably their equal. But British cycling never had the environment in which their talent could blossom, and do so regularly. The recent environment has allowed riders to develop their full potential and enabled medals to be won in numbers.

But even David Brailsford couldn't have done what he has done, and gone on doing it, without money, although he was very clever in the way he spent it, especially at the beginning when there wasn't much. Money from the National Lottery was made available for sport towards the end of the 1990s, and the criterion for funding was Olympic success. If you won medals you got more money. It was as simple as that.

The man whose embryo plan Brailsford carried forward and saw to fruition was Peter Keen, a talented and highly qualified cycling coach and sports scientist. A few years earlier Keen had worked with Chris Boardman, and in 1992 they delivered a gold medal at the Barcelona Olympic Games.

Boardman did it in the individual pursuit, an event that's no longer in the Olympic cycling programme, but which in many ways is the purest test of endurance cycling. It's a prolonged burst of high speed over 4,000 metres that requires sprint and endurance power. It also transfers very well to road racing. In fact old professional road race team managers used to say, "Give me a world pursuit champion and in a few years' time I'll give you back a world road race champion." There's no better example of this than Bradley Wiggins, whose track specialities were the individual and team pursuits. He's been Olympic champion at both, and now he's won the biggest road race in the world.

Track racing, and particularly the individual pursuit, is pure physics. There are no tactics really, it's just a matter of getting the start right so the rider is up to speed quickly, which is a skill that can be taught then practised. Then it's a question of going as fast as possible without fading for the whole distance. The track is flat, and modern international track competitions are always held indoors, so even wind direction isn't a factor.

That means that the pursuit can be expressed in numbers, the most basic of which is the rider's power output divided by their aerodynamic drag. So if a cyclist can hold a certain power output, measured in watts, for the pursuit distance, and his or her riding position is made as aerodynamic as possible, the same going for the bike, then the rider will achieve a certain time. The times needed to win gold medals are known, or thereabouts, because they are there for all to see in competition, so if a rider and his or her coach work on increasing power output and reducing drag they can progress towards the goal time. Provided of course the rider has the innate ability to produce the power required.

Before Bradley Wiggins won the gold medal in the individual pursuit in Beijing he revealed that he could even predict what time he would achieve for the full 4,000-metre distance by looking at his power outputs during certain key training sessions that were nowhere near that distance.

"It's simple really. We have so much data that I know what my power output is for doing a 4 minutes 15 pursuit, and I know what power output I'm able to do in various interval training sessions when I'm in condition to do that time. One of the sessions I do that really brings on form but is also a good test of how I'm going is ten times 30 seconds on the turbo trainer in the riding position I use on the track with one minute in between. If I see 600 to 700 watts in those intervals, then I'm going to ride 4:15 on the track or faster," he said.

Nothing illustrates the power of numbers better than that. If you have the ability, and Chris Boardman had, you can work on all the physical requirements to achieve a measurable performance. Peter Keen worked on realizing Boardman's innate talent by using the latest coaching technology, while working with a manufacturer who was developing the most aerodynamic bike in the world. They refined Boardman's riding position too, and he won the gold medal in Barcelona and set a world hour record as well.

In doing that, Boardman also provided a template for British Cycling to use when lottery funding was available. There wasn't much at first, but there would be more if British cyclists could win medals. That's why first Keen, who was the head of performance at BC before Brailsford and is now the driving force behind Team GB's entire Olympic effort, and then Brailsford decided to spend what money they had on track cycling.

They were both criticized by cycling fans and by some cyclists. Track cycling and road cycling are like two different sports in terms of the interest they create. Road is seen by fans and most of those inside the sport as far and away the pinnacle of cycling.

All the most famous cycling events are road races. But, as Brailsford knew, track abilities are transferable to the road; it was part of his long-term plan. He's a cyclist at heart, a former road racer, he understands the sport and loves it, and he always appreciated the importance of road racing. Also, it was always his aim to work towards a British winner of the Tour de France, and he announced that target when Team Sky was created. By that time he had won the right to be taken very seriously, but even then there were plenty who didn't believe it was possible. It was certainly an ambitious project.

The professional road racing season lasts most of the year. Men's pro road racing starts in Australia in January each year with the Tour Down Under. It's a relatively new race, first held in 1999, and it was and still is part of the International Cycling Union's (UCI) initiative to grow cycling from a mainly European sport into a worldwide one.

In response to that initiative the best teams – still mainly European, although there are American and Australian squads in the top flight now, and African and Asian teams are shaping up – treated the race with the respect it deserved. It was given plenty of ranking points and ranking points are important. The UCI's World Tour is the umbrella covering the top events: the Grand Tours, the single-day Classics and a few other races. Teams need ranking points to stay in the World Tour, so the teams went to Australia and they got stuck in. Past winners of the Tour Down Under are split almost 50/50 between Europe and Australia, which you wouldn't expect as it's held during the European winter. There hasn't been a British winner yet, although Team Sky's Geraint Thomas came close in 2013.

Immediately after the Tour Down Under the focus shifts to the Tour of Oman and the Tour of Qatar. They aren't World Tour events yet but the top teams ride them, and as they are going on there are some older races of equal status in the warmer parts of Europe, such as the Tour of the Mediterranean. They are the traditional prologue to the European racing season, which starts with a bang in Belgium on the last weekend of February, or the first in March depending which fits better, with two big single-day races.

Next up are two stage races, Paris–Nice and Tirreno–Adriatico (between Italy's two coasts), for which the World Tour teams send different squads of riders. The first single-day classic, Milan–San Remo, comes after them, and then the World Tour splits: the teams send their best single-day racers to northern Europe, while the best stage racers and the guys who are best suited to supporting them ride stage races in Spain.

The northern races are the cobbled Classics: Ghent–Wevelgem, the Tour of Flanders and Paris–Roubaix, also known as the "Hell of the North"; and the Ardennes Classics: the Amstel Gold Race, the Flèche Wallonne and Liège–Bastogne–Liège. These races are old-school cycling, races which go back a long way and have produced many great stories. Liège–Bastogne–Liège was first run as a pro race in 1894, Paris–Roubaix started in 1896, the Tour of Flanders in 1913, the Flèche Wallonne in 1936, Ghent–Wevelgem in 1945; the most recent is the Amstel Gold Race, which was first held in 1966.

But all European bike races are fairly old, and the schedule for the season in Europe can almost seem to be set in stone. After the Classics, attention turns to stage races with the Tour of Romandie in Switzerland, and then it's the first Grand Tour of the year, the Tour of Italy.

Grand Tours are three-week races and there are three of them in cycling: the Tour of Italy, the Tour de France and the Tour of Spain. The Tour of Italy, or Giro d'Italia – it's more commonly known in cycling by its Italian name – was born in 1909 and is now the first Grand Tour each year. That honour used to fall to the Tour of Spain, but for a number of reasons it got pushed back to a late August start in the 1990s. That was a controversial move, and the biggest change there has ever been in the pro cycling calendar.

Racers will sometimes ride two Grand Tours, but rarely three in the same year. Pro racers who haven't done the Giro will either ride the Critérium du Dauphiné in France or the Tour of Switzerland. Both are mountainous and the Dauphiné usually contains an element of what's in store for everyone in that year's Tour de France, which basically occupies the whole of world cycling's attention for July.

The rest of the men's pro racing year is taken up with the Tour of Spain – called the Vuelta a Espana in Spain and referred to simply as the Vuelta by most of the rest of cycling – some stage races that the UCI want to build up, and a couple of single-day races they want to do the same for in Canada, plus one in Spain and one in Germany that are both on their way to Classic status.

The Road World Championships are held shortly after the Vuelta. Then come the end-of-season Classics, Paris–Tours and Il Lombardia, which up until 2012 was called the Tour of Lombardy. The World Tour ends in China in mid October with the Tour of Beijing.

That's how the men's pro road season unfolds, ticking along like a clock, counting down the days and years with little change, and bike fans love it. Historically pro road racing is where British riders have struggled to make an impression, although a few individuals made big ones. That is changing now, and the change is set to go on.

International women's road racing follows a similar pattern through the year to men's racing now, especially early on, with some single-day races on similar routes to the men's, only shorter. Women's racing is growing, but it's subject to growing pains. It has had its equivalents to the Tour of Italy and Tour de France, but it's struggling to get a solidly established big stage race at the moment, which is frustrating as it provides exciting, high-quality sport. The women's Olympic road race in London was a fascinating struggle marked by aggression, attack and counter-attack, whereas the men's race was a dull, tactical affair that sparked into life only near the end.

The problem for women's road racing is TV coverage, without which it's difficult to get the sponsorship needed to provide continuity and a solid platform to build on. The answer seems to be running races in conjunction with the men's races. Whenever organizers do that, the races are high points of the women's road race calendar, because the TV coverage is already there.

It's particularly unfortunate for Britain that women's cycling isn't a bigger sport worldwide, because British women have always been at the forefront of international road racing. From the great Beryl Burton, who was arguably one of the best female athletes in any sport, through Mandy Jones to Nicole Cooke, who won every major race in the world at least once, and Lizzie Armitstead, British women's cycling history is a glorious one.

Back in the early days of lottery funding, however, Brailsford didn't spend money on road racing, because there are too many variables in that side of the sport, and in the case of men's top-level road racing it costs too much to break in. You need a huge amount of money to take part in World Tour races. The teams that do so are big, maybe 25 to 30 riders with mechanics and other support staff as well as managers. A top-flight road team costs millions of pounds, and Brailsford didn't have millions. He needed to invest what he did have in an area of cycling where he'd get the greatest return. Therefore, because it's so quantifiable, a sport where you can measure what the money you spend provides in return, the choice Brailsford made was to invest British Cycling's money and effort at first almost exclusively in track racing.

Because it takes place indoors, international track racing has become a sport of the European winter. It revolves around the World Cup, which has rounds on all the continents, and culminates each year with the World Championships, which are usually held in March.

The World Cup and World Championships track cycling programme is bigger than the one for the Olympics; it has title races for both sexes in the match sprint, team sprint, keirin, 1,000 metres time trial, individual and team pursuits, scratch race and points race, and there is also a Madison for men. There is nothing on the track that British racers haven't won.

Mountain biking and BMX are recent additions to the Olympic programme. They are also the area of the sport where British riders haven't had the consistent success they've had in track racing and more recently on the road. Neither attracted the funding that track did in the early days of Brailsford's push, but they do now and it's only a matter of time before British mountain bikers start winning elite world titles and Olympic medals. The same goes for BMX, where but for bad luck Britain's great star Shanaze Reade would have already won an Olympic medal.

Adventurous cyclists have always ridden off-road, and cyclo-cross – riding adapted road bikes across country – was invented as a way for road racers to keep fit during the winter back in the 1920s and 30s. It became a sport in its own right in the forties, and the first world cyclo-cross championships were held in Paris in 1950. Britain has won one elite medal in the World Championships, although British riders have had slightly more success at junior level. The problem now is not any lack of talent but the fact that it's not an Olympic sport, so it doesn't get lottery funding.

BMX and mountain bike racing, at least in the form we know it today, both began in America at about the same time, while appealing to slightly different age groups. BMX began in the early 1970s in Southern California when groups of kids, inspired by motocross racing, began racing whatever bikes they had on dirt tracks. The trend went nationwide when a documentary film about motocross racing, *On Any Sunday*, opened with kids riding Schwinn Sting-Ray bikes on dirt trails. Sting-Rays were the preferred bike of the first BMXers, but by the mid-seventies bike manufacturers were making bikes suited to the kind of off-road riding the kids were doing, and the BMX bike was born.

There are different forms of BMX, but it's racing on constructed tracks that received Olympic status in 2008. Britain's number one BMX star is Shanaze Reade, who has been world champion three times, and since the Olympic BMX event is essentially a sprint, she has also won two gold medals and one silver medal in the team sprint at the Track World Championships.

The World Championships, the Supercross World Cup and Olympic Games make up the international BMX programme, and British racers feature in them all. It's only a matter of time before they deliver Olympic medals.

Mountain biking started the same way as BMX, but with older riders adapting the bikes they owned to ride the trails around Crested Butte in Colorado and Cupertino in California. The bikes, known as cruisers, were heavy things with fat tyres and coaster hub brakes that were better suited to freewheeling downhill than pedalling up. It's understandable then why the first races were downhill races. The most famous was called the Repack, because after each run the riders had to repack their crude brakes with grease – the heavy braking involved having caused it to burn up.

All sorts of bikes were used at first, adapted and created out of bits of other bikes, until Joe Breeze designed and produced the first custom-made mountain bike in 1978. Tom Ritchey,

Gary Fisher and Charley Kelly followed suit, creating a small mountain bike manufacturing industry in America, and in 1979 a motorbike trials rider, Geoff Apps, produced a lightweight bike purpose built for riding in muddy conditions in the UK.

The sport of mountain biking splits into cross-country and downhill racing, of which the latter has a few off-shoots such as four-cross, but only cross-country made it into the Olympics. That happened in 1996 and British riders are edging closer to the medals.

The mountain bike season revolves around a World Cup with rounds on different continents, and the World Championships. We'll look in detail later at how this branch of cycling has developed, and at the British riders who played a part in that, notably the downhill world champion Steve Peat, and at the cross-country racers who've come close to world championship honours and those who will do that and more in the future.

There are some other forms of cycling, such as cycle speedway and cycle polo, but mainstream cycling consists of road racing, track cycling, BMX and mountain bike racing. British racers have made their mark in them all, ever since the time, soon after the bicycle was invented, when somebody said, "Let's have a race."

CHAPTER 1

WINNING AND LOSING

The British were closely involved with the development of the bicycle from the outset. It was a Briton who first gave it pedals, and when the first cycle race was held in Paris, it was won by a young man from Suffolk.

The first bicycle was introduced in Paris in 1817 by a German, Baron Karl Friedrich Drais von Sauerbronn. The Draisine, as it became known, was a wooden two-wheeler with a saddle, but had to be propelled by the rider's legs. It was patented in the UK by Denis Johnson in 1819 and became very popular with Regency dandies, earning the name hobby-horse or dandy-horse. However, it could only be used on the flat until a Scottish blacksmith called Kirkpatrick Macmillan built a version with foot-powered treadles to drive the rear wheel. By being the first to break the contact of the rider's feet with the floor, Macmillan effectively invented cycling.

The next development was in France, and it was the one that led to cycling becoming a sport. In 1861 Pierre Michaux, a French blacksmith, attached pedals and cranks to the front wheel of a dandy-horse and called his invention a "vélocipede". People could travel relatively long distances on them, but on the cobbled roads or stony tracks of the time they were extremely uncomfortable because their wooden wheels were shod with metal tyres, and they were nicknamed "boneshakers". Nevertheless they caught on and soon Michaux's wooden velocipedes were being mass produced. They were very popular with young Parisians, who rode the city streets and in the parks, where they could show off their skills. There was none keener than James Moore, a young Englishman living in Paris. Growing up near the Michaux home he owned a velocipede from the age of 16 and was taught to perform cycling tricks by performers at the nearby Cirque d'Eté.

The number of velocipede manufacturers grew throughout the 1860s, and in 1868 the Olivier brothers, who owned the Compagnie Parisienne, decided it was time to put on a race.

The so-called first-ever bicycle race was held on May 31, 1868. The venue was the Parc St Cloud but there's a fair amount of uncertainty as to who actually took part, how many races there were, and even if this race was the very first. Some historians say there was just one race that day, others that there were two or three. Some even claim that other races in Paris pre-dated the May 31 event. Whatever the truth, until recently there was a plaque outside the park that read "On May 31st, 1868, James Moore became the winner of the first race for vélocipedes in France." Nobody knows where the plaque is now.

It's possible that there were other races in Paris before the St Cloud event, and it seems almost certain that before Moore's race in the park there was another for smaller wheeled bikes, and therefore slower ones, than he rode. It may be that Moore's was remembered more widely because it was the main event. One thing is certain: James Moore must have been a very good rider, because he won the next big milestone in cycling, the first bike race on the open road.

Again organized by the Olivier brothers, the race was held on November 7, 1869, and it ran from the Arc de Triomphe in Paris to the centre of Rouen, a distance of 81 miles (130km). By this time bikes had developed a bit. Metal frames with metal spoked wheels had replaced wooden ones. Bikes also had tyres made of solid rubber, not metal, and the hubs ran on ball bearings. Wheels had grown in size too, or at least the front one had.

With the pedals attached directly to the front wheel, riding speed is determined by how fast riders can spin their legs, and anyone who has ridden a bike knows there's a limit to that. The solution was to make the front wheel bigger, because a bigger wheel travels further per pedal revolution. The bike ridden by Moore in the Paris to Rouen race, made by the Surihey company, had a 48.25-inch diameter front wheel and a 15.75-inch diameter rear wheel.

Cycling had been enjoying a boom by then. Not only were people riding their bikes in parks and around towns; adventurous sorts were seeing just how far the new invention could take them. The Michaux brothers had ridden from Paris to Avignon in 1865, and during the same year they started exporting velocipedes to America. It was only a matter of time before the distance capacity of bikes was combined with their speed potential in a long-distance race. Paris to Rouen was that race.

The first prize was 1,000 francs, and 325 starters, including a few women, set off at seven o'clock in the morning. Moore won the race in a time of 10 hours 25 minutes, an average of eight miles per hour (13 kph), but given the poor roads and the low gear he was pedalling it was a fantastic achievement.

The next finishers were 15 minutes behind Moore. Another 35 contestants made it to Rouen inside the 24-hour time limit, with the only female finisher taking 22nd place when she arrived at dawn the next day. Cycling was regarded as a little bit scandalous for girls, so she called herself Miss America to avoid bringing shame on her family by revealing her real name, which was never recorded. Moore's Paris–Rouen winning bike has since disappeared, but the one on which he won the Parc St Cloud race is displayed at the museum in Ely, Suffolk. Moore was born in Bury St Edmunds.

Moore won other races, including a circuit event in a park at Le Neubourg in 1868 and the Grand Prix Cognac and Grand Prix Vésinet in 1869. The Franco-Prussian War of 1870 stopped the development of bike racing for a while, but afterwards racing began in the UK as well as in France, and Moore won on both sides of the Channel.

He set a world record by riding 14 miles 880 yards in one hour at the Molyneux Grounds in Wolverhampton, and he won the MacGregor Cup, which was held all over France and regarded as the world championships of the era, from 1872 to 1875 and again in 1877. Moore then retired from racing to study and eventually qualify as a vet.

With new races springing up all over the place the quest for speed saw front wheels grow to alarming sizes, ending with the development of the "ordinary" bicycle, better known as the "penny-farthing" because it had a huge front wheel and a tiny rear one. These were the bikes on which James Moore won his later races.

Penny-farthing races were mostly held on big flat cinder tracks. One of the most famous was the Lillie Bridge track in London, where the most common wheel size was 54-inch diameter, but a taller rider could use a bigger and potentially faster wheel. The first cycling match between Oxford and Cambridge universities was held at Lillie Bridge in 1874.

These bikes were difficult to ride, something that reduced their desirability to people other than daring young racers. Some of the ordinary bikes were over five feet high from the saddle to the floor, and in 1875 the Hon. Ion Keith Falconer raced at Lillie Bridge on a bike with a 60-inch diameter front wheel. To make bicycles usable by the general public they needed smaller wheels as well as a way of matching the speed of an ordinary bike. The answer was the "safety" bicycle.

It had a chain-driven rear wheel. The chain was turned by a large chainwheel, to which pedals and cranks were attached. Turning the cranks drove a smaller sprocket on the rear wheel, which made several revolutions per revolution of the cranks, so now gearing did the job of the penny-farthing's huge front wheel. The safety bicycle had equal-sized wheels and a double diamond frame, which is basically the blueprint for the bikes we ride today.

Early safety bicycles had solid rubber tyres, but during the 1880s John Boyd Dunlop developed the pneumatic tyre, and they soon found their way on to bikes. This development made riding on the open road more attractive, but the growth of racing, in Europe at least, was also driven by bike manufacturers.

There's no better way to prove the durability of a machine than by testing it against others in a long race, and the races soon became very long indeed. Bordeaux to Paris at 356 miles (572km) and Paris–Brest–Paris at 750 miles (1,200km) were absolute marathons, and they were tackled all in one go. The clock started when the riders started and only stopped when they finished. British racers were among the best.

George Pilkington Mills won the first Bordeaux–Paris in 1891 in a time of 26 hours 36 minutes, with Montague Holbein in second place and H. B. Bates in fourth. The British were amateurs, and before they allowed them to take part the British cycling authorities asked the French organizers to only allow amateurs to compete against them, which caused the beginnings of a rift between the UK and the rest of Europe.

That rift got bigger a few years later as a result of a traffic accident. In 1894, during a 50-mile race just north of London, the horses drawing a lady in her carriage were frightened when the riders sped past her. The horses shied and several of the riders were knocked off their bikes. The lady was unhurt, but her carriage got bashed around a bit, and she complained to the police.

The position of cyclists on the roads of England and Wales had not been established by the end of the nineteenth century, and some police forces objected to racing. The UK cycling governing body at the time was called the National Cycling Union (NCU), and fearing that all cycling, even leisure riding, might be banned from the open road if the police got involved, they voluntarily banned bunched racing, or massed-start road racing as it was called then, as a gesture. In doing so, however, with one flourish of a pen they cut off British cycling from the development of road racing in Europe, and consigned generations of potential big international road race winners, if not to exile, then to starting European road races at a massive disadvantage.

Meanwhile road racing flourished in Europe. Today's great single-day Classics such as Liège–Bastogne–Liège and Paris–Roubaix started during the last decade of the nineteenth century. The first Tour de France was held in 1903 and the first Tour of Italy in 1909, but after winning many of the early European races British riders were prevented from taking part, partly because of the bunched race ban at home but partly also because the big road races of Europe were for professionals, and cycling in the UK was largely an amateur sport.

With the benefit of hindsight, what the NCU did looks now like a piece of bureaucratic vandalism, but at the time they genuinely believed that they were protecting cycling as a whole. Relationships between cyclists and the police were bad. Race organizers tried to find quiet country roads for their competitions, but there were still reports of police charging at riders on horseback and throwing sticks at them.

The NCU asked clubs to only hold races on closed tracks, but a few rebels started a rival organization that encouraged riders to compete on the road but in a different form of racing. Frederick Thomas Bidlake was one of the rebels, founding the Road Records Association (RRA) in 1888, and he set several of their records, although he preferred to ride a tricycle rather than a bike. He was also one of the racers involved in the 1894 carriage incident.

The key tenet of the RRA is that records are set alone and un-paced, and Bidlake applied this model to his form of road racing. Following Bidlake's code, races took place early in the morning on isolated stretches of road deep in the countryside. The location of the races was only given in code, so secrecy could be maintained. Competitors also had to dress from head to toe in black, so as to attract as little attention as possible. For the same reason, riders started at one-minute intervals. If any rider was caught by the one behind they had to drop back, so there was no pacing and definitely no bunches. To the casual observer a race looked like a number of cyclists who just happened to choose the same stretch of road to ride on. Competitors didn't wear numbers and their bikes were equipped with a bell to warn of their approach.

The first race under these rules was over 50 miles and organized by the North Road Cycling Club on October 5, 1895. It wasn't the first-ever time trial, because time trials had been organized by the NCU before this date, but it was the first under this new "private and confidential" code, one that was to dominate British road racing until 1942, and cause a huge rift for many years after that. The time trial organization became known as the Road Time Trials Council (RTTC) and, after being seen at first as a rebel body, was accepted by the NCU and became allied to it, especially in the road racing conflict to come.

Time trials grew in popularity, soon settling into five forms: set distances of 25 miles, 50 and 100 miles, plus races to see how many miles could be ridden in 12 and 24 hours. The events threw up some remarkable athletes. In 1911 Freddy Grubb set a record of 220.5 miles ridden in 12 hours. H. H. Gayler beat that with 223.5 miles in 1913 before being killed during the First World War. It took a while for racing to get going again after the war, but by 1927 Jack Lauterwasser had increased the 12-hour record to 240 miles, an average of 20 miles per hour. Then in 1935 three riders, Jackie Bone, James McKechnie and Maurice Clark, all rode more than 240 miles in separate races on the same day.

Other formidable records were set at 25, 50 and 100 miles and in the 24-hour. British time trials produced some strong athletes, and when road racing was introduced to the World Championship in 1921, which was only for amateurs at first – a professional world title race wasn't introduced until 1927 – British riders dominated the first two editions, because those races were time trials too.

The first was held in Copenhagen over a distance of 190 kilometres and Charles Davy took the bronze medal. The titles moved to Liverpool the following year and Team GB got a one–two–three, with Dave Marsh winning, William Burkhill second and Charles Davy filling the bronze medal slot again. That result flatters the British racers slightly, however, because not many foreign riders took part and it was run on a well-established "secret" course, that of the Anfield Cycling Club's 100-mile time trial, which was definitely a home advantage.

After that the World Championship changed to a bunch road race and Great Britain didn't provide another men's medallist for over forty years. The reason was simple: British road racers were strong, they could ride all day against the clock, but they weren't adept at riding in a bunch and they couldn't cope with the changes of pace involved in bunched road racing as it was practised on the continent.

Road racing developed a lot by the 1920s. At the time when the Tour de France and the Classics started, bikes were basic and roads were so bad that races were a trial of strength in which the field was spread out over many hours, but as roads and equipment improved, road race tactics changed. A bunch of riders, or the peloton as it's almost universally called, became the mobile base of operations in most races. And as professional cycling grew, teamwork began to be seen, even if some race organizers were dead against it. Road racing slowly became an alien experience for British racers trying to compete at world championship level, and they were outclassed.

It wasn't due to lack of ability, but isolation – an isolation that wasn't helped by the British stance on professionals in sport. Professionals were seen by UK sports administrators as second-class citizens, not just in cycling but in most sports.

In Europe, meanwhile, particularly as the twentieth century moved on, professional cycling was seen as the pinnacle of the sport, and amateur honours, including Olympic medals, were a means of gaining a better pro contract and more money from a pro team.

The political landscape of cycling had been formed in the early 1890s. The sport's first international governing body, the International Cycling Association (ICA), had a strong British contingent on its board, including the president, Henry Sturmey – whose name lives on in Sturmey Archer hub gears. From its foundation in 1892, amateurism was high on the agenda.

The objective of the ICA was to promote an official annual World Championships, which started in 1893 in Chicago with three track races over one mile, ten miles and 100 kilometres. In the latter the competitors were paced by riders on tandems. However, in the first championships a dispute arose when the largely British race jury excluded the Italian team because they had sold some trophies they won earlier in the year, in contravention of the amateur code.

As the title races continued, a gulf began to emerge between Britain and the rest of Europe on the question of professionalism. Pro titles were introduced in 1895 in Cologne in response to the growing popularity of pro racing in Europe, but the Brits didn't like it. And to back their cause they cited the fact that the amateur stance of the ICA served cycling well when it was included in the first modern Olympic Games in 1896. But the Europeans weren't listening, and things reached a head in 1900 when they broke away over British insistence that each country that made up the United Kingdom had a voting delegate on the ICA board.

The Europeans formed the Union Cyclisme International (UCI), the body that still governs cycling today, and the UK was barred from membership at first, which widened the gulf still further because resentment at the snub filtered down into grassroots racing in the UK. It was unfortunate, because Britain had some great riders at the time, including the nation's first world cycling champion, Jimmy Michael, from the Rhymney valley in South Wales.

He was born in 1876, and by the time he was a teenager cycling had caught on so much that nearly every town had a cinder track. Michael started racing locally and was an instant success, winning the Welsh Championships at five miles and 50 miles on the Newport track when he was only 17.

His national titles brought an invitation to ride the Surrey 100 at the Herne Hill track in South London, a version of which still exists today, many of the other tracks used during this era having gone. There were 27 riders in the race and they were described in the pre-race build-up as "the cream of the cracks at the distance". Michael was five feet tall and weighed seven stone two pounds, but he won the race, breaking clear in the second quarter to lap the field by half way. He continued to lap them too, running out the winner by seven minutes in a time of 4 hours 19 minutes.

That was it for Jimmy Michael. He was offered contracts to ride in prestigious races all over Europe, and at 18 he went to live in Paris, where a number of Welsh cyclists lived, including multiple world record holder Arthur Linton. They were professionals and they were trained by "Choppy" Warburton, a former runner who knew all the tricks there were in this fast-growing circuit of pro races. Warburton always carried a doctor's bag with him, and it seems certain his little black bag contained stuff a lot stronger than smelling salts to revive tired riders and make them faster.

There have always been two sorts of track cyclists: sprinters and endurance racers. Linton and Michael were endurance racers, and the most popular endurance races in their time were ones where the riders were paced either by tandems or triplets or other multi-seated bikes, with each of the "crack" riders sitting in his pace crew's slipstream. The principle of pacing was that two or more sets of legs could go faster than one, and the pace bikes would change within an event, so fresh legs would take over throughout each race. The object was to increase the race speed to create a better spectacle. It worked, and people flocked to the tracks in their thousands to watch the paced races.

The first professional world track title race over 100 kilometres took place in Cologne. Each of the competitors in the race was paced by seven men riding a quadruplet bike (four riders) followed by a triplet (three riders). A capacity crowd saw Michael win for Great Britain. His time was 2 hours 24 minutes and he lapped the next racer 12 times.

A tour of American tracks followed, then Michael set a human-paced hour record of 28 miles 1,072 yards. He was in demand at tracks all over Europe, who paid up to £200 to get him on their bill in front of up to 20,000 paying fans. Michael didn't win another world title; he didn't need to as he was making so much money on both sides of the Atlantic. He was a genuine star and was even painted by Henri Toulouse-Lautrec for an advertising poster, of which a copy can be seen at the National Museum of Wales. Then in 1898 Michael signed a contract that guaranteed him 2,500 dollars per race for a series of ten match races.

He earned it, though. As the cycling evolved, human pacers were replaced by motorcycles, which increased the race speeds to dangerous levels. Racers didn't wear crash helmets either in those early days. In April 1902 Michael was leading a race on the steeply banked wooden track in Berlin. He'd done 57 miles in 58 minutes, at an average of nearly 60 miles per hour, when the rear wheel of the motorbike that was pacing him collapsed. Michael crashed, fracturing his skull and suffering multiple injuries. He was never the same rider after that and died in November 1904 while aboard a transatlantic liner. Jimmy Michael, Britain's first-ever world cycling champion, is buried in Brooklyn.

Maybe the British authorities were right to steer cycling away from professionalism; motor-paced races were dangerous, and race distances on both track and road bordered on being inhuman and exacted an enormous physical toll. For example, in 1896 Michael's compatriot Arthur Linton, who was an established pro when Michael won his first race, won Bordeaux–Paris. He hadn't ridden so well the previous year, which increased his determination this time. He decided to compete in a long-distance race every weekend from March until Bordeaux–Paris in order to toughen up, and he had some good results, like fourth in Paris–Roubaix, but instead of getting stronger he was all but dead on his feet when he started Bordeaux–Paris.

He crashed several times, at one point breaking his bike and having to walk for ten kilometres until he could get it repaired. More crashes followed, but Linton battled though to Paris in first place – with help, according to reports made at the time, from Choppy Warburton's little black bag. That was it, though, for Linton. He couldn't start several races after Bordeaux–Paris and he died of typhoid a few months later.

Some claim his death was due to doping, but it can't be attributed directly to that, even though it was clearly going on back then. Track racers like Linton and Michael could earn big money, but they had to ride incredibly hard to do it. And as road teams grew there was pressure from sponsors to win.

Where those conditions exist, all you need to add is ambitious young men and there will always be somebody prepared to break the rules to help them. Cycling history is littered with such characters, from Choppy Warburton to Doctors Michele Ferrari and Eufamiano Fuentes.

*   *   *   *   *

British road racers were protected from that side of professional sport, at least in the beginning, and nowadays top-level pro cycling seems to be changing for the better. Anyway, there was very little money in UK cycling at the beginning of the twentieth century, and although this reduced a GB rider's chances of winning international honours, the first half of the century is widely regarded as a golden era for cycling in this country.

An insight into British cycling as it was back then is provided by the story of Charles Davey. He was a rider who did achieve some results internationally, albeit when the world road titles were time trials. He was a runner first, winning races on road and track until 1906, when he bought his first bike for 25 shillings – which is now £1.25. He started riding with his local club, then entered the Addiscombe Tradesmen's Sports Day grass track meeting. He won everything and was hooked.

Davey joined the Vegetarian Cycling Club and raced in time trials and on the track, all on the same bike, because that's what almost everybody did. They rode a fixed gear, which is what's required for track racing, on the road, and kept a selection of sprockets so they had the right gear for each sort of race. They also rode their bikes to and from races, while the richer riders would have a set of light race wheels which they carried on detachable mounts bolted to their forks.

Tyres were tubulars, which meant the inner tube was encased in a treated cotton cover. This was stitched together around its inner circumference and had a rubber tread stuck to the outer circumference. The tyres weren't very good and road surfaces were poor, so punctures were common. Davey carried three spares on a long race, one strapped under his saddle, one strapped to his handlebars and the other looped and knotted around his shoulders. He didn't fit brakes to his bike until 1910, because with a fixed gear you can stop by letting your legs resist the pedals, although it takes time.

Davey was selected for the Stockholm Olympics in 1912, where the only cycling event was a road race run as a time trial over 200 miles. The course was incredibly rough, and British time trial rules weren't observed because any rider caught by the man who started behind him was allowed to sit in the catcher's slipstream, although with five minutes separating each rider it probably didn't skew the results too much. Britain's Freddy Grubb took the silver medal, and with Davey backing him Team GB won the team silver medal.

Davey saw service in the Royal Navy Air Service during the First World War, and resumed racing after it. He was reserve for the Antwerp Olympics, but the following year was selected for the first post-war world road race championships. They were in Stockholm but over a better course than the Olympics had been and the distance was cut to "only" 123 miles. He won a bronze medal that year, and another in 1922.

Davey turned professional in 1923, but it wasn't to ride big European road races, it was to do something British time triallists would do many times over the coming years: attack road records. Sponsoring a professional was a good way for bike manufacturers to advertise, because amateurs weren't allowed to carry the manufacturer's name anywhere on their bikes, although the more imaginative manufacturers got around that by producing very distinctive frames.

Hetchins made bikes with curved seatstays and chainstays, Bates bikes had a distinctive fork rake (effectively the amount by which the fork curves forwards), Baines a distinctive arrangement of their frame tubes, whereas Carlton's Flyer bike had very steep frame angles and very little fork rake. The manufacturers also allied themselves with certain cycling clubs, providing bikes and in some cases unofficial cash payments. Still, the best advert was to employ a pro and crack out some records. Davey set several, including Land's End to London, London to Portsmouth and back, and London to Bath and back, before retiring from competition at the age of 40.

Thousands turned out to witness these records. Cycling clubs were booming all over the country with people not only taking part in races, but going on organized club runs and adventurous tours of the countryside. Cycling grew as a pastime as well as a sport; couples met through cycling, and ordinary people began to use it to explore where they lived and enjoy the wider countryside.

Also, although road racing was developing in Europe in a totally different way from the UK, the cycling clubs kept producing champions who could more than hold their own internationally on the track, and on the road too if it was in a long-distance time trial. The next major character was just such a rider, another South Londoner called Frank Southall.

Southall was a record breaker on road and track, the best British time triallist of his generation and one of the best in the world. He proved that in the 1928 Olympics in Amsterdam, where the road race was run as a time trial again. Southall won the silver medal, and it would have been gold if a protest by the British officials had been successful. They claimed that the winner, Harry

Hansen of Denmark, had cut the course. They didn't see him do it but their logic was simple: Southall was 90 seconds behind the Dane after 50 kilometres of the 165-kilometre course, but 34 kilometres later he had lost a further seven minutes to Hansen. Southall hadn't slowed, and the Dane gained no more time over the remaining 82 kilometres.

Southall also did the track team pursuit in the same Olympics, setting a world record of 5 minutes 1.6 seconds, but the team didn't win a medal. That came at the next Olympics in Los Angeles where Southall took bronze in the team pursuit with William Harvell, Ernest Johnson and Charles Holland. Southall doubled up in the road race again, which was another time trial, but took sixth. Holland was 15th and Harvell 19th, so the team narrowly missed a bronze in the road team classification.

While Southall turned professional in 1934 and spent the rest of his racing career breaking road records, his Olympic team-mate Charles Holland was soon to take a monumental step in British cycling history. He would become the first British cyclist to ride the Tour de France.

Holland came from the West Midlands. His father was a keen cyclist and Charles went on family cycle-touring holidays from the age of 12, but didn't race until he was 18. That was in 1927, and five years later at Los Angeles he won an Olympic bronze medal. In 1934 Holland finished fourth in the World Amateur Road Race Championships, which was a proper bunched race by then, despite the fact that his normal race diet was time trials and the track. And he might have taken a medal if he hadn't been using a single-geared bike – the others in the winning breakaway move were all on multi-geared bikes.

Holland also rode the first Olympic road race that took the form of a bunched race. It was in Berlin in 1936, but on a flat course the race ended in a big bunch sprint and Holland just missed out on a medal. The 1936 Olympics were a strange experience for everyone, and Holland later told of a brush he had with Adolf Hitler when out on a training ride. Holland had stopped on a bridge over an autobahn when a motorcade drove right under him. Hitler was right in the middle of it, sitting in the back of an open-topped Mercedes. Holland later observed that he could have prevented the Second World War right then by dropping a bomb into Hitler's lap.

To round off his 1936 racing, Holland won a competition that had grown into the mainstay of British time trialling, the British Best All-Rounder competition, or BBAR. It still exists today, but is much less important than it used to be. It's basically a national ranking calculated on speed over 50 miles, 100 miles and 12-hour time trials. The events can be anywhere in the country, provided they meet BBAR standard, and the idea is that someone who races in Scotland could be measured against and compete with someone who races in Cornwall, for example. It never worked out quite like that, because some parts of the country have faster time trial courses than others, so the best riders had to travel to the fast courses if they were to have any chance of finishing high in the standings. Holland was the first BBAR winner to beat a 22 mph average over the three distances.

Having done most of what he could do as an amateur, Holland turned professional in 1937, but it wasn't just to attack road records as most Brits did. Holland wanted to compete in a type of race that was very popular in Europe and in America at the time. Six-day track racing had recently returned to London, and the 1937 event was to be held inside the Empire Pool building in Wembley on a steeply banked track that was built specially for the occasion.

Six-day races had been going since 1878, and they started in London. Not that the six-day races of the thirties were anything like the original, which was held at the Agricultural Hall in Islington, as the result of a bet. A professional racer called David Stanton was the gambler, and he bet one of his backers that he could ride 1,000 miles inside six days. A flat oval track was marked out inside the hall, and Stanton started riding his penny-farthing bike around it. He did 172 miles the first day, and 160 on each of the subsequent ones, to hit 1,000 miles with just 27 minutes to spare before the six days were up. His total riding time was 73.5 hours, giving an average speed of 13.5 miles per hour.

Watching a man ride round in circles on a big bike at 13.5 mph might not sound like a spectacle now, but Londoners flocked to the hall to see it. Another six-day race was put together, but to spice things up there were more competitors, including a Mexican who rode a horse. He won with 969 miles in the time allowed. The first cyclist was 59 miles behind him, but the cyclists were unhappy because the jockey was allowed to change horses. It was the humane thing to do, but at the same time it was unfair to the human competitors.

The race was another crowd-pleaser, though, and the next six-day race was planned, without any horses, and with the field boosted to ten, including a Frenchman, Charles Terront. A Sheffield rider, W. Cann, won with 1,060.5 miles and took the first prize of £100. The public were hooked, and in April 1879 a six-day world championship was held at the same venue. George Waller of Newcastle won with 1,172 miles, including 261 miles done on the first day. Events came thick and fast after that, and as the six-day distance record grew and grew, so did the fame of these races. Soon there were six-day races in other British cities and in both Europe and America.

Bikes developed, race speeds increased and banked tracks had to be built for the racers or they would have crashed on each bend. Some tracks were so tiny and their banks so steep that they looked like walls of death. At first people just wanted to see the riders suffer as the week went on, but then they wanted faster racing, which meant having fresher riders because competitions had turned into a battle hinging on who could stay awake the longest. Two-man teams were introduced, with one rider racing and then, when he wanted a break, relaying his partner into the fray with a hefty shove on his backside. This type of racing is basically the track event known today as the Madison, named after Madison Square Garden in New York, where it was invented.

London 1937 was a Madison-based six-day, and Holland knew that a lot of his competitors would be adept at riding Madisons, whereas he wasn't. He therefore went to Belgium to train, but he crashed and broke his collar bone on the first night of the London race. However, by then another race that Holland had heard about in Belgium had captured his imagination. He wanted to ride the Tour de France.

He'd won bunched races on the Isle of Man, where bunched racing was allowed on the open road, so Holland felt he had the experience, but by the 1930s it was no longer possible to enter the Tour de France as an individual. Still, the intrepid Englishman contacted the Tour's organizers, who said they were interested. Eventually they accepted Holland for the 1937 Tour so long as he competed with another British entrant, Bill Burl, and one from Canada, Pierre Gachon, in a British Empire team.

The team was given white jerseys with Union Jacks on each sleeve in which to ride, but by the end of day two of the Tour they were down to just one rider, Charlie Holland. He battled on for several stages until punctures and a useless bike pump put him out during a stage in the Pyrenees. Of the 98 starters only 46 reached the end in Paris, but Holland was bitter about his performance because he thought the organizers hadn't given him enough support. "They didn't provide us with a manager and you cannot look after yourself in a race like that. I think the organizers got all the publicity they wanted out of me first, then they didn't want me to finish. How would it have looked if an individual rider with no support had finished their race?" he said in an interview in the 1980s.

While Holland spent the rest of his career breaking road records, the Tour de France ceased to run after 1938 and only started again in 1947. By that time there was a movement to get road racing allowed on the open roads in the UK, and that led to more ambitious men like Holland having a go at the Tour. The man behind the movement, the man who lit the fuse that burned until Bradley Wiggins won the 2012 Tour de France, was an argumentative, driven and slightly cantankerous man from Wolverhampton called Percy Stallard.

Stallard started racing the British way, mixing time trials with grass- and hard-track racing, but his enthusiasm was truly ignited when he took part in a series of bunched races on the Brooklands car racing and test circuit in 1933. They were organized in response to the decision by the UCI to run the 1936 Olympic road race as a bunched race, not as a time trial. The NCU tried to get the UCI to reconsider, but they wouldn't, so they asked a club local to Brooklands to organize some bunched races at the venue.

The series culminated in a 100-kilometre bunched race that served as the selection trial for the GB team for the world road race championships in France. Stallard did well in it, got selected then finished 11th in the worlds, the best of the British riders. However, he still found it difficult to deal with the changes of pace in the lead group when attacks were made towards the end of the race. He also saw that his bike and equipment were out of date, and that he didn't know anything about road race tactics. "I learned more in that one trip to France than I had in six years as a time triallist," he said afterwards.

Stallard improved the following year, when he was seventh in the world title race on a very flat circuit in Leipzig. Then in 1936 he raced in a bunched race around the famous motorcycle TT road circuit on the Isle of Man. The island authorities received dispensation from their police and the race grew into a very successful Isle of Man cycling week later on. It was the first time that almost all of the British riders had raced in a bunch through town and village streets, and the first time they had raced up and down a mountain. Stallard finished 17th and although he continued to compete at Brooklands and in NCU-sanctioned bunched races around the outside of airfields, he felt they were a shadow of real road racing, and he could see no logical reason why it shouldn't be allowed in the UK. His chance came during the Second World War.

There was very little traffic on the roads during the war (owing to petrol rationing), so Stallard wrote to the NCU requesting permission to put on a bunched road race. He pointed out that there would be no need to close the roads, and there would be very little disruption, if any. The NCU wouldn't entertain the idea, so Stallard went ahead without their permission. He approached the police, putting forward his plan for a race from Llangollen to Wolverhampton, and they not only didn't object but promised to help. Stallard announced at Easter that his race would take place on June 7, 1942.

The race went ahead with 40 riders but it plunged British cycling into what slowly became a war. The NCU banned Stallard

from competing in any of their events before his race had even
started, and the body that governed time trials, the Road Time
Trials Council (RTTC), did the same. But the race went ahead
without incident, and a big crowd turned out in Wolverhampton
to see a local rider, E. A. Price, claim victory.

The police helped with marshals and provided motorcycle
outriders, but that worried the NCU too – they feared that
racing and permission for races could get put in police hands and
that would affect all cyclists' freedom to compete. Their reaction
was draconian: all 15 of the Llangollen to Wolverhampton race
finishers were suspended from competing in NCU and RTTC
events, and Stallard's suspension was made indefinite, pending
appeal – but he never appealed.

Instead Stallard created the British League of Racing Cyclists
(BLRC) and organized a national road race championships,
which he won. British cycling was torn in half; clubs could
affiliate to the BLRC, and many did, or the NCU, but not both.
The BLRC was painted as a renegade organization by cycling's
establishment, but that just made it and road racing more
attractive to young riders.

Cycling's war continued long after the Second World War ended,
and it continues into the next chapter of this book to become linked
with the stories of young British racers who discovered the allure of
racing in Europe. Meanwhile there was another cycling discipline
where British racers have always been good.

*   *   *   *   *

British track racers had competed without disadvantage all through
the twenties, thirties and forties, and by the latter decade a track
racer was the first British cyclist to be a household name in this

country. The medal tally for the period is impressive. Team GB cyclists won Olympic team pursuit gold in 1908, silver in 1920, bronze in 1928, 1932, 1936 and 1948. They won the sprint silver medal and the bronze in 1920, then silver in 1928. They won tandem gold in 1920, silver in 1928 and bronze in 1932. Plus they won a hatful of medals at distances and in events, like the tandem, that are long gone from the Olympic programme. GB track racing has a glorious Olympic CV, which declined slowly through the second half of the century, then began to build again and turn into total domination after 2000.

The 1948 Olympiad is important to the story of British cycling, not just because it was the last London Games before 2012, but because it introduces the important figure of Reginald Hargreaves Harris.

Harris was a true force of nature. In 1936 he won the first race he ever took part in and by 1937 he only needed to work during the winter, because he picked up enough track racing prizes, which he sold, to support himself in the summer. Harris was a formidable sprinter who would become the best in the world at this discipline, but he could also ride and win endurance events on the track, as most other sprinters could in his day.

Harris's first world championship selection came in 1939, when the track events were to be held in Milan. However, while the British team were getting familiar with the Vigorelli track, war broke out and they had to go straight home. Harris saw action in North Africa as a tank driver with the 10th Hussars, but was wounded and invalided out of the army in 1943, so he started training again.

A run of six national track titles saw Harris selected for the 1947 World Amateur Sprint Championships, which he won with ease, becoming the red-hot favourite to win gold in each of the sprint disciplines in the London Games: the sprint, the tandem sprint and the 1,000-metre time trial. Unfortunately a road accident resulting in two fractured vertebrae, and another fracture sustained in a track race at Fallowfield in Manchester forced Harris to complete his Olympic training in a specially made plaster cast. It was a miracle that Harris even raced in London, let alone took two silver medals, but it said much about his tough and uncompromising personality.

Tommy Godwin was the other big name to emerge from the cycling events in London. Born in America but brought up in the Midlands after his parents moved back there, Godwin competed in the team pursuit and the 1,000-metre time trial and won a bronze medal in each one. Not as driven as Harris – few people are – Godwin was a true amateur in the spirit that de Coubertin intended for the first modern Olympic Games. He worked full time as an electrician and years later recalled the austerity but also the warmth of the 1948 Olympics. "There was no athletes' village. After the medal ceremony I walked back to the house we were staying at, where I'd got my mum to come down and cook for us, I had a cup of Horlicks then went to bed. We lived by the Olympic motto really, which was 'Bring the youth of the world together to meet and make friends.' That's what the Olympic Games were for in those days." Godwin, who later became the first paid British national cycling coach, died shortly after the London 2012 Games, aged 91. He was highly respected inside British cycling, and so was Reg Harris, but for different reasons.

Harris was a winner. Sport wasn't part of his life, it was his life. Right from the outset he saw it as the way he could achieve fame and fortune, and he was right. He pushed the boundaries of 1940s amateurism, and by 1948 it was common knowledge that although he was employed by the cycle company Claud Butler, the only work he did for them was ride a bike. Harris turned professional for Raleigh at the end of 1949, and took the pro sprint world by storm.

In the early days of racing, professional sprinters were the best-known cyclists in the world. Road racing had grown enormously in stature by Harris's time in the sport, but pro sprinters were still held in high regard and their contests in various Grand Prix events held in major cities throughout Europe and in the world title races could pack stadiums to the roof. Most Western European amateur sprinters wanted to become professionals and break into their highly paid circuit. However, places in it were jealously protected and the professional sprint tour contained some of the toughest and fastest athletes you could find at any time in any sport.

Reg Harris ruled the pro sprint world from 1949 until 1954, winning four consecutive world titles. This is when he became a household name, and the advertising slogan "Reg Rides a Raleigh" was seen on hoardings and on the sides of buses up and down the country. Harris earned well over £12,000 a year during this period, when the average yearly wage was around £500. He was voted Sportsman of the Year in 1949 and he won the Sportswriter's Sportsman of the Year award in 1950. He mixed with other sports stars of his era, such as Sir Stirling Moss, and was awarded an OBE in 1958.

Harris raced until 1957 and was able to invest the money he earned in various businesses, none of them successful. He loved cycling, and kept himself fit by continuing to train around the Cheshire lanes where he lived, but maybe he loved it too much. The cut and thrust of physical competition was Harris's strength, and he couldn't seem to channel it into business. He even made a comeback to racing in 1971, when he won a bronze medal in the British professional sprint championships, and in 1974 when he won the British title at the age of 54, but pro sprinting was a shadow of what it had been by then, and Harris looked totally out of place. He died in 1992 and is buried in Chelford churchyard in Cheshire.

*   *   *   *   *

As the 1950s began cycling was on the whole an amateur sport in Britain. It was mostly a working-class sport too; it was an escape from factory and mine, from steel and from textiles, and from the tedious work done by legions of office clerks, which in those pre-computer days represented the largest single workforce in the country.

Cycling in the rest of Europe was very different. There it was dominated by professionals, and bunched road racing was part of the fabric of everyday life. Road racing touched most people's lives, because in the great European hotbeds of cycling, Flanders, Northern France, Britanny, the Basque Country, and Northern Italy and Tuscany there was a road race somewhere almost every day of the year between April and September, and the great races, the Classics and Grand Tours, were legends in these regions. So were the riders who rode them. Every town and almost every village had a pro racer at some time, and when his career ended he still meant something in his neighbourhood.

Not having top pro road racers as national heroes, Britain was a world away from the continent. Out of this separation, however, something grew in Britain, something that was unique to the UK until the worldwide explosion in leisure and sports and fitness cycling we see today: the British cycling club.

A diet of time trial races over set distances might have left our top riders at a disadvantage when they competed in international road races, but British time trialling was and still is a very accessible sport. Time trials are sometimes called the race of truth. They are a simple, straightforward battle, you against the clock, with few tactics and little opportunity for finesse. In a time trial the strongest and fittest man or woman usually wins, whereas in a road race your strength can be used by others who shoot past in the final sprint.

Time trials over set distances also have another appeal: instead of talking about the position you finished in a race you can talk about your time. It means that although only one person can win, everybody else in a time trial has something to race for; they want to beat their personal best for the distance, or at least their best on that course, or the best time done at their current age. That's why time trials grew to be the mainstay of racing in the UK, and it's one of the reasons why cycling clubs grew so big. The other big reason is the social aspect of cycling.

By the start of the twentieth century working people had more leisure, and for the first time they had an affordable means of personal transport, the bicycle, to explore the countryside. Cycling clubs formed as much to meet this need as they did to participate in sport, but those two sides fitted well anyway.

The cycling club staple was the Sunday run. These were all-day affairs covering epic distances with stops for lunch and tea. Few concessions were made to younger members or novices; they held on to the pack for as long as they could, then would either carry on solo and maybe catch up with the rest when they stopped for lunch somewhere; or they went home. Many of them got lost, many were lost to cycling, but at least the apparently heartless way they were treated was a good incentive to get fit and stick with the pack.

This hard riding attitude was good training for time trials, to which competitors rarely travelled by car because so few had a car. This is Ron Kitching, a Yorkshireman who became an excellent long-distance racer, then as a cycle dealer and importer played a huge part in the development of road racing in this country, describing his first-ever race in 1934. "I wasn't really bothered about racing to be honest, I enjoyed the club runs, but most of the club were riding to the event and going on somewhere afterwards, so I thought why not take part? We rode from Harrogate to Wetherby then stripped the mudguards off our bikes and stuffed them, extra clothing and our saddlebags under a hedge. The better off changed in the Three Legs pub.

"It was the Yorkshire Century club's 25-mile time trial on the Old Great North Road, starting from just north of Wetherby and going up to Boroughbridge, where you rode around a marshal stood in the middle of the road at exactly 12 and a half miles. Then you rode the 12 and a half miles back to the start. I did one hour nine minutes on my ordinary bike with heavy tyres, and the way I did the race had been no different to the way we did the last leg of every club run. It was just a matter of riding eye-balls out for 25 miles.

"We changed afterwards, reassembled our bikes into standard club trim with saddlebags and mudguards, then set off for more riding. But to me, living on the edge of the Yorkshire Dales, the race cut into the time I could spend exploring them, so it was back to the club runs the following week and I didn't race again for another two months."

Kitching eventually got a taste for competition, especially 12-hour events which fitted his full-day-out ideal anyway, and he became a good racer. He would have won the 1939 BBAR, but the competition was annulled, with him leading, owing to the start of the Second World War, and he did win many great time trials. Kitching also took part in road races, including a short stint in Belgium, and he became a staunch supporter of the BLRC.

Kitching always rode the biggest time trials when he could, races like the Bath Road 100 and the Andy Wilson Memorial 50. These were the highlights of the British racing calendar in their day, and it was an honour to be selected to ride them, as there were only places for the fastest 120 entries. Cyclists turned out in their thousands to watch them, just as they did for events held on some of the faster courses, which always attracted the stars of the era because they wanted to see if they could set a competition record.

That's what British time triallists called the fastest times set at each distance, and the words competition (or simply "comp") record still have a magical ring to them. The hour for 25 miles was the first invisible speed barrier to go. It was beaten for the first time on British roads by an Irish rider, Ralph Dougherty, in 1939. He'd already done it in Ireland earlier that year, and so had the British rider George Fleming, who went on to beat two hours for 50 miles for the first time in Britain after the war.

So was there something special about Irish roads at the time that made them faster than British ones? No, it was what competitors were allowed to wear that made racing faster there. In line with the "at all costs be inconspicuous" ethos of time trials, the rule in Britain was that racers had to be dressed neck to toe in black, which meant black wool tights and a black alpaca jacket with a shirt underneath. The jackets were fairly light, but still bulky, and they flapped about in the wind, about as far removed from the one-piece skinsuits used in time trials today as possible, and a lot slower than shorts and a cycling-specific racing top. That's what riders in Ireland were allowed to wear for riding on the road, and that's why the 25 mph barrier was broken there first.

But the finest record-breaking performance of this era, and one of the best ever, was set in 1956 by a gangly, studious-looking electrician from Nottingham called Ray Booty. Roger Bannister had broken the four-minute-mile barrier in athletics in 1954, but cycling had a barrier too. The 25-mile record had dropped into mid-fifty-minute territory; 50 miles in under two hours was a regular occurrence; but nobody had broken four hours for 100 miles. Then in 1956 Ray Booty went close by winning the national 100-mile title in 4 hours 1 minute 52 seconds. The next big 100-mile time trial was the classic Bath Road event, held every August Bank Holiday on an out-and-back course starting just west of Reading.

Thousands rode out to see if Booty could break four hours. And in typical British club rider style he rode all the way to Reading too, the previous day, clocking up a nice round 100 miles from his home in Nottingham. He set out on a still morning, pedalling an 84-inch fixed gear. Gear size in those days was expressed as the diameter of a penny-farthing wheel that would be equivalent to a particular ratio, whereas on the continent it was expressed as the distance the bike covered during one pedal revolution in that particular ratio. Now cyclists almost universally express gear sizes by the simplest formula, the number of teeth on the chainring by the number of teeth on the sprocket. To give some feel for Booty's gear, 50 x 16 would give a gear of 84.4 inches.

It was the perfect choice for the conditions and Booty never faltered, pedalling with a style that sports journalists of the day described as swan-like, all serenity in his upper body as he crouched over his Raleigh Record Ace bike to be as aerodynamic as possible, and pedalling furiously to a new record of 3 hours 58 minutes 28 seconds.

Booty was an amazing athlete, a superb time triallist, who was also the Commonwealth Games road race champion in 1958. After being helped by Raleigh unofficially for years, Booty repaid them with another incredible 100 miles, the fastest time in one direction of 3 hours 28 minutes – again riding a Record Ace, but with a Sturmey Archer three-speed fixed gear. It was 34 years before Ian Cammish beat that one.

INTO EUROPE

The BLRC could easily have withered under the NCU's policy of suspending anyone who competed in their events – rendering them unavailable for selection for official GB teams – but instead the League grew. Riders joined, clubs switched allegiance, and when fellow BLRC members were spotted on the road they would be greeted with shouts of "Up the Leaguers!"

In 1944 BLRC clubs organized 25 road races on open roads, including regional and national championships, as well as place-to-place events such as Morecambe to Bradford and the first-ever stage race held in Britain, the Southern Grand Prix, which was held in Kent in August.

BLRC race winners included Stallard, who took the national title; Ernie Clements, who won the Tour of the Peaks, the Midlands championships and the Tour of the Clees; Geoff Clark, who won Morecambe to Bradford, and Ron Kitching, the winner of the Craven Dales road race in his beloved Yorkshire Dales.

By then Kitching was a member of the Bradford Racing Cycling Club, a breakaway group formed by members of the Yorkshire Road Club who approved of what the BLRC were doing and wanted to get involved. The cycling press held entirely the opposite view, with the predecessor of the current *Cycling Weekly* magazine stridently supporting the NCU.

This is what they said in a 1943 editorial. "Our leniency towards the riders who support the BLRC should have a time limit, from now until the date of the next illegal promotion. After which the mischief-makers should be kept right outside our sport. We can do without men who are thus jeopardising the whole road game at a time when those away from home look to cyclists who are still able to carry on with their sport, to preserve it with a level-headed and sound policy that will ensure its future." It was a vitriolic attack on the BLRC and what it was trying to do, and mentioning cyclists away at the war was a cheap shot, but it shows how entrenched the situation became.

It is difficult now to imagine what it felt like to be part of that conflict, but the bitterness towards officialdom that some BLRC pioneers felt then, and in some cases still feel, was and is both warranted and genuine. The NCU and BLRC did finally, grudgingly, combine to form one body in 1959 called the British Cycling Federation (BCF), but BLRC officials weren't given much of a role to play in it, even though they had driven road racing in this country from humble beginnings in 1942 to a sport we would recognize today.

In the course of 1944 the number of BLRC races grew, and in 1945 Jimmy Kain put on the Victory Cycling Marathon.

Designed to celebrate the end of the war, it ran from Brighton to Glasgow in five stages and set out with a budget of £174, which ran out in Bradford. In an interview years later Kain described his simple solution: "I got my hat out and had a whip-round among the crowd at the stage finish; they contributed another 26 quid, which got us to Glasgow."

The race was hugely popular and attracted massive crowds, but the competitors had a really hard time. Some stages were miles longer than billed, accommodation was difficult to find and in some cases impossible, so competitors slept in barns or under hedges. The winner was a Frenchman, Robert Babot, who also represented a non-mainstream cycling body, the communist-inspired Fédération Sport et Gymnastique du Travail (FSGT), a workers' sports association that's still going strong today.

The event grew amid the conflict, while remaining highly unstable. One moment it was an attractive sponsor proposition; then sponsors would be put off because of the constant bickering going on in cycling. The *News of the World* gave the race £500 in 1947, then pulled out the following year. The *Daily Express* got involved but went the same way, as did Butlins holiday camps. Meanwhile the race developed into a Tour of Britain, although some years it was called the Circuit of Britain. Sponsorship stability only came the year before the NCU and BLRC amalgamation, when a Derbyshire racer called Dave Orford persuaded the Milk Marketing Board to take over and the Tour of Britain became the Milk Race.

The bickering definitely held back the development of road racing in the UK, but apart from some understandable intransigence on the part of people who had been burned by the NCU, none of the blame can be laid at the door of the BLRC. On the contrary, they created a wonderful blueprint for racing in this country, and they sent teams to compete abroad too, either in races not affiliated to the UCI or by arrangement with individual race organizers. For example, from 1948 the BLRC sent a team to the biggest bike race in Eastern Europe, the Peace Race, or Berlin–Warsaw–Prague as it was called then, the invitation coming though the BLRC's association with the communist FSGT.

That Britain had talented road racers was shown when Ian Steel won the Peace Race in 1952. It was a really hard race, usually dominated by the Russian, Polish and Czech National teams, who were all soldiers, although 90 per cent of their soldiering was done out training and racing on their bikes. The race ran through Eastern Europe's most populated and industrial regions, where the roads were terrible.

Vin Denson, who later rode the Tour de France several times and was the first UK rider to win a stage in the Tour of Italy, rode the 1959 Peace Race. He recalls: "Most stages were a blur of cobbled city roads and tram lines, interspersed with bumpy highways and giant potholes. You bounced around, jumped your bike up on to the smoother pavements, where the crowd allowed you to. Millions came out to watch it, they must have been starved of entertainment, and crashes were frequent. It was madness."

The Peace Race was extremely tough, and the pro teams, especially French ones, set great store by it when dishing out contracts, as Scotland's Billy Bilsland remembers. "When I turned pro at the end of 1969 I'd won a lot of big amateur races in France that year and raced for the top club in Paris, but all the Peugeot-BP team wanted to know was had I won a race in Belgium and had I won a stage of the Peace Race. I answered yes to both questions and that was it, I was in the team."

The BLRC widened British cyclists' horizons, not just by their Peace Race exploits, but by modelling their races in the UK on European ones. Even the way the riders dressed was inspired by European pro road racers. Like them the BLRC riders raced in short-sleeved cycling tops, shorts and white ankle socks, and wore little cycling casquette caps and crochet-backed track mitts. On training rides they wore plus fours with long, patterned woollen socks and cycling-specific jumpers, an outfit sometimes topped off with a black beret. The young British racers had seen pictures in French and Italian cycling magazines, some in colour, of famous pros racing in the Alps, the Pyrenees, the Dolomites and across the plains of France and Flanders, and they were hooked.

Seeing those pictures was why Brian Robinson wanted to break into continental road racing. He was a good rider, and the photos he saw in his brother's cycling magazines set him on the path to becoming the first British cyclist to make a place in European pro cycling. Brian Robinson, who is 82 now but still riding his bike when he can, is a legend in his native Yorkshire. In fact Robinson was one of the local cycling heroes who played a part in Yorkshire's successful bid to host the start of the 2014 Tour de France.

"My older brother, Des, raced in Europe and he brought some magazines back. It was the early fifties and I was a keen rider with the Huddersfield Road Club, but my father wouldn't let me race until I was 18, so all I could do until then was look at pictures. They held some sort of fascination for me, though," he says.

When Robinson turned 18 in 1947, he started, as all British racers did, by riding time trials. He wanted to do road races, but being ambitious he also wanted to ride in the Olympics, so he had to steer clear of the BLRC and focused on NCU massed-start races and time trials. Then in the spring of 1952 he got the chance to ride in Europe in a race called the Route de France, then regarded as an amateur Tour de France.

"I was doing my national service and the Army was invited to send a joint team to France with the NCU. I was lying fifth with three days to go, then we got to the Pyrenees and I'd never seen anything like it. The only mountain I knew was Holme Moss, which is about 2,000 feet high, but the big Pyrenean climbs are over 8,000 feet. I'll never forget the day we were in the valley riding towards the Peyresourde, and you can see the road zig-zagging up that climb, although I didn't know it then, all I saw was a zig-zag line of what looked like lights going up the mountain. I asked the rider next to me what they were, and he told me it was the sun reflecting off the windscreens of the cars parked along the route."

Robinson was a bit out of his depth on climbs that size, or at least he was then, and he dropped down to 40th overall by the end of the race. However, he was selected for the Olympic road race in Helsinki, where he finished 27th, one place behind his brother. France's Jacques Anquetil, who became the first man to win five Tours de France, was 12th in that road race. A few weeks later Robinson finished equal eighth alongside Anquetil in the amateur world championships. Next year they were both professionals. Well, Anquetil was; Robinson was really a semi-pro in the Ellis Briggs team, working in the winter and racing full-time for parts of the summer.

Ellis Briggs was a Yorkshire bike shop and pretty typical of the early British pro team sponsors, who were mostly bike or bike component manufacturers or shops, with one or two bigger brand names thrown in, such as Ovaltine. The team took part in the BLRC-created pro road race circuit in the UK, including the Tour of Britain, in which Robinson was fourth in 1953 and runner-up in 1954, but things were about to change for him.

The bike manufacturer Hercules now decided they needed to do more to boost their brand than just sponsor a team in UK races, so they hatched an ambitious plan to ride the Tour de France. Thanks to the experience of their manager, former pro sprinter Syd Cozens, who knew how hard European racing was from competing with road pros in the old six-day races, Hercules realized they couldn't just rock up at the Tour and expect to compete. To give themselves a chance of getting through to the finish, they decided to decamp to Europe for several months to do all the races the other Tour riders would do in the run-up to the Tour.

The Tour was still for national teams in those days, but Hercules weren't put off. By 1955 they had recruited most of the top British road pros, so the Great Britain selection would be dominated by their riders anyway. They set up camp at Les Issambres in the South of France in early February, with Robinson, a good little sprinter called Dave Bedwell, Derek Buttle, Arthur Ilsley, Ken Joy, Clive Parker, Freddy Krebs, Dennis Talbot and Bernard Pusey. The idea was to train in the Riviera warmth, as the other European pros did, and be as ready as they could be for the start of the European racing season in March. It was a good plan, but some riders felt homesick almost as soon as they got there, and couldn't adapt to the change of lifestyle.

"The Hercules team was a good set-up," Robinson says. "We had a good wage and it should have been the start for a lot of British riders on the continent, but to my mind the others weren't dedicated enough. They didn't get down to it. We were in France, so my philosophy was you had to live like a Frenchman, but the others were always thinking of home, saying things like 'I wish we could get some Yorkshire pudding.' That was no good. You were in France, you had to put thoughts of home out of your mind and get on with it."

Robinson got on with it. This quiet man, while powerful in his racing prime, did not appear physically outstanding, but his understated exterior hides a core of steel. "Being away from home didn't affect me. Maybe I was lucky but I could live anywhere. After Hercules folded I stayed in France, I couldn't afford to come home for a visit. If I came home that might have been the end of racing in Europe for me, so I stayed, I stuck it out for the rest of the 1955 season, when with no team I had to win prizes in races just so I could eat."

During that first season Robinson finished eighth overall in Paris–Nice, his first pro stage race, and fourth in the Flèche Wallonne, one of the first Classics he ever rode. New riders at this level dream about a debut like that, and here was an Englishman achieving those remarkable results. It was unheard of. The only problem was that a lot of the other Hercules riders went home long before the Tour de France started. "By the time the Great Britain team was selected there wasn't enough Hercules riders left to fill it, so they recruited men from other teams," Robinson says. Only two of them got to Paris: Robinson finished a very creditable 29th and Tony Hoar struggled valiantly to finish last, but even he did better than a lot of seasoned Euro-pros, who dropped out. The Tour de France was longer and harder in those days, and always had a high dropout rate.

Living and racing in Europe back then cannot have been easy for Robinson. No British racer had lived all year in France and been part of a big pro team. Robinson had no template, no one to ask, no one to follow. He had to hit the ground running, carve out a life for himself with no back-up and hardly any contact with home. He couldn't ring up, as he rarely had access to a phone and most people in the UK didn't have them back then anyway. The only way to communicate was by letter, but it was a while before Robinson even had a fixed address in France to send one to.

His solution was simple: "I learned French, one phrase a day, every day, until I was fluent. Then I showed I could work in a team, and I could take my chance if it was given. I also raced as much as possible, especially in stage races, which suited my style of racing anyway, but when you are doing stage races the team pays your living costs. I didn't even rent a place to live in until my second year in Europe; I didn't need to, because I lived in hotels on races or I lodged with French friends in between."

Robinson's ability as a bike racer and his ability to adapt to racing in Europe won him a contract with the St Raphael pro team for 1956, when he finished 14th overall in the Tour de France. He was third in the 1957 Milan–San Remo, then made history in 1958 by taking the first-ever stage victory by a British rider in the Tour de France. Just as important as winning was the fact that Robinson fitted into European pro cycling. He understood the importance of teamwork, and he knew how to do it. He was tactically astute, and he could take his chance when it came.

He was also very good at making chances for himself and then delivering a result, as when he won his second Tour de France stage in 1959. "It was the day before the time trial, so I knew all the favourites would want an easy day. I decided to do my time trial a day early and got the mechanic to fit my 28-spoke time trial wheels with light tyres instead of the normal road wheels and tyres we used. The plan was to attack at some point, quite a way out, build up a big lead and hang on. But when my team-mate Gérard Saint asked me to lead him out for some King of the Mountains points, I decided that was the right time. I led him out, he got the points and I kept going.

"I went down the other side of this hill really fast, with Jean Dotto behind me shouting 'Wait, wait.' Well, Dotto might have been the first French winner of the Tour of Spain, but he was a terrible descender. So I kept at it and rode flat out, even though the descent had a loose surface with stones all over it, and I had my nine-ounce silk tubular tyres on."

There were still 130 kilometres to go. Once off the climb, Robinson went into time trial mode and kept pulling away on the undulating roads until he was 20 minutes and six seconds clear at the stage finish in Chalon-sur-Saône. And what did he think about for all those kilometres alone at the head of the Tour de France? "The big contract for next year that was dangling like a carrot just in front of me."

By 1959 Robinson was an established and well-respected member of the European pro peloton, the first British rider ever to achieve that status. He spent the whole cycling season, February to October, in Europe, and even had a flat in Paris – at a time when, as he says, "Not many British people travelled abroad, not even for holidays, and it was well before the age of the package tour."

Robinson is an astute man and he quickly understood what European pro racing was all about. "Cycling is a job for a pro in Europe, and the team winning is more important than individual success. Anyway, the team shares the prizes, and in my day contract money, your monthly wage from the team, wasn't as big as it is now. The prizes were good, and if you were a good team rider who could win a bit you got contracts for criterium races, where riders were paid to start. The top riders had a big say in who got contracts for criteriums, so if you fitted in and they respected you, you got contracts," he says.

Robinson considers the 1961 Critérium du Dauphiné stage race as his best victory. "That was a solid win. Any one of five riders from our team could have won it, but I got in a break during an early stage. I was policing it really, riding at the back so the team was represented, but then my *directeur sportif*, Raymond Louviot, came alongside in the team car and said, 'You can work a bit.' That was his vote of confidence – he was saying I could go for the overall, and the team would back me."

The world is now a very different place from what it was in the late fifties and early Sixties, but the cycling characteristics of the various countries haven't changed much. Robinson enjoyed racing in France the most, although even then he found the Tour de France big and slightly intimidating. "I liked the Tour, it suited me, but I found the crowds and the noise of the Tour a bit much at times. Paris–Nice was a good race too. I liked racing in Italy, but I didn't like Belgium, at least not Flanders, even though I was once fourth in Het Volk. Racing there is hard, but the people are hard too, and brash."

Robinson competed with two of the greatest pro road racers of all time, and he studied them at close quarters. That was part of his racing skill; he would notice when a rider exhibited certain characteristics that might show he was going well or struggling a bit – not that these two ever struggled. "I raced against the two French masters Louison Bobet and Jacques Anquetil. Bobet had an aura around him, a sort of star quality. I remember a criterium in Brittany, which is where Bobet comes from, and I won every prime [the prize given to the first across the finish line each lap], but coming into the finish Bobet tapped me on the shoulders and said, 'This one is for me.' And it was, he won. I was more in Anquetil's age group and I was friendlier with him. I did my best ever time trial around Lake Geneva and was still three minutes behind Jacques. That's how good he was."

Robinson's professional career lasted until the end of 1962, when he was still a force to be reckoned with; and he had a place in a team for 1963, but he decided it was in his and in his family's best interests to bring the adventure to a close. He returned to Yorkshire to work in the family building business, but he is still actively involved in cycling today. His daughter Louise is a top cyclo-cross racer, the only British rider to have won a senior world championship medal in the discipline. And now his grandson, Jake Womersley, is winning races and looks like keeping the family tradition going.

Even before his career ended, however, Robinson played a crucial role at the start of the following chapter in the British cycling story. Robinson opened the doors of world pro road racing for Great Britain, and the next rider to step inside, Tom Simpson, blew the doors off.

He was the best British road racer ever until Bradley Wiggins, Mark Cavendish and Chris Froome came along, and even they haven't won some of the races Simpson did. His first pro road race was the 1959 World Championships, and he finished fourth in it. To put that into context, only Cavendish and Simpson himself have done better. In 1964 Simpson was fourth again and in 1965 he became Britain's first-ever world professional road race champion. Simpson also won three of the five single-day Classics called the Monuments of Cycling, while Cavendish is still the only other British winner of one, and so far he's only won one.

Simpson was the first British rider to wear the yellow jersey in the Tour de France, in 1962. With his sixth place that year he was also the highest British finisher until Robert Millar, arguably a better stage racer, finished fourth in 1984.

Simpson's achievements would be spectacular even today when British cyclists dominate many aspects of world cycling, but they came without the carefully planned and lottery-funded national development programme that brought success in the twenty-first century. In fact, when Simpson was winning there was no programme at all.

He was a prodigy. He started racing at 14, started winning at 16, and took an Olympic bronze medal in the team pursuit a few days after his 19th birthday. Simpson stayed in Britain for two more years, winning national titles and a Commonwealth Games silver medal, and then he went to Europe to fulfil his destiny. He lived in France and then in Belgium, but although he still has the best spread of results of any British road racer, he achieved it at the head of teams who were never fully committed to him.

A British winner was an alien concept in a sport dominated by European racers and European teams, and furthermore success in pro road racing depends a lot on teamwork. One man wins, but the team help him do it. There were no British teams when Simpson raced, and he had to fight to impose his will on the French teams he raced for before he could even think about winning. It compromised his tactics, as he always had to attack early, but it makes what he achieved even more remarkable.

And maybe it made him try too hard. Good cyclists are praised for their will to win, but Simpson had more: he had a need to win. From childhood onwards he had to succeed at whatever he did. Committed to making early attacks in races so his team were left with no choice but to back him, Simpson often rode to a state of complete exhaustion to make his tactic work. Sometimes it paid off, and sometimes it didn't. Alongside the victories, Simpson's career is littered with races in which he dominated but then faltered in the final stages.

Brian Robinson helped Simpson get his first pro contract. "I knew about Tom. He lived in South Yorkshire as an amateur and as well as being a good international track rider he had a reputation as an attacking rider on the road, and he'd won a lot of races. I also knew he'd gone to France, to Brittany, and he won there too. I'd met him a few times; then during the 1959 Tour de France Tom came to visit the British team, so I introduced him to my trade team manager, Raymond Louviot, and a deal was done for Tom to join our team, St Raphael, for 1960."

Early in 1960 Robinson picked Simpson up at his home in Harworth, near Doncaster, and they travelled to Narbonne in southern France to start training for the first races. After that Simpson shared Robinson's flat in Paris. Robinson helped Simpson a lot and was a big influence on him, although it was hard work at times.

"Tom talked a lot, he was always chattering away when we shared rooms, and I must admit I prefer a bit of peace and quiet. He wasn't very tidy either, or organized, at least at first, and he'd chat away to people at the end of a stage for hours if you let him. But I told him he had to be organized, he had to plan ahead, know where all his kit was so he didn't waste energy looking for things. He had to get to his hotel quickly after a stage, sort himself out there quickly so he could rest and recover. All these things are crucial on a stage race. If you get more rest than the next man you'll stay stronger.

"Tom learned, he calmed down a bit, he got more organized, although he was never very careful with money. I remember him going well in the 1960 Paris–Roubaix, then he won a big stage race. He'd got some extra money, prizes and bonuses, so I said to him, 'Now Tom, you want to save that.' And as ever he nodded and looked like he was listening, but I knew he wasn't. Next thing, I came back to the flat after a race somewhere and there's an Aston Martin parked outside, left-hand drive too. Tom had blown all his extra cash on it." Robinson shakes his head when he tells this story, but then he smiles and says, "But do you know what? I'd have swapped all of my discipline and organization for a little bit of Tom's talent."

Today we take live cycling on the TV for granted, but the 1960 Paris–Roubaix mentioned by Robinson was the first race ever to be televised live on Eurovision. They only covered the final hour, but for 56 minutes of that hour everybody who was watching saw a young Englishman alone in the lead. Simpson had attacked early – because, he said in typical style at the end, he wasn't confident when riding on the cobblestones in a group.

One minute he was looking like the winner, the next he blew, completely, and he was caught at the gates of the velodrome in Roubaix. Eight men passed him on the track there, so he finished an exhausted ninth. He'd tried so hard, holding off the best racers in the world across all the terrible cobblestones of the Hell of the North. The skinny 22-year-old was besieged by reporters in the track centre Roubaix, and using bits of language he'd picked up he gave interviews to any TV stations, radio and newspapers who wanted them. Next day Simpson was a household name all over Europe.

The overnight effect is summed up by Jean Bobet, a former racer, winner of Paris–Nice, and brother of three-time Tour de France winner Louison, but then a journalist and radio commentator with RTL and now an award-winning author. "Before that Sunday the continent did not really know much about British cycling. Sure enough, we had heard of Reg Harris, but there had always been something unreal about him. Harris was a wonderful athlete who rode two or three laps of the track then disappeared for months on end. His name was printed on the world record tables but not in the hearts of people. And then Simpson came along."

After Roubaix, Simpson won the Mont Faron hill climb, beating the 1958 Tour de France winner, the legendary Charly Gaul, the man they called the Angel of the Mountains. Simpson was seventh in the Flèche Wallonne, 11th in Liège–Bastogne–Liège, and then he won the Tour du Sud-Est, with no small help from Brian Robinson.

"I think he was tired for the first two days," Robinson remembers, "because he'd done a lot of racing that spring, so he kept saying he wanted to stop, but I kept telling him to stick at it, that it would get easier. Eventually he worked his way up the overall standings, then he won the last stage, a really hilly one, on his own by enough time to win the race overall as well."

Then Simpson rode the 1960 Tour de France, which perhaps he shouldn't have at such a young age. It wasn't a bad debut, though, finishing 29th overall after being close to the lead early on. The Tour was still for national teams in 1960, and Robinson was the only other British finisher in 21st place. But the Tour is a tall order for any 22-year-old and Simpson was shattered afterwards. He was tired for the rest of the year, which affected his earnings.

That winter he got married. This, Brian Robinson says, was "just Tom being impulsive again". But maybe that's what drove

Simpson to win; he kept raising his personal bar higher, then getting into situations where he had to raise it some more. And Helen Sherburn was the making of him.

It was a whirlwind romance and a tale of coincidence. Tom and Helen lived only 15 miles apart in England, but they never met there. That happened in 1959 in Brittany, when Helen mistook Tom for a Frenchman, and she couldn't believe it when it turned out he lived just down the road from her in the UK. "He thought I was a snooper come to look at him sitting in the garden, which in a way I was," she says. "Talk of the 'coureur anglais' who was winning all the races was a big story in St Brieuc, where Tom was staying with a family of cyclists and I worked as an au pair for another family, so I went round to introduce myself. I saw this sun-tanned, dark-haired young chap in their garden and thought he was French, so I spoke to him in French, asking him if the young Englishman was in, and he told me to bugger off in English!"

The confusion was soon cleared up, they had a good laugh, and that was it. They went out occasionally but didn't see each other all that much at first. They kept in touch, however, then fell in love and were married just after Christmas 1960. They couldn't have been a better match really. Helen was adventurous and self-reliant. She spoke fluent French and German, and when they later moved to Belgium, because it was cheaper than living in France, she soon got to grips with Flemish. By that time Tom was one of the biggest names in Belgian cycling, because in 1961 he won the Tour of Flanders.

The Ronde van Vlaanderen, as Flemish-speaking people call it, is Belgium's biggest race. Liège–Bastogne–Liège is another monument, and older, so it's just as important in world cycling, but Liège–Bastogne–Liège is in the French-speaking part of

Belgium and cycling isn't as popular there as it is in Flanders. Actually, the word popular doesn't do the feeling and emotion justice; Flanders is mad about cycling.

To the many Flemish people who see Flanders as a country with its own heritage, the Ronde is their race and it expresses something of that heritage. One of the cobbled Classics, it's tough, uncompromising and it favours an attacking spirit and a hard worker. Tom won from a break of two, out-sprinting the Italian national champion, Nino Defilippis. Behind them were Belgian legends like Rik Van Looy, Arthur de Cabooter and Jos Planckaert. It was Tom's first time in the race, and he was 23. Even Tom Boonen, the great cobbled Classics star of today, perhaps one of the greatest ever, couldn't win Flanders at 23. Simpson was a star now, at least for cycling fans.

A British cycling star was unheard of, and some of the most established European riders found it hard to take. As a result Simpson's Classic victory didn't give him access to the top table in the way that it would today. He had to fight even harder over the next 18 months, but eventually he broke through.

He took the yellow jersey in the 1962 Tour de France when the race entered the Pyrenees, lost it, dropped down the classification, then fought back up to third overall in the Alps, only to crash on the final mountain descent of the race to finish sixth in Paris. The following year Simpson not only won Bordeaux–Paris but also had a string of podium places in other big races. They saw him take second place in the season-long Super Prestige Pernod competition behind Jacques Anquetil, which meant effectively that by the end of the 1963 season Tom Simpson was the world number two in professional cycling.

Finally, that got him accepted. Simpson was acknowledged as one of the very best riders of his day. A fierce rival was Belgium's

Rik Van Looy, the best Classics rider of that generation, one of the best from any generation and still the only man ever to have won every Classic race. When I interviewed Van Looy in 2005, this is how he rated Simpson: "I considered Tom the man to beat in the Classics, he was very good and always attacking, always a threat. In fact I think he should have focused on the Classics instead of trying to win the Tour de France. I understand why he did that, because there was a time when I was the same age that for a while I thought I could win a Grand Tour.

"The thing you have to remember with Tom is he didn't have long. He won Flanders in April 1961 and died in July 1967. If he had lived I think he could have done what I did and won every Classic. Of the ones he didn't win, he definitely had the ability to win the Flèche Wallonne and Liège–Bastogne–Liège because their routes suited him. He was second in Paris–Tours, and in Ghent–Wevelgem too, so he could have won both of those in time. The only Classic that maybe didn't suit him was Paris–Roubaix, but I know he was sixth behind me in 1965 and he was in the first ten on other occasions. If you can finish sixth you can win Roubaix. He had the potential if he'd had the opportunities."

It's a glowing assessment from a man who doesn't throw compliments around lightly. Simpson underlined his status in world cycling with a masterful victory in the 1964 Milan–San Remo, ahead of France's Raymond Poulidor. But while he'd been making his way as a pro, a growing band of British racers had followed Simpson over the Channel, and by the time he won in Italy a handful had filtered into the pro ranks.

The best of them were Alan Ramsbottom from Clayton-le-Moors in Lancashire, Vin Denson from Chester, and Barry Hoban, a Yorkshireman from Stanley near Wakefield. Ramsbottom and Denson had been good road racers in the UK, a fact that Ramsbottom, the quiet man of this story, underlined with 16th place in the 1963 Tour de France. Hoban was more like Simpson: a track rider first, then a road racer with a rapid sprint and a very shrewd racing brain.

Denson and Ramsbottom were part of the French Pelforth-Lejeune team in 1964, where Denson earned a reputation as a strong team rider, the kind that is called a super-domestique in pro racing. He was recruited later by the teams of the two top sixties racers, Rik Van Looy and Jacques Anquetil, and was due to ride for Simpson in an Italian squad in 1968. However, Simpson's death hit him badly and his appetite for pro racing had almost gone by then.

Ramsbottom appeared to fall between two schools. He was a very good climber, capable of performing in the Ardennes Classics, as eighth in the 1963 Liège–Bastogne–Liège shows, and capable of winning shorter stage races, like the Tour de Haute-Loire in 1964, but he wasn't as driven as Simpson. It seemed that a misunderstanding kept him out of the Pelforth team for the 1964 Tour de France, but in all probability the team leader, Henri Anglade, didn't want Ramsbottom because he thought he'd work for Simpson as he was due to join his Peugeot BP team in 1965. Ramsbottom had moved to Belgium by then, but neither the life nor the racing there suited him and he returned to the UK and his job as a sewing machine technician in 1966.

That was a shame, because Ramsbottom had the talent to be a good pro, and he would have been a very good pro if he was racing now. But in the sixties if you were British it wasn't enough just to be good; you had to be twice as good as a Belgian or a Frenchman or an Italian, and you had to be a bit bloody-minded. Looking back, the only British riders who made money from top-level road racing during the sixties were Denson, because of his value as a domestique, Simpson, because he was one of the best of the whole era, and Hoban, because he was a winner and he had enormous drive. And even Hoban had to wait until the latter part of the decade and into the seventies to realize his potential, because of what he went through in his first professional year.

"I turned pro for Mercier-BP for 21 pounds a week basic salary, which was great in those days, when Manchester United footballers only got paid 20 per week. On top of that there were bonus payments, and a share of the prize money, so I was making 60 or 70 pounds a week. I was single and had a good bit of cash saved by the end of 1964, but boy I had to work for it. I rode all of the Classics, then the Tour of Spain, which was from late April to early May back then. I won two stages in it, so I was the first British rider to win a Vuelta stage. Then my team manager, Antonin Magne, put me in Bordeaux–Paris, which took preparation and recovery to cope with well, and I got neither.

"I was so trusting. I had to travel for two days by train to get to Bordeaux, so I asked Magne what I should do to cope with the journey and make sure my legs weren't in bits at the end of it, and he told me to only eat apples. So I sat there chomping through a whole bag of apples all the way down France.

"I wanted to ride the Tour de France that year, but to give me a little leg stretcher before it Magne made me ride the Midi Libre stage race. I was tired before the Tour de France but got through, and I nearly won a stage in Bordeaux, but I was done in after that and it took me until the end of the following year and into 1966 before I felt myself again. Magne still put me in the end of season Classics, though."

It was as though Brits were a commodity to be used by European pro cycling, and that attitude lasted for a long time. Even Simpson said, "It's a dog eat dog world," but then added something that encapsulates his character: "But if you are one of the top dogs earning ten thousand pounds or more per year it's not so bad." And Simpson was earning that and more by 1965, when he had his biggest ever pay day and probably tripled his year's takings. But before looking at what was to be glory of Simpson's career, it's worth considering the state of cycling back in Britain.

*   *   *   *   *

For a start Britain had another bright international star in Beryl Burton. Born Beryl Charnock in Leeds, she grew up and lived for the rest of her life in Morley. She suffered from rheumatic fever as a child and was warned against doing any form of exercise, but she was incredibly determined and decided to do what she wanted, despite the doctors' advice and despite a heart arrhythmia she had all her life.

Burton was introduced to cycling in 1955 by her husband Charlie, who says: "She was handy from the start but not that competent. We used to have to push her round a bit. Slowly she got better. By the second year she was one of the lads and could ride with any of us. By the third year she was going out in front and leading us all. By then it was 1957 and Beryl decided to do a bit of time trialling because I was dabbling at it."

That was how it worked in cycling clubs then. The club run was still the main thing, racing was second – at least it was for Charlie. Beryl had talent, and in 1957, when she won her first national title in the 100-mile time trial, Charlie decided to dedicate himself totally to backing his wife's racing career.

They became a two-person Team GB. They travelled everywhere together, Charlie doing logistics and getting the bikes ready, Beryl racing and winning. She won the world pursuit title in Amsterdam in 1959. Then they travelled behind the Iron Curtain to Leipzig in 1960, getting into all sorts of scrapes to do it, and Beryl won the road race and track pursuit world titles. She won the pursuit title twice more in 1962 and 1963, and took silver medals in 1961 and 1964. Burton's career continued from strength to strength and, as we shall see later, it became more remarkable as it did so.

Time trialling was going through a change, one that may have boosted interest but also one that some believe held Britain back internationally. Up until the early sixties the best short-distance time triallists, those who won national titles and set records at distances up to 50 miles, were mostly track riders and they did time trials on a fixed gear too. Then, as the decade progressed, riders like Dave Bonner and Charlie McCoy switched to time trialling on multi-geared bikes. Courses changed too, moving to duel carriageways in search of faster times, which were possible not just because their better road surfaces were faster but also because of the dragging effect from passing traffic. Gear ratios got bigger, so riders could exploit the speed potential of these new courses, and a new kind of time triallist was born, men and women capable of churning away at a huge gear ratio. However, they weren't as adept in other branches of the sport, and often didn't ride anything but time trials, which meant that these specialists could still be beaten by track-trained and road racing rivals in national title races.

The formation of the British Cycling Federation in 1959 meant that road racing was no longer seen by the establishment as an outlaw sport, and it grew as a result. With secure sponsorship in place, the Milk Race went from strength to strength, and professional road racing blossomed for a while in the UK, although the rules kept changing as to whether the racers were called professionals or independents and whether amateurs could race with them or not. It was a very confusing situation; suffice it to say there were some good races, many of which were created by the BLRC, although they never got the credit for it, and even some Europeans took part in them.

The Manx Trophy was one, a pro race that used to be part of the much missed Isle of Man Cycling Week. Fausto Coppi raced in the Manx Premier, as did Jacques Anquetil and Rik Van Looy. Tom Simpson won it in 1963 and again in 1967. Other great races included the Vaux Grand Prix in the North Pennines and the London to Holyhead race, a Percy Stallard creation from 1951, which he modelled on the super-long Bordeaux–Paris. Riders started at Marble Arch in London at 5 a.m. and raced the 261 miles along the A5 to the far north-west of Wales in a single day.

Tom Simpson won London–Holyhead in 1965, just before crashing in the Tour de France and then having to retire with a badly poisoned hand. That poor performance left Simpson with very few contracts for the lucrative after-Tour criterium circuit, where riders were paid a contract fee to ride races all over Europe during August and part of September. The criteriums aren't as important now as they used to be, but for pros in the 1960s they were like Christmas for a shopkeeper and a big proportion of the year's takings could be gathered in just a few weeks. However, not riding them did at least allow Simpson to prepare fully for the world road race title, which was held on a hilly circuit near San Sebastian in northern Spain.

Simpson arrived in good form and told the Great Britain team he was up for winning. They were up for helping, too, because on top of the patriotic desire to stick it to the Europeans, Simpson promised them a cash bonus if he won. Most of them did what they could, even if some were playing in a league well above what they were used to, but Barry Hoban's riding more than made up for that.

"The Spaniards attacked from the off," Hoban recalls, "and Tom told me to go with anything that looked promising. I got in a break on the second lap with some Spaniards, Arie Den Hartog and Peter Post from Holland. Franco Balmamion was there from Italy, Roger Swerts from Belgium, and a few others, and although some of them were sitting on, the rest worked well together and we quickly gained some time. Every big cycling nation but the French were there, so Tom quite rightly thought that this was the move, and within a few laps he'd bridged over to us with another Spaniard and the German rider, Rudi Altig. That was my signal to start working and I didn't miss a turn, really pulling so we gained time. But as the race wore on, some of the riders stopped contributing as much, and Balmamion hadn't done much work anyway. Tom started to get worried, and I'll never forget him riding alongside me and saying, 'Barry, if you feel like falling off then fall off in front of Balmamion.' I could tell he was thinking about attacking."

And attack he did. With two and a half laps to go Simpson shifted into his top gear, 54 x 14, and went hard all the way up Hernani Hill without once looking behind him. He saved that for the top, where he saw that Rudi Altig was the only one with him. He couldn't have had anyone better. Altig was a good track racer, a former world pursuit champion, and a generous rider who worked hard if he had a sniff of victory. He was the better rider on the flat, Simpson a bit faster uphill, but they complemented each other and they stayed away to the finish.

Altig must have fancied his chances, being a good sprinter, but Simpson was too. According to Barry Hoban, who later became one of the best road sprinters in the game, "You took Tom to a sprint at the end of a hard race at your peril. He was very fast, he'd been a good track pursuiter and was one of the fastest six-day riders, but the thing is he didn't lose his sprint after a long race. I wasn't at all surprised when he beat Altig."

Simpson was world champion. A few weeks later he won another monument, the Tour of Lombardy, now called Il Lombardia. It's a hilly race in northern Italy and Simpson took apart Gianni Motta, one of the best Italian racers of his generation, in a two-man break, eventually dropping him to win in Como. It was beautiful, a British racer wearing the rainbow jersey of world champion winning one of the world's biggest races, with the world's best riders chasing behind but still finishing three minutes in arrears.

His success fired the imaginations of young British racers, who for several years had been coming to Europe to race, mostly to the Ghent area where Simpson lived. Many lodged in the Café den Engel, a bar-cum-boarding house run by one of Simpson's most loyal supporters, Albert Beurick, and his mother, referred to affectionately by the young Brits as Fat Albert and Ma Beurick.

It was a hard way to do things. The staple form of racing was the amateur *kermesse*, originating from Belgium, which was a race held in a town or village, usually on the same day as the local festival, where everybody was under 25 and hell bent on winning the cash prizes to keep the dream going. That dream was to turn pro, and if they hadn't done so by 25 they stopped racing and got a job. The races were desperate affairs, fast, furious and with all sorts of illicit deals and tricky practices going on, but some of the better Brits like Keith Butler made it through this tough school and raced as pros.

It was preferable to go to France, but French racing was more regulated and it was difficult to get into a French amateur team. One who did was a teenage time trial prodigy, the youngest-ever winner of the BBAR at 18, Peter Hill. He was given a place in the AC Sotteville club just outside Rouen, where he was coached by Jacques Anquetil's coach, André Boucher. Hill won or was highly placed in several big French amateur races and graduated to a place in the Peugeot BP pro team, alongside Simpson, in 1967.

*   *   *   *   *

Going back to 1965, Simpson's heyday was a wonderful time for British cycling. The sport had many loyal followers and a good few participants, but it wasn't a mainstream one; then Simpson's story struck a chord with the media. Here was a working-class lad who went abroad and beat the locals at their own game in their own back yard. One journalist likened it to a kid from rural France travelling to the UK to become our best cricketer.

But when they interviewed Simpson they found out there was more. He was intelligent, witty and had an air of continental chic that made him extra interesting. Simpson was voted the Daily Express Sportsman of the Year, the Sports Journalists' Association's Sportsman of the Year and the BBC Sports Personality of the Year, beating football's Bobby Moore – and you couldn't get more mainstream than that in the mid-sixties.

Simpson was a star and he loved it. He was huge in Europe, where they loved him for his Britishness, and big in Britain, where they loved him for beating the Europeans but also just for being that little bit European himself. And in that he represented something important for the country at the time.

Then England won the football World Cup, and Simpson was left needing to do something bigger to grab centre stage again. He had to win the Tour de France, but in 1966 that was out of the question. He broke his leg in a skiing accident and played catch-up all year; 1967 had to be different.

The Tour returned to national teams that year, and with no Jacques Anquetil in it, Simpson would lead a British assault on the Tour with a good chance of winning. There was just one minor problem. Whereas nowadays Great Britain could field a good Tour de France team, in 1967 only half of the British riders who started the Tour were full-time professionals in Europe. They were absolutely committed to Simpson, but there were limits to what they could do to help when the race got going. It was the best deal Simpson was going to get, however, so he went for it.

He moved up the overall standings on the two important stages during the first week, and lay in sixth place overall when the race entered the Alps. He was behind the eventual winner, but ahead of the two who finished second and third in Paris, so a podium was likely, and of course Simpson still thought he could win. The British team was down to six from 12 starters, but their leader could cope with that. What he couldn't cope with was the stomach bug that hit him on the hardest day in the Alps.

Simpson lost a lot of time, but during the next two stages he fought back to seventh overall, even though he wasn't able to eat solid food and was only kept going on glucose drips administered by the Italian team's doctor. Simpson should have dropped out of that Tour, but that would have been giving in, and he never did that.

The 13th stage, held on July 13, ran from Marseilles to Carpentras by way of Mont Ventoux. In the summer of 1967 the whole of Europe basked under a heatwave; people as far north as Belgium had died from heat stress; and the Ventoux's white top was a solar furnace. It would be the crux of the stage, and for three-quarters of the climb Simpson kept his place near the front and kept his hopes alive. Then he faltered.

He began to weave all over the road. Simpson's team car stopped and the mechanic, Harry Hall, got out, caught him and said, "It's over, Tom." But Simpson replied, "No, Harry, get me straight, tighten my toe straps and push." Hall did, and Simpson rode a few hundred metres further, then fell. He was two kilometres from the summit.

Simpson was unconscious. Hall tried what he knew of first aid, then the Tour de France doctor arrived and took over. Nothing happened. They flew the fallen racer to hospital in Avignon, trying to revive him all the way, but he was dead already.

There was an autopsy. Amphetamines were found in Simpson's body, and that, and what happened that day, has haunted British cycling up until very recently. Simpson became the man every promising racer was compared with. The race he died in, and the desperate measures he took to try to win it, and in all probability other races as well, had the effect of making the great European races seem bigger and more daunting than they really were for generations of British racers, even if only subconsciously. It was an attitude that lasted, with some notable exceptions, until the great revolution in British cycling that started with Chris Boardman in 1992 and led to Bradley Wiggins winning the Tour de France 20 years later.

CHAPTER 3

FLYING THE FLAG

Simpson's death did not put an end to British cycling success, but did change its trajectory. The numbers who followed his template and moved to Europe to race as amateurs dropped dramatically for a while. So much so that for a time during the 1970s Barry Hoban was the only UK rider in big races, although that didn't stop him winning.

But before Hoban really came into his own and became the long-time standard bearer of British cycling in Europe – and in contrast to the tragedy of that year's Tour de France – Great Britain had its best-ever Road World Championships in 1967, taking two world titles through Beryl Burton and Graham Webb.

Webb had the raw power to be a great cyclist. He was physically gifted, single-minded and uncompromising, but his story shows how, even with all that going for him, European pro cycling wasn't going out of its way to include British riders back then. In two years Webb went from being a new pro with a salary that was twice what Eddy Merckx got when he turned pro three years earlier, to working as a crane driver in a Belgian factory.

Webb had a hard start in life. He was born in Birmingham in 1944, the youngest of five children, and his father was killed in the war shortly afterwards. His family were poor and Webb's health suffered. He was given the last rites twice as a child but he pulled through, got a bike and fell in love for ever.

"I started doing crazy long rides, 100 miles from Birmingham to Gloucester and back, trying to do it non-stop, and I managed it the third time I did it," he says. It was the sort of training that makes or breaks young cyclists, but it made Webb, and he grew into a phenomenal physical specimen. He won his first race at 17, nearly beating the hour for 25 miles when not many did that, and nobody did it on an old sports bike like the one Webb was riding.

Webb's physique was perfect for cycling. Once when he was examined by a Belgian sports doctor he broke the lung capacity machine. "I blew down this tube like they told me to and the cylinders came out of the top. They couldn't believe it, so they made me do it again, and the same thing happened," he says.

He won time trials, he won on the track, he set records and he won road races. Like Robinson, Simpson and Hoban, Webb's talent was too big for racing in the UK, so in 1967 he moved to Holland and started winning there. He was excellent at the fast, round-the-houses street races they have, not just winning but lapping the field, on one memorable occasion several times. But as well as racing Webb trained like crazy too, as he recalls.

"When I was an amateur living in Holland I raced three evenings a week on the track but I still trained 200 to 300 kilometres during the day. I've always liked pushing myself, and I could do that in the endless landscape up there. It grows on you after a while."

Webb even rode from Ghent to Herleen for the world title races, where he dominated the amateur event. He played with the opposition really, getting in an early break then dropping back to pace a team-mate to the front. When Webb got there he found the break had split, so he just rode up to the leaders then accelerated rather than sprinted out of the final corner to win by lengths. Behind him was the promising French rider Claude Guyot, as well as Rini Pijnen, who went on to have a good pro career, and Roger De Vlaeminck, who went on to be a cycling legend.

When Webb was offered a place in the Mercier-BP team for 1968 on good money he looked set for life. But contracts in pro cycling, especially back then, aren't awarded for what a rider has done, they are awarded for what they are expected to do, and the expectations on Webb were high. There was no settling-in period and no room for mistakes.

A few years ago I visited Webb at his home in Wachtebeke in Northern Flanders, and this is how he described what happened to him next all those years ago. "I trained in Sardinia in January 1968 but got stuck there because of a transport strike, so I missed the team's first races in February in the South of France. Then all my bikes, clothing and equipment got pinched out of my car while going back to Belgium. Losing the bikes wasn't a problem, but losing my shoes was. It took a year to break in new shoes back then. I raced in Het Volk the day after I got back to Belgium and my toe straps fell apart on the first climb. Next day in Kuurne–Brussels–Kuurne my knee went on a climb. Then it went again during the first stage of Paris–Nice.

"And that was it for my team. I don't think they ever forgave me. It was like they were waiting to say, 'Oh here's another world champion who was a one-day wonder.' A registered letter came saying they'd stop paying me until my results improved. I won four pro races in 1968, and I sent them the results, but they still didn't pay me. I was left with the choice of racing for nothing or taking them to court. If I did that I knew no French team would ever touch me again. But in the end I had to, and I won my case."

Webb's hero to zero journey went like lightning. He was due to race for a Belgian team in 1969, but then their manager told him that the sponsor had no money. "He said I could keep my bike and continue racing, so I picked it up, handed it to him and said, 'If you think I'm racing for you for nothing, then you can think again,' and that was it. I turned my back on it. Next day I got a job in a furniture factory, and eventually I ended up with a good job in Belgium as a crane driver."

With no job, deep in debt, Webb could have high-tailed it back to Britain, but he didn't. "No, there was nothing for me there, only bad memories. Anyway, when I first came to Europe I thought I was on holiday, and I still do," he says.

And there will always be his world title; nothing can take Webb's rainbow bands away from him, because in bike-mad Flanders they really mean something. In the streets of Wachtebeke, where he's lived for over 30 years, people still come up to say hello and make a fuss and ask his opinion on the races today. To them Graham Webb will always be a Wereldkampion first, and a crane driver second.

These days Webb doesn't ride his bike as often or as far, since his aorta ruptured a few years ago, but I went with him on a short ride and he soon settled down to a good pace going north towards

Holland. "I love this flat landscape, but it's an acquired taste. It's timeless and it slowly gets into your blood," he told me.

In the eighties, Webb got the urge to race again. He says that he feels more Flemish than British. "I even dream in Flemish, and my wife says that when I talk in my sleep it's in Flemish," he says. His adoption was sealed when he won four Belgian track titles with the non-UCI federation he raced under.

Webb isn't the slightest bit bitter about his pro racing career not working out, despite the talent he had. "It happens. It happens in show business too. Sometimes talented people don't make it. Anyway, so many good things have happened to me outside of cycling, so you won't find me complaining," he says.

*   *   *   *   *

In 1967 Beryl Burton was also a class apart at the World Championships in Holland. Having just lost out in the pursuit title earlier in the week to Ludmilla Zadorozhnaya, she set about the road race as though there was nobody else in it. Burton shook the peloton until only Zadorozhnaya could follow her, then left her as well, completing what had virtually been a time trial to win by 1 minute 47 seconds from the Russian and nearly six minutes ahead of the rider in third place.

Later that year Burton was invited to compete in the Grand Prix des Nations, a time trial event for professionals that ran through the Chevreuse valley just south of Paris and into the city. She completed the 73.5-kilometre course at an average speed of 41.55 kph. The winner, the 1965 Tour de France winner Felice Gimondi, averaged 47.5 kph, and although Burton was the last of the 13 invited riders, it wasn't by much. Her presence must have terrified some of the slower men in the event.

It was vintage Burton, the Yorkshire woman was at the height of her powers in 1967, and she achieved something that year that was even bigger than the world title. She set a record for the 12-hour time trial that is still the best-ever performance in the UK by a woman, which is quite amazing, but at the time it was also faster than the men's record set in the same race, which is incredible.

There are very few sports calling for strength and endurance in which a woman out-performs the men, although it does happen in ultra endurance events. However, the 12-hour isn't ultra endurance; it's a long bike ride but it requires strength and speed and not just the ability to keep going. What makes this story better is that the man Burton beat was a friend, Mike McNamara, and the fact that when she caught McNamara early in the race, she offered him a liquorice allsorts sweet, which he accepted. The other important thing is that although she won, Burton did not become the national 12-hour champion. The title went to McNamara, because it was then the men's title race, not an open title as it is now.

This story has become Burton's signature, and it rather suggests that she breezed through life offering everybody sweets, which is not true. She was very down to earth, and chomping on liquorice allsorts while setting a record is in no way out of character for a woman who got her knitting out to relax after events and even during tea stops on the Morley club runs. But Burton could be blunt at times, and didn't like young men who gave up work to train to be better cyclists, observing that they often got slower "because they are messing about all day on their bikes instead of training on them".

She didn't mess about. Her training was a diet of hard miles squeezed in between housework, being a mother and doing farm work for a friend. Burton would also get incredibly nervous before a race, often being sick, and she was ultra competitive, once refusing to attend the medal ceremony or even talk to her daughter Denise after being beaten by her to the national road race title. By then Burton was in her forties and near the end of her racing career, while Denise Burton was getting to the peak of hers. It sounds like terrible sour grapes, but Burton senior was angry with herself for losing, rather than for being beaten by Denise, and angry with her daughter for not contributing to their breakaway move. It wasn't a family thing; it was a bike racing thing.

Awarded an MBE in 1964 and an OBE in 1968, Burton carried on riding her bike all her life. She died in 1996, while out on her bike delivering invitations to her 59th birthday party. The cause of death was heart failure, and it may be that the arrhythmia finally caught up with her, but her daughter thinks otherwise. "Her competitiveness and relentless drive eventually wore her body out."

The last British world champion of the sixties scored a silver medal in the Amateur Pursuit Championships in 1967, turned professional and won gold in the pro pursuit the following year. His name is Hugh Porter and until recently he was best known by many viewers as the BBC's voice of cycling, who commentated on the run of recent British Olympic and world championship success. Now in his later years, he is a master of words – and probably unique in having quoted a Russian proverb in a cycling commentary: "They say let a man be judged by his deeds not by his words. Well, Bradley Wiggins's legs have just spoken."

But there was a time when Porter's legs spoke volumes too. He turned professional to ride the new London six-day race in 1967, held inside Earls Court on a tiny prefabricated track with very steep 50-degree bankings. The event was meant to be a showcase for Tom

Simpson, who as well as a top road racer was one of the best six-day riders of the time, but that wasn't to be. Porter crashed and broke his collar bone, but the Earls Court six-day was still a big success, and when the event moved to Wembley, where a much better track was used, it provided many years of exciting racing.

In the days before racing went open, so there was one elite pursuit title, the professional pursuit was over 5,000 metres, and the amateur event was over 4,000, as the elite is now. The longer distance suited Porter better, as he explains: "I wasn't as explosive as some pursuiters are, so it took me longer to get going, but the extra kilometre the pros did allowed me to make good any early losses."

His 1968 world title came on a big outdoor track, the former Olympic velodrome in Rome, and the following winter saw Porter break into six-days in a more serious way. "They were very hard, not as hard as they had been with somebody on the track for the whole six days and long neutralized periods so one of each team could sleep, but when I rode the sixes the racing sometimes went on into the early hours of the morning, especially in Germany.

"The big killers, though, were the long Madisons. They have one-hour Madisons in the six-days now, with maybe a shorter one earlier in the evening, but when I did them, 100-kilometre Madisons were common, and you might get three Madisons in one evening in some sixes. It was a hard life but we had fun doing it. There were some characters on the six-day circuit back then, and I remember fights and some pretty good after-race parties," he says.

The final person to move this story on from the sixties is Barry Hoban. He won the Tour de France stage that was given to the British team by the Tour peloton the day after Tom Simpson died. There's been a dispute between Hoban and Vin Denson ever since about how that happened, but it was clearly the right result because Hoban took the British torch from Simpson on the continent, and also he married Simpson's widow, and took on his young family, so in a sense he's been living with Simpson's ghost ever since. Hoban was the right man to win.

Hoban and Simpson weren't close friends, but they have sometimes been portrayed as such. Simpson was closer to Denson, which is not surprising. Denson is easy-going, affable and good company. Hoban wasn't easy-going when he was racing; he was competitive, he could be prickly, and he was ambitious. For Simpson he was a bit too much like Cassius to his Julius Caesar; Hoban had a lean and hungry look and he needed watching.

Hoban is 72 now, semi-retired and as affable as anyone. "I admired Tom, but I wanted to beat him too. He was a class act. Tom achieved the record he did because he attacked so many times, and because of that he got into a lot of winning situations. And when Tom was in a winning situation he could look after himself. He was a great role model, but we weren't close friends. I remember once I was away in a break and Tom got Altig and a few of his pals to help him chase me down, and I asked him afterwards why he'd done it. He just looked at me and said, 'Barry, you need to remember that I'm the number-one British rider on the continent, not you.'"

Hoban was fifth in the 1967 Tour of Flanders and came very close to landing a classic when he lost Paris–Tours by a hair's breadth in a sprint with Rik Van Looy. It was a bitter disappointment but a good lesson. "It changed the way I sprinted after that. Coming into the finish Van Looy knew I was the fastest of a small group that contested the finish, and I was glued to his back wheel. Then with 500 metres to go he stopped pedalling. I did too but the rest were riding away from us, so I panicked and shot past Van Looy, who quickly locked on to my back wheel. Now he had the element of surprise, and when he went with 200 to go he got a bike length in the time it took me to react. I gained on him with every pedal rev after that, but I was still just behind him on the line."

The Tour de France was for national teams again in 1968, the last time this ever happened, although a return is often talked about. Hoban led the GB team, but there was no feeling that he was going to win the Tour, as there had been with Simpson the year before. "We were aiming for stage wins and I started the race with good form, attacking like crazy on the stage that went through Flanders to Roubaix," he says.

"My life in Europe began in Northern France in 1962, and by 1968 I was based near Ghent in Belgium, so it was incredible to break away and win the King of the Mountains points at the top of the Muur van Geraardsbergen. I climbed past two solid walls of people, the noise they made was immense, the authorities reckoned one million people stood by the roadside to watch that stage go by."

Hoban's break was caught before Roubaix, but he continued attacking and continued coming close to adding another stage victory to the one he won in 1967. It was bound to happen, and when it did the victory was historic.

That year Hoban won Britain's first-ever Tour de France mountain stage. It was in the Alps, a 200-kilometre stage from Grenoble to Sallanches-Cordon. Hoban attacked on the descent of the Champ Laurent climb. "I was lying third in the intermediate sprints competition, and a sprint was coming up in Albertville. It was early in the stage and the overall contenders weren't racing yet on the climbs, so I thought I'd make certain of getting the sprint points by going early for them. The problem was a Spanish rider, Andres Gandarias, came with me. He was fifth overall and I knew I'd not stop away if he came with me, because everybody would chase him. So I told him I was only going for the sprint points and wouldn't work in a break after that," Hoban says.

Gandarias took the hint and dropped back, but Hoban had pulled the wool over his eyes – he kept going after picking up the sprint points. He climbed the Col d'Aravis, and then he carried on to the foot of the Col de la Colombière. "I had some climbers chasing me, but I was good downhill and they weren't so good. My plan was to gain time going down and keep my cool going up. Anyway, the Colombière south side was my kind of climb, wide and with an even gradient. I dropped into my lowest gear at the start of it, then shifted up until the gear matched my natural climbing rhythm. I was riding within myself; riding, hopefully, to stay away until the finish."

Hoban reached the top of the Colombière with a six-minute lead. He dropped down the north side like a stone, gaining more time, then made a time trial effort along the Arve valley to Sallanches, but still not giving it full gas. "I used my 14 sprocket in the valley, not the 13. I needed to preserve as much as possible in my legs for the last climb."

Hoban duly powered up the steep but short Sallanches-Cordon climb under the shadow of Mont Blanc to win the stage by four minutes, and become the first British rider to take a mountain stage in the Tour de France. "With my mountains points, the Desgrange prize, the stage prize and a cow called Estelle, I won £1,200 during that stage – not a bad pay day in 1968," says Hoban, who sold Estelle that night to a local farmer but still has her bell on his study wall.

Hoban finished the 1968 Tour in 33rd place overall with one stage win; he was sixth in the points classification, sixth in the King of the Mountains competition and third in the intermediate sprints race, behind compatriot Michael Wright.

Wright was something of a one-off in the British cycling story. He was a good rider, winner of three stages in the Tour de France and four in the Vuelta a Espana, and finished fifth overall in the 1969 Vuelta, which at that time was the highest ever finish by a Brit in a Grand Tour – but he hardly spoke a word of English. He was born British, in Bishop's Stortford in Hertfordshire in 1941, but his father was killed in action during the Second World War and his mother married a Belgian soldier. When Wright was three the family emigrated to Belgium and he grew up in Liège speaking French.

There were a few other British pros around in Europe as Hoban's career marched on. Derek Harrison improved through the latter part of the decade, winning some good races. He was part of the GB team in the 1968 Tour de France. Then when the race returned to trade teams in 1969 he was there in the French squad, Frimatic-Viva-De Gribaldy, finishing third on a stage to Maastricht and in 32nd place overall. But Hoban was the British star. He won two Tour de France stages back to back in what was a cracking season.

Hoban started out the year by underlining his Classics credentials with third place in Liège–Bastogne–Liège and seventh in the Tour of Flanders, two races won by Eddy Merckx when he was literally in the form of his life. "I'll never forget Flanders that year when Merckx climbed the Muur van Geraardsbergen. I was with him in the break at the bottom of the Muur. He didn't attack, instead Merckx just hammered up those cobbles going faster and faster. Soon there was a gap behind him to Franco Bitossi, then another gap to me, then one between me and Felice Gimondi, then one between him and a few other riders, and we all just about held station all the way up the climb by going as hard as we could, literally eyeballs out. Then at the top Merckx kept going. Bitossi moved over and looked back at me, I did the same to Gimondi and he did the same to the guys behind him. We were all smashed and Merckx just kept going. Gimondi jumped away near the end to finish five and a half minutes behind Merckx, and we were another two and a half behind Gimondi."

The win that started Hoban's Tour de France double was especially sweet. "It was on the velodrome in Bordeaux, where in my first Tour de France in 1964 I got beaten into second place by André Darrigade, who was a great sprinter but he'd got an almighty push from a team-mate to get past me. I was in a break in 1969, and I liked track finishes because I'd ridden the track a lot as an amateur. I latched on to Harm Ottenbross, who went early, then moved up the banking slightly and used its slope to zoom past him.

"Next day was a similar-length stage to the Bordeaux one; it was 200 kilometres to Brive. The route was hillier and I didn't expect to feature, but I got in another breakaway. I had to be a bit crafty, though. I wasn't going as well as the day before, and Jos Spruyt from Eddy Merckx's team told me that if I wasn't going to work he'd stop working too. I explained I didn't feel good but promised him that if he attacked I wouldn't chase him. He did attack, I didn't chase but the others did, and when they caught him that set me up perfectly to take the sprint."

Hoban would eventually win eight Tour de France stages, six of which he won with his fearsome sprint. That fact has caused some journalists to compare Hoban to Mark Cavendish, but it doesn't bear examination, and Hoban is the first to admit it.

"We aren't alike," he says. "For a start I wouldn't class myself as a sprinter. I was more of a Classics rider. I did win Tour stages in bunch sprints, beating some of the fastest riders of my day, but I didn't win every bunch sprint, where Mark wins a bunch sprint almost every time he's in with a chance. The bigger difference between us, though, is I won from breakaway groups, and I could win on my own," Hoban says.

Hoban crashed out of the 1970 Tour de France early on, but the big cycling news in Britain that year was that the World Championships were held in Leicester. It was the first time Britain had hosted a modern world cycling championships. The track events were held on the concrete 333-metre velodrome at the Saffron Lane Sports Centre, the 100-kilometre team time trial was based on the Six Hills dual carriageway to the north of the city, and the road races were held on an undulating circuit based on the Mallory Park motor race track.

The track events went well for Great Britain, with Hugh Porter taking his second gold medal in the professional pursuit, while Ian Hallam rode to a silver medal in the amateur pursuit and Beryl Burton completed a full set of pursuit medals by taking the women's bronze. But the star performer really was Les West in the professional road race.

West won the 1965 and 1967 Milk Races, but he shot to world fame when he took the silver medal behind Evert Dolman in the 1966 amateur world road race championships, held at the Nurburgring in Germany. West was promised a place in Jacques Anquetil's Bic team for 1967, but for some reason the contract never turned up.

He stayed in the UK and set his sights on the 1968 Olympic road race in Mexico City, but had a disaster there when he punctured early on in the race then had to wait an age before a service car arrived to help him. West chased alone for 30 miles, during which time he had to change bikes twice, before giving in to the inevitable and abandoning the race.

ABOVE: The British were winning major cycling races from the earliest days of serious competition. Here, Leon Meredith, Ernest Payne, Charles Kingsbury and Benjamin Jones take gold in the team pursuit at the 1908 London Olympics.

BELOW: The British men's cycling team from the 1956 Olympics in Melbourne. The team came away with a silver medal in the team road race and two bronze medals – in the 4,000m team pursuit and the individual road race.

LEFT: Reg Harris at the track they named after him in Fallowfield, Manchester. The track has gone now but Harris's records still live on, having become world professional sprint champion four times, as well as winning two Olympic silver medals.

BELOW: Tom Simpson racing in the 1966 Tour de France. Simpson was Britain's first professional road World Champion and winner of three of the five monuments of cycling – Milan-San Remo, the Tour of Flanders and the Giro di Lombardia.

ABOVE: Barry Hoban after scoring his second consecutive stage win in the 1969 Tour de France, on stage 19. This was the first time a British rider had won two stages in a row on the Tour, a feat that was not repeated until Mark Cavendish bettered it in 2008.

LEFT: The Tour de France first visited the UK in 1974 when a stage was held on the newly built Plympton bypass in Devon. The next time the Tour visited the UK was when London staged the prologue of the 2007 race – a considerably more high-profile event.

ABOVE: Robert Millar wins the 1984 King of the Mountains competition to become the first British rider to win a Tour de France jersey outright. His fourth place overall was the best British performance until Bradley Wiggins matched it in 2009 (later promoted to third).

ABOVE: Sean Yates cornering on his way to victory in the stage six time trial of the 1988 Tour de France. In 1994, he went on to be only the third British rider to wear the yellow jersey, after Tom Simpson and Chris Boardman.

ABOVE: Tim Gould takes a drink after the Canmore, Alberta leg of the 1998 mountain bike World Cup. A year later, he was inducted into the Mountain Bike Hall of Fame in Colorado.

BELOW: Downhill racer Steve Peat celebrates on the podium after picking up the World Champion's rainbow jersey in Mount Stromlo in Canberra in 2009.

ABOVE: Bike design genius and incredible athlete, Graeme Obree crouches over the bike he designed and built on his way to setting a new world hour record in July 1993. He broke the record again in 1994 and was twice the 4,000m pursuit World Champion.

ABOVE: Chris Boardman takes his first yellow jersey in the prologue of his first-ever Tour de France in 1994, riding a road version of the Lotus bike he rode to the 1992 Olympic individual pursuit title.

West turned professional in 1969 for the British-based Holdsworth team. "More for the change in competition really," he says. "I bet my earnings and winnings added together as an amateur were more than most pros got back then." There was a reasonable circuit of pro races in the UK by 1969, and it grew during the seventies with West as one of its stars. However, his true worth was proved on those Leicester roads back in 1970, where West got into the winning move with some of the best road racers in the world. They were Jean-Pierre Monseré of Belgium, the Dane Leif Mortensen, the Italian Felice Gimondi, and West, and that was their order over the line, where West's sprint was compromised by cramp.

It was an amazing performance, though, especially as it was done on a diet of British pro races that were shorter and much slower than their continental counterparts. To this day only Tom Simpson and Mark Cavendish have finished higher than West. He's still riding and still winning too. In 2003 West added a National Masters Road Race title to the ones he won as an amateur and as a professional.

It's interesting to compare how riders trained between the generations. Reg Harris did a lot of road riding for a track sprinter, much more than Sir Chris Hoy did and sprinters do today. But when Harris was training to get into shape for the World Championships his road miles were all done on fixed gear, and his track training was simple. He would warm up at the Fallowfield track, which in his heyday was renamed the Harris Stadium, then do five flat-out sprints with long rest periods between them. That's a surprisingly modern approach, because we now know that the anaerobic mechanisms in the body that power sprinting take a long time to recharge.

Tom Simpson was very up to date. He experimented with interval training and trained behind a motorized Derny pacing bike. He was also very meticulous with his diet; he tried to eat as little processed food as possible and would drink vast quantities of liquidized vegetables and fruit, which ensured he got plenty of vitamins and anti-oxidants but in a form that was easy to digest. Liquidizing fruit and veg is something the Team Sky chef does now so that Sky riders get the nutrients they need without loading their stomachs with bulk that has to be broken down before the nutrients are released.

Barry Hoban was less fussy with his diet, but he started the training build-up to each season with a three-day fast. "I believed it forced my body to burn up all the rubbish and toxins that accumulate there," he says. What it in fact probably did was switch on a gene response that made his body burn fat for fuel at higher exercise intensities. Fasting, and training in a fasted state, is something endurance athletes do today to provoke the same response.

Hoban wasn't a believer in doing lots of steady state riding. "We only needed to train regularly during January each year, because we rode so many races; the riding we did between them was mostly to recover. Even when I trained for the Classics, which are well over 200 kilometres, the maximum I did was four hours, but I rode hard. I had my circuits and I knew how fast I should do each leg if I was going well. In Belgium I'd ride down to the Tour of Flanders hills and ride hard up a few of them," he says.

Hugh Porter was a good road racer as well as a track rider, so he spent most of his time training for road races. Then he altered his training slightly in the run-up to the world track title races. "What I did then was ride for three hours on the road every morning but in a low gear, really spinning my legs to get the suppleness and fluid pedalling you need on the track. Then in the afternoon I'd train on my local open-air track, riding behind a Derny at well over my pursuit speed," he says.

*   *   *   *   *

Britain hit an uncharacteristic dry patch in Olympic track cycling during the 1960s, with no medals from three Games, but the team pursuit riders bounced back in Munich in 1972 when Ian Hallam, Willi Moore, Mick Bennett and Ron Keeble took the bronze medal. The road race was a revelation too, with Phil Edwards and Phil Bayton finishing fourth and fifth in front of the likes of Freddy Maertens and Francesco Moser, who went on to be two of the best pro road racers of their generation. Bayton and Edwards became professionals too, as did Dave Lloyd, another Munich Olympian. Lloyd, like Bayton, was involved in what began as a British plan to win the Tour de France on a British bike, but ended up with a Dutchman winning it on one.

Raleigh industries bought Carlton Cycles towards the end of the 1960s. Carlton made quality race bikes and sponsored a pro team that took part in British pro races. In 1971 the team became a bit more ambitious and competed in some European pro races ui. der the name of TI Carlton, TI being Raleigh's parent company. Then in 1972 the name changed to TI Raleigh and they widened their racing remit a bit more because Raleigh began a sales campaign in Europe. A pro team was the obvious way to do it, so why not try to be the best pro team in the world while they were at it? At least that was the remit the Raleigh board gave to David Duffield, the man in charge of the project, whose voice would later become familiar to viewers of cycling on Eurosport.

Raleigh dipped their toes in the water during 1972 and 1973 with British racers, including Bayton and Lloyd, and a British manager, George Shaw, but their budget was nowhere near big enough to make an impression. "It was crazy," says Lloyd. "We did things like go over to Belgium to ride Ghent–Wevelgem and come back on the same day. You can't do that and have any hope of success."

Duffield needed more money, which he got from Raleigh, and he decided to spend some of it on hiring a more experienced manager who would then recruit the riders. "I commentated at the London six-day – the Skol Six as it was called, because it was sponsored by Skol lager – so I'd seen Peter Post work as a rider and as a director. I can sum up what I thought about him leading the Raleigh team by saying that he was a winner, I'd seen that, but he also had something else. He was a tough racer, and he was respected for it, but he had a certain something, a natural authority if you like. I just thought that here was a man who would be equal to any challenge," Duffield says.

So the former Dutch star took over the team for 1974 and moved the whole thing to Europe. Post brought in some Dutch pros, then started making life as difficult as possible for the Brits, although he always denied that. It's become accepted in British cycling that Post got rid of the Brits because of prejudice. The story goes that he failed to support them, gave them inferior equipment, was sarcastic and bullied them. Phil Bayton came home, as did Sid Barras and all the rest, apart from Dave Lloyd.

Bayton and Barras could both have made it in Europe. Bayton was super strong and Barras had a fearsome sprint, as he showed when he won a stage in the 1973 Tour of Switzerland when riding for a small British team called Bantel. But there were other issues involved in that decision, as Barras points out: "I saw what was going on with doping over there, I mean generally in European racing, and I didn't want to go down that road."

Still, Post admits he was hard on the Brits, over-hard, goading them into stand-up arguments at the dinner table, but he says he had his reasons. "I didn't do it because they were bad riders, I just needed to get into their heads what European racing was about, what a pro team was about. It's not about individuals trying their best and trusting to luck. It's about having a plan and executing it so you win the race. Barras was very good, very fast, but he didn't have the right attitude and I couldn't change him," Post told me shortly before his death in 2011.

Only one British racer made it through the Post purge of 1974 to become part of what Post called "the first true year of TI Raleigh in 1975", and that was Dave Lloyd. He is firmly in the "Post was a bastard" school, but he was inside the team and saw how Post worked. "Post was bad to the Brits," Lloyd recalls, "but not necessarily just because they were British. He picked on a young Dutch rider called Wim de Waal too, who was very talented and well-educated. Wim liked a joke and had a really nice, pleasant, outgoing nature. Post didn't like that. He was a grim bastard and thought all bike riders should be the same. He would rip into Wim so badly that he had him in tears, and he did it in front of everybody. Wim didn't fit in the mould Post carried in his head of what a bike racer should be."

Lloyd proved to Post both his seriousness and his worth as a team rider. Post meanwhile signed Hennie Kuiper for 1976 and a solid attempt to win the Tour de France, where Kuiper, the 1975 world and 1972 Olympic road race champion, had all the credentials of a contender. "I was roughly the same height as Hennie," says Lloyd. "We rode the same-sized bikes and I could climb. I was told I'd be in the Tour de France team for

1976, and one of the team's most respected riders, Jan Raas, kept telling me, 'Hennie will need you to stick with him as long as possible in the mountains.'"

In 1975 Lloyd did valued team work all year and scored some high places, like 11th overall in the Tour of Switzerland when Post forced him to wait for team-mate Dietrich Thurau even though Lloyd was in the winning break on a crucial stage; but during the year he began to have heart trouble. "It would seem to suddenly do an extra beat then start beating very fast," says Lloyd. He was diagnosed with an ectopic heartbeat and was unable to take his place in the 1976 Tour.

Lloyd eventually returned to racing as an amateur and won national time trial championships, while coping fine with his crazy heartbeat, but you have to wonder how much the stress of working for Peter Post contributed to that condition. Post signed the 1976 Milk Race winner Bill Nickson for 1977 and 1978, but he lasted about 18 months of his two-year contract. Then Post didn't recruit another Brit until Robert Millar joined his Panasonic team in the eighties – and that wasn't an easy relationship either.

Meanwhile Barry Hoban's career reached its zenith. He was unlucky not to win Paris–Roubaix in 1972. "I went through the Arenberg Forest with the leaders, then I punctured. I had to wait two and a half minutes for a team-mate to give me a wheel, and it was buckled. I closed the gap and got away again with eight good riders, but my wheel was on the verge of collapse. So I had to stop again, but as I did, Roger De Vlaeminck attacked.

"I lost another minute waiting for another wheel but I chased the group down again. I caught them just as Andre Dierickx attacked to take second place behind De Vlaeminck. I got my breath back and went again with about five kilometres to go. I closed on them but I couldn't catch them. Ifs and buts don't win races – that was one of Tom Simpson's favourite sayings – but De Vlaeminck never beat me in a sprint, so if I hadn't punctured, well, what then?" he says.

What indeed. Hoban won two more Tour de France stages in 1973 to take his running total to six, but with third in Liège–Bastogne–Liège and third in Paris–Roubaix, plus other top-ten places, victory in a Classic had to come. And it did in the 1974 Ghent–Wevelgem. To do it Hoban beat Eddy Merckx and Roger De Vlaeminck in a sprint finish. "OK, it's not one of the monuments, and I would have loved to have won one of those, but in those days Ghent–Wevelgem was 250 kilometres long, that's real Classic length, and we did 44 kph average.

"Over the Kemmelberg for the last time it nearly didn't happen, though. Those friction gears we had were notorious for slipping, and my chain was skittering in the big sprocket. I remember praying for it to stay put. I had to back off the power a bit so it did, then when I could change up I chased and got back to the front. I had two team-mates in the finale, Alain Santy and Raymond Poulidor, and boy I used them. There was loads of attacking, but my team-mates helped close gaps and I won in the end."

British participation in the Tour de France and other big European races had dwindled by 1974, when Hoban added another Tour stage to his record. For the first part of the decade only Hoban and Michael Wright started the race. Then it was only Hoban in 1975, but he scored what he feels was his best Tour sprint victory. "It was in Bordeaux again. The sprints had been really hairy that year, Jacques Esclassan and Rik Van Linden both had bad crashes, but I was always extra motivated for a finish in Bordeaux and it was on the track again, so I used my track craft to swoop down off the banking just before 200 metres to go to fly by everybody," he says.

Hoban would have loved to win the final stage that year, because it was the first on the Champs-Elysées, but he was fifth. He was also 35 and began to suffer with back problems. He missed the 1976 Tour but started alongside Bill Nickson in 1977 and was able to help Paul Sherwen get through his first Tour de France the following year. It was also Hoban's last. He raced for two more seasons then moved back to Britain after nearly 20 years of living in Europe to work in the cycle industry. He should have been offered the job of national team coach, but there was neither the money nor the will to get him involved.

How do you describe Barry Hoban, and how did he have such a long career in what was still another world for British cyclists back then? Forthright, determined, talented; he's all of those, but above all he's tough. Knock him down and he gets right back up. "I'm resilient," he agrees. "One of my strengths, one of the reasons I had such a long career was because I had good health. I could eat anything, I was adaptable and self-sufficient, and if you raced on the continent in my day those things mattered.

"They were more important than talent. Britain has always had talented bike riders, but until now they had to up sticks and live abroad. That meant adapting to continental ways, eating different foods, learning new languages, giving up home comforts. I'll never forget the first time I drank coffee in France. Back home in Yorkshire coffee was a milky drink, nothing like the bitter black stuff they put in front of me where we stayed, but I drank it and I adapted to it," he says. Hoban didn't just adapt, though; he was assimilated into European bike racing, becoming an integral part of it.

*　*　*　*　*

Hoban was not the only British cycling celebrity at this time. The most British branch of cycling, set-distance time trialling, had a star who was just as famous, just as iconic, albeit in a much smaller world, as Hoban. It had Alf Engers, or "King Alf" as his supporters called him. The affection wasn't universal.

Engers was a young North London time trial ace who broke the competition record for 25 miles in 1959 when he was just 19. He took out an independent licence in the early sixties, so as far as the authorities were concerned he became a professional, but pro racing was still in its infancy back then and beset by procedural problems, so Engers applied to be reinstated as an amateur. He was refused, so he reapplied, seven times in seven years. No wonder Engers thought somebody in authority didn't like him.

That's how it was back then. Many sports officials in the UK thought themselves to be the guardians of amateurism; they thought being a pro tainted an athlete, despite the fact that these "pros" often earned less than some amateurs with their under-the-counter cash deals and their ability to sell off valuable prizes. On top of that, some cycling officials simply didn't like Engers's style; he wasn't the archetypal, clean-cut British sportsman they admired, and they seemed jealous of his popularity.

He was eventually allowed to compete again in 1968 and won the 1,000 metres time trial on the track. He then dominated short-distance time trials for the next ten years, winning five national 25-mile titles. And during that time Engers turned time trialling into a spectator sport.

Thousands turned up to watch Engers compete, especially if he was on one of the fast courses needed as he became obsessed with breaking 50 minutes for 25 miles. Engers focused on it like a laser. He used every bit of cycling science known. His time trial bikes were like track bikes with five gears on; then when he realized he only used three sprockets he binned the other two. He used ultra-thin silk track tyres inflated to incredible pressures. He raced in a silk track jersey, tucked inside silk shorts. His bikes were cut, shaved and drilled so much to make them lighter that they whistled as he sped along the road. Brakes and brake levers were hidden to take them out of the air flow. Handlebars were welded to their stem to remove the clamp bolt. Engers even had patent leather shoes made, because their shiny surface might be faster, and once they were on he would gaffer-tape the laces down.

It was all very fascinating, especially for bike geeks, but not enough in itself to bring out thousands. They didn't come to see Engers's bike, they came to see his rock star persona. He grew his frizzy hair long so he looked like a pale, introspective Jimi Hendrix; and he wore long Afghan coats that trailed to the ground, hippy T-shirts and wide flares. He gave few interviews, said little in those he did give, and that was mostly about meditation, mental focus and carp fishing.

And of course there was his disdain of those officials, whom he hated as much as they hated him, and who frequently tried to get him banned. Young people identified with that, and for them Engers carried the whiff of teenage rebellion, despite being 38 when he finally achieved his cycling goal. On August 5, 1978 Alf Engers raced around a 25-mile course based on the A12 near Chelmsford in Essex in 49 minutes 24 seconds. And that was cycling over for him. Engers more or less disappeared after that, and has spent the time since trying to catch a carp as big as his 30-mph-plus record.

CHAPTER 4

BRAVEHEART

The end of the 1970s saw a mini boom in cycling in the UK. Pro racing was a growing presence on British roads, with stars like Sid Barras, Keith Lambert and Phil Bayton leading the way, and there were good races, some that even attracted European professionals. But it was also a time when a growing number of ambitious and talented young amateurs began looking to race in Europe once more and carve out careers with the big pro teams there, like Robinson, Simpson and Hoban before them.

It was an Irishman, Sean Kelly, who in many respects led the charge over the Channel. He raced for an amateur club in Metz, eastern France, in 1976, and made an instant impression, winning 18 out of the 25 races he rode, as well as winning the amateur version of the professional classic, the Tour of Lombardy. Those performances brought Kelly a place in the Belgian pro team Flandria for 1977, when Kelly rode his first Tour de France, winning a stage.

In 1976 Paul Sherwen won the season-long Pernod Trophy, which was a points competition run over the best amateur races in Britain, and he was offered a place in the big Parisian club, Athletic Club de Boulogne-Billancourt (ACBB), for 1977. There Sherwen rode the ACBB colours to second place in the season-long Palme d'Or competition for amateurs, despite having time out to continue his university studies in the UK. It was a successful start, good enough to get Sherwen a place in the Fiat pro team for 1978, and good enough for ACBB to want another British rider.

"Fiat had been Eddy Merckx's team in 1977," says Sherwen, "but he took all the riders with him to form another team at the end of the year, leaving Fiat with a two-year commitment to cycling but hardly any riders to fill it. In fact there was probably more places available than good riders to fill them, and in the end we were not a team of big hitters," he says modestly.

He went on to build a solid career as a pro racer in Europe, although Sherwen is more famous now for his much longer career as one of the British voices of the Tour de France in his commentary double act with Phil Liggett. But when he gets time away from looking after his other business interests, one of which is a gold mine in Africa, Sherwen looks back on his racing career with fondness and pride.

"The first year was an experience. Our manager was Raphael Geminiani, who'd been a great rider, but great riders don't always make great managers. Geminiani was very old school, so much so that he frowned on arm warmers and wouldn't supply the team with the waterproof tops we called racing capes back then. He just said, 'You can't race with your coat on,' and that was it. 'Gem' had spoken, so no capes.

"I also remember my first Tour de France vividly. It was in 1978, my first pro year, and the start was in Holland with a prologue time trial in Leiden. It ended up not counting towards the overall race, because there was a huge downpour for part of the time it was on and some team managers argued that their riders had been affected but not others. Anyway, next day there was two stages, and I must have got some time bonuses or something in the morning which gave me an outside chance of taking the yellow jersey if I could get some time on those around me in the overall classification during the afternoon stage. I went crazy. I was attacking all over the place, trying desperately to get away in a break. Then Barry Hoban rode up alongside me and said, 'What are you doing, Paul? There are three more Sundays in the Tour de France.' Three more Sundays, imagine that. Barry saying that suddenly brought home to me just how long the Tour was, how big it was, and seeing those three Sundays stretching out in front of me calmed me down no end. I'd have been wrecked in a week if I'd carried on like I started. It wasn't the last time Barry helped me that year either," he says.

Sherwen finished the Tour in 70th place, 2 hours 18 minutes behind a young Frenchman called Bernard Hinault who was winning the first of his eventual five Tours. Eight men finished behind Sherwen; Hoban was five places in front. Meanwhile Sherwen's training partner from Manchester had moved to Paris and was racing for ACBB.

Graham Jones was one of four riders trained by Harold Nelson from the South Manchester area who would become pro racers over the next few years, three of them with big European teams. A year younger than Sherwen, Jones was a talented all-round sportsman who had a trial for Manchester United when he was at school, but he loved cycling more than football. "Another kid at school used to get *International Cycle Sport* magazine, and I remember being fascinated by a technical drawing of Eddy Merckx's bike in there. I think that's what sparked me off, the bikes," says Jones.

"Harold Nelson gave us a good start; me, Paul Sherwen then John Herety. Harold, or H as we called him, was way ahead of his time and seemed to know things intuitively that sports scientists later discovered. H understood that training near your steady state limit was a really potent way to build fitness, but it was years later when scientists discovered the anaerobic threshold, which is the same thing as H used, and learned how to use it. Anyway, when Paul Sherwen left ACBB to turn pro at the end of 1977 the club asked him if he knew another British rider who could take his place, and Paul recommended me."

Jones spent the 1977 racing season in Belgium, where he made a big impression, and he went one better than Sherwen with ACBB because he won the season-long Palme d'Or competition. He won the two big amateur time trials as well: the GP des Nations and GP de France, which is a big marker for any pro team because a potential stage race winner has to be a good time triallist. Jones also won Paris–Evreux, a top-ranked single-day race.

"Paul turned pro for Fiat, but I was the first to go to the Peugeot team, and from that point ACBB became a feeder club for Peugeot. Robert Millar was next from ACBB, then Stephen Roche, then Sean Yates, then Allan Peiper."

As with Paul Sherwen, Barry Hoban was a big influence on Jones. He said: "Barry was still racing when I turned pro, but there'd been a long gap, with only him in the Tour de France and other big races until we came along.

"I really don't think Barry gets the credit he deserves for his career either. Not just for what he did in the Tour de France, winning eight stages, but for what he did in the Classics and races like the Midi Libre. But he was also quite hard on us and he could be unduly critical. When Sherwen punctured in a race once, Barry just told him that he should look where he was going, because punctures are a rider's fault for not seeing hazards in the road."

Graham Jones had what it takes to win big races, but the way his career unfolded reveals a bit about how the European pro teams regarded British riders, and gives an insight into what life was like then for a new professional. Most teams viewed riders as a commodity to use, and they only invested in developing riders who stood out because of their talent and their attitude. Jones had the talent, but maybe not the attitude to go with it. "Very few riders were nurtured or had their careers planned, unless they were extra special," Jones says, "but even then it was because they were extra strong and durable or they didn't allow themselves to be used. For most riders life was a succession of races, and any rest during the season only came when you were ill or injured."

Jones made a good pro debut in 1979, and then a fantastic Tour de France debut in 1980. Towards the end of the three-week race he was lying in 11th place overall, with just one mountain stage and a time trial to go. "I think I was the only rider up till then to win the two classic amateur time trials, the GP de France and GP des Nations in the same year. So with a time trial left, and I was going OK in the mountains, I was confident of getting into the first ten by Paris. But then several of us in the Peugeot team caught some sort of stomach bug, and next day I was dropped early in the stage and rode 100 kilometres on my own off the back." Jones made it to Paris in 49th place, but says, "My career would have been different if I'd got that top-ten place."

It was a crossroads. Top ten in his first Tour would have put Jones on a different trajectory, one where he had a say in choosing the races he rode. It didn't happen, and Jones had another thing that worked against him: he could ride well anywhere and in any kind of race. Riders like that tended to get overused by teams in those days.

Jones's true strength, though, lay in stage races. In 1981 he finished second in the Tour of the Mediterranean, beating Bernard Hinault. He nearly had Hinault again in the Critérium International, a two-day, three-stage race, when Hinault led overall and looked to have the race in his pocket. "I went away in the morning road stage on the second day," he recalls. "It was really hilly and I was flying. All Hinault's team chased after me but they couldn't catch me. I kept pulling ahead and got to where I was the race leader overall on the road, so if I'd have stayed at that and I'd done a good time trial I could have won the race. Instead I was knocked off my bike on a descent by a TV motorbike."

As well as racing hard in the summer Jones trained hard each winter. "I spent every winter in the UK and always started training for the following year on November the first after a couple of weeks' rest. I did at least two days in the week riding in the Peak District from November the first, sometimes more, and then I rode both days at the weekend. Then on January the second I'd meet Paul Sherwen and we would train every day, putting in lots of miles in the Peak District or around Cheshire. We were lucky too because even for mid-week sessions there was a good group to ride with: me and Paul, John Herety and Ian Binder, plus some top-class amateurs like the Williams brothers. Our training was all about doing the miles, but with good riders and in hilly terrain we were making hard efforts too, so there was an element of interval training in it."

The group trained in all weathers, which led to Jones crashing on some black ice early in 1982 and fracturing his femur. The enforced lay-off seemed to do him no harm, because Jones finished second in the 1982 Het Volk, the first of the Belgian Classics, but underneath his apparent good showing he was tired. "Het Volk suited me, but by then I was racing too much and it was having an effect. Peugeot had me down to ride everything, and it was the same when I moved on to the Wolber team. Looking back now, I should have been awkward, like Robert Millar was. I was too willing and too easy to pick for a race. Robert stuck up for himself, refusing to ride some races he was picked for. He wasn't always a popular team-mate, but it meant he got to ride the races that suited him, and he developed because of it," Jones says.

By 1984 the excessive workload of up to 150 racing days a year got to Jones and he was exhausted. He returned to Britain to race in the growing number of pro events here, but the fire had gone out, although the occasional good result showed that the class was still there. Still, with hindsight Jones says that racing in Britain was a backward step: "I shouldn't have come back here. It was my biggest mistake. I should have stuck it out in Europe, taken a leaf out of Robert Millar's book and tried to do the races that suited me, the ones that would help me, rather than always agreeing to be there to help the team. My big influence in cycling when I was a kid was Tom Simpson's book, *Cycling is My Life*, and in it I underlined something Tom wrote about there always being another day to fight, but in the end I didn't follow that advice and stick it out. My head had gone."

* * * * *

The British pro racing that Jones returned to might have been a step down for him, as any European country's bread and butter pro racing is for a rider with the sort of international talent Jones had, but it was good racing with a growing list of events. These days the top level in men's pro road racing is the World Tour, in which the best teams take part. Teams at the next level down may get into the occasional World Tour race if they are offered a wild card place, but they tend to focus on races in their own countries, which is where their sponsors' interests lie anyway. The pro teams in Britain were a bit like that in the 1980s.

Pro road racing developed in Britain through the second half of the seventies until there were some good races. Among them was the Empire Stores London to Bradford Marathon in 1979, which was brought in to replace London–Holyhead. At 260 miles, it was billed as the world's longest road race and attracted French, Dutch, Belgian and Swedish riders from several European teams, as well as the best British-based pros. It also provided a fitting stage for the end of Barry Hoban's cycling story.

Hoban was 39 years old and in his last year racing for a big pro team. The wet ride from London to Yorkshire was his homecoming in every respect. The race started from Hampstead at 5 a.m. and went through Milton Keynes, Atherstone and Market Drayton to the Stoke area, where the hills started. Lucrative prizes were on offer in each town along the route, and there was some aggressive racing to win them, but the deciding move came in Oldham. Hoban attacked, caught and passed a local pro, Ian Greenhalgh, then time trialled his way across the Pennines into Yorkshire. The rain poured, but Hoban was oblivious to it, winning by nearly seven minutes in front of 8,000 spectators who stood cold and wet in Bradford's Odsal stadium to welcome Hoban home.

The race was a success, but it showed the gulf between British and continental racing. Even though there were races for the pros here, they weren't as long as big European races, and because they had smaller fields they weren't as fast. British road races definitely weren't good preparation for something as long as London–Bradford. On top of that, several British-based pros grumbled about the foreigners from different teams combining to set Hoban up for the win, which was probably true. A "them and us" theme, the European-based Brits versus the British-based Brits, has always run through British pro cycling. It provided a back story to the national championships later that year, in which Hoban took part for the first time in his career because he wasn't selected by his team for the Tour de France. He was outgunned by the Brits ganging up, but it still took a sprinter of the calibre of Sid Barras to beat him.

The rivalry has bubbled on for years, and it's still alive today when Team Sky does the national road race championships, the one race they are allowed to ride in the UK each year. The whole field tries to beat them, but the Sky riders are better prepared, and the team have mopped up the best British riders anyway, so they always win, often packing the podium with their riders.

But one place where British-based pros could always hold their own is in circuit races in city centres, and by the early eighties this formula of exciting one-hour street races had hit British TV screens in the Kellogg's Series. It was helped by ground-breaking TV coverage. Static cameras dotted at key points around the short circuits, combined with a motorbike-mounted cameraman who rode in a separate lane but right next to the riders, followed every bit of the action. The circuits were well planned; people finding they had free entertainment on their doorsteps piled into the city centres and out of the pubs to create a wonderful atmosphere; and knowledgeable TV commentary from Phil Liggett turned British criterium specialists like Sid Barras, Phil Bayton and Phil Thomas into household names. However, the British-based pros guarded their new status jealously, which led to the odd fight in later years when some of the top European stars were paid to make guest appearances in the Kellogg's races.

One of them was Robert Millar, and he packed people into the centre of Glasgow when the Kellogg's Series went there. In 1984, after he became Britain's most successful Tour de France rider to date – which he remained until Bradley Wiggins won the race in 2012 – he even appeared in TV advertisements for a new cereal called Kellogg's Start.

Robert Millar was born in 1958 in a more industrial Glasgow to the one that exists today. He spent his early life in an area known as the Gorbals, just about the toughest place in a tough city, and he grew up as single-minded as a kid could be. It wasn't a terrible childhood, though. In fact Millar used to take offence when journalists tried to paint a picture of a young boy growing up in a deprived area, once remarking, when he'd heard something written about him, "Anyone would think I lived in a cave when you read what they write."

But cycling can be a loner's sport, or at least one where you need to feel comfortable being alone, because pro bike racers are alone a lot when training and travelling. They need to be confident and self-reliant to make their way in the business. It's true that top-level pro cycling is a team sport, or at least a sport where the team produces a winner, but to get into it, survive it and make a place in it, a person must be self-motivated and self-reliant. Robert Millar is both of those things, and then some.

He won the Scottish junior road race title in 1976, he was Scottish senior hill climb champion the following year, then he blew away the best British amateurs in the 1978 British road title race held on a hilly course based on Caistor in North Lincolnshire. Millar was still 19 but very mature. He controlled the race against better-known, older and far more experienced opposition, and on the last lap he simply rode away from his breakaway partner Steve Lawrence towards the top of Caistor Hill. It looked easy, he had enormous potential, and the only place to develop it in those days was in Europe.

Millar took Graham Jones's place in ACBB for the 1979 French road season. He won five big races there, retained the British road race title, and he won the season-long points competition to find the best amateur rider in France. Millar was also fourth in the world amateur road race championships, the highest British finisher since Graham Webb, and but for bad luck he would have won a medal. Near the finish he pulled his foot out of the toe-clips and straps that riders used back then to pull as well as push on the pedals.

More important, Millar emerged as a true climber, and that's a rare talent. It's not just a question of having a high power to low weight ratio – power to weight is just the starting point. True climbers must also have a way of pedalling, a certain style and facility, that helps them change pace and make killing attacks uphill. Millar had that gift, and he knew how to develop it.

Millar turned pro for Peugeot in 1980 but didn't allow himself to be used in the way that Graham Jones was. His first three years are a lesson in development and steady improvement. Millar tried to ride the races that would help him, and when he had the chance to do well he took it deftly. By 1983 he was ready to move up a gear, he was ready to ride the Tour de France.

Second place to Greg Lemond in the Critérium du Dauphiné, the traditional warm-up to the Tour, saw Millar selected for the Peugeot team. He crashed on stage 3 and lost a lot of time, which put a really high overall place out of reach – although he would still finish 14th. Meanwhile he still had the mountains.

There was only one stage in the Pyrenees in the 1983 Tour de France, but it was a big one and Millar won it. He attacked on the early slopes of the final climb, the legendary Col du Tourmalet, caught a lone breakaway rider and rode straight past him to take the Souvenir Desgrange prize, which is awarded each year at the top of the highest climb. Millar continued down the other side, descending with great skill to cross the finish line in Luchon six seconds ahead of Pedro Delgado of Spain.

Millar was even better in 1984. He had high places in Paris–Nice, the Tour of Romandie, in Switzerland, and the Midi Libre, winning or finishing well on all the key mountain stages in those races. He won the 11th stage of the Tour de France at Guzet-Neige in the Pyrenees, took the King of the Mountains title to Paris and finished fourth overall. He had surpassed Tom Simpson's Tour de France performance of 1962, and Millar's 1984 Tour would be the best by any British rider until Bradley Wiggins won in 2012. But Millar wasn't just the best British Grand Tour rider in 1984, he was one of the best of his generation, and he really should have won the 1985 Vuelta a Espana.

The Vuelta started in April back then. Millar worked his way towards the race lead and took it and the amarillo jersey on stage 10, holding on to it until the penultimate day. His lead wasn't big, just ten seconds ahead of Francisco Rodriguez and 1 minute 15 seconds ahead of Pello Ruiz Cabestany. Neither was a good enough climber to distance Millar, and although Rodriguez tried to, he couldn't drop the Scot. However, a plot was soon to develop.

Millar punctured at the foot of a climb, and when he caught back up to the riders he'd been with they congratulated him for doing so and acknowledged that he would be the overall winner. A largish group had formed, but nobody told Millar that two riders had attacked and left it. It wasn't announced on race radio, and it wasn't on any of the marshals' blackboards that were used to inform the peloton of the state of the race in those days before rider radios. Even Millar's team manager Roland Berland, following the Millar group in the Peugeot team car, didn't know about the attack at first.

The attackers were Spaniards, José Recio and Pedro Delgado. The stage covered some of Delgado's home roads, and he was lying sixth overall, six minutes behind Millar. Delgado gained most of that time back before Millar and Berland found out what was happening, and when they did nobody in Millar's group would help him chase. Recio helped Delgado, for which Delgado gave his compatriot the stage, and Delgado won the Vuelta by 36 seconds.

Speaking after losing the race lead, Millar showed how disgusted he was with the way the Spanish riders rode and with his entire reception in Spain. "The crowds throw things at you and spit at you because they want a Spaniard to win. But I don't let them affect me; I still get on and race. The other night, though, at the hotel in Albacete I blew my top. We had been waiting an hour for dinner, and when it came it was food you wouldn't give your dog. The others couldn't believe it when I stormed out. I went down to the cake shop and stuffed myself.

"Next day the whole Fagor team attacked with Delgado at the first feed because they thought I was hungry. I had planned for our team to ride through both feeds to make the others hungry, but the guys said they were hot and wanted their feeds. The Fagor riders also rode against me on the stage to Tremp. If they hadn't done that, we would have finished two or three minutes ahead. They have lost the race for me. But I'll get my own back on them. In the criteriums there are those who like to win their local race. As a 'named' rider on the publicity posters for races like that, I am allowed to show myself off at the front for a few laps. When I can I will just carry on and lap the field; that will show them," Millar said – revealing, in case anybody in cycling didn't know by then, that he was a tough cookie and not to be messed with.

Millar was also very upset with Berland, and criticized him for not offering to pay some non-Spanish riders in the group to help him chase Delgado and Recio, as was the usual practice in pro racing in similar situations. And there was the feeling that Peugeot hadn't really backed Millar right from the start of the Vuelta. They even had to fly a special time trial bike out to Spain for him when he was defending the leader's jersey. Millar's contract with Peugeot was up for renewal anyway, so he signed for Peter Post's Panasonic team.

Panasonic was a much more professional and better-organized outfit than Peugeot, and it was a successful move for Millar. He wasn't a good fit with Post, however, because the two rubbed each other up the wrong way. According to Allan Peiper, who moved to Panasonic with Millar, "Post respected Robert, but Robert didn't fit his mould. He was different to the average bike rider in the same way that Cadel Evans is different today, only more so. And Post couldn't get to Robert either. If Post had one of his famous tantrums, Robert just stood there looking at him without saying a word. Then, when Post had finished, Robert just shrugged his shoulders, turned around and walked out. Post couldn't get to Robert, but he admired his ability and his professionalism and they had some good results together."

Millar had started working on his weakness in time trials, so he could be a better overall stage race rider. He changed his training to include long time trial type interval efforts during which he used a high gear, higher than necessary, and kept his upper body stock still while he did so. The idea was to build up power in the time trial position while keeping the upper body still, so it creates less drag.

Cycling was changing around this time. When Francesco Moser broke Eddy Merckx's hour record in 1984, to general surprise because Moser was past his prime by then, he used new training methods, and even a new "low-profile" bike with disc wheels, and he beat the record by a lot. The bike and wheels Moser used and the skin-tight clothing he wore improved his aerodynamics. One of Moser's training methods was the kind of over-geared interval training that Millar adopted. Moser also used a heart rate monitor and underwent tests to establish where his performance thresholds were: two things that Millar's generation experimented with and that are available for anybody to use today.

Despite saying he would never race in Spain again, Millar lined up for the 1986 Vuelta bent on revenge. He won the sixth stage to the mountain-top Lagos de Covadonga and took over the race lead, but then he lost it to Alvaro Pino in an uphill time trial. Millar wasn't too worried; he planned to attack on stage 17, which finished on the Sierra Nevada climb at over 2,500 metres.

On the day Millar attacked early because he needed to get as much time as possible, and Pino cracked, leaving Millar to forge on alone for 18 kilometres. However, a concerted effort from a number of different Spanish teams, including most notably Marino Lejarreta, who on paper was Pino's rival, hauled Pino back to Millar six kilometres from the summit. Millar later admitted that he attacked too early, but the Spanish teams had again colluded to prevent him from winning. Millar finished second overall in the Vuelta for the second year running.

*   *   *   *   *

Sean Yates was the next to put on ACBB's grey and orange racing top. "My ambition as an amateur was always to ride the Olympics, which I did in 1980, but once I'd done it, it was a case of 'where to now?'. I felt I owed it to my dad, who'd given me so much support, to push onwards and upwards. But in those days, when there was still a distinction between amateurs and professionals, and the Olympics were only for amateurs and were the biggest thing an amateur could do, onwards and upwards meant turning professional. And with no disrespect to the British-based pros, it meant turning professional in Europe.

"So I asked Tony Mills, who supplied my bikes through Emperor Sport and who had a lot of contacts abroad, if he could get me in some races in France. Time trialling was my thing, so Tony got me an invitation to the amateur and the GP des Nations. I came second, beaten by Stephen Roche who was riding for ACBB then and who already had a place in the Peugeot pro team for the following year. That got me into ACBB," Yates says.

With the success of Sherwen, Jones and then Millar, as well as Irishman Stephen Roche, the French club were hooked on British riders and they took four in 1981, as Yates recalls. "There was me, John Herety, Jeff Williams and Kevin Reilly that year, and having them there with me really helped. We were a group of young guys tackling the same problems. The club supplied us with bikes, with an apartment, and they took us to all our races. It was a lot better for us than the first British riders who went abroad. I did OK; I won the GP de France time trial, which was really important back then, and a pro contract with Peugeot sort of fell into my lap."

Just how important the GP de France was is shown by its list of winners. The first in 1952 was Jacques Anquetil, who went on to be a cycling superstar. Most winners down the years had good pro careers, while the race has had its fair share of British winners. Peter Hill won in 1965; and Peter Head won in 1968 before becoming a pro in Belgium and training and racing under the wing of the legendary Flemish hard man Frans Verbeek. Phil Bayton won in 1972, Graham Jones in 1978 and David Akam the year after Yates in 1982. The last British winner of the GP de France was Chris Boardman in 1989.

David Akam, from south London, was also an ACBB rider when he won. He turned pro in 1984 for the Italian Gis-TUC-Lu team, falling into the role of a domestique for Francesco Moser. In doing so he followed an earlier path set by Bristol's Phil Edwards who, after ploughing a lone furrow in Italy racing for an amateur team, turned pro in 1976 for Sanson and rode in support of Moser until 1980. Edwards chose Italy instead of France to develop his cycling career because his mother was Italian and his family had business interests there. Edwards and Akam were British one-offs in Italy until British Cycling set up the road race side of its under-23 academy in Quaratta in Tuscany, where the likes of Mark Cavendish and Geraint Thomas developed their skills in the tough school of Italian amateur racing, the dilettante class.

John Herety graduated with Yates into the pro ranks in 1982, and Herety went to the Co-op Mercier team. Sean Yates explains why: "That must have been to do with quotas, because I think the ACBB manager Micky Weigant got some money for every rider he recommended to Peugeot. It was a good earner for him, so long as he didn't send anyone who was terrible, and John wasn't that. But pro teams were only allowed a certain ratio of foreigners to riders from their own country, the country where the team was registered, and Peugeot already had Phil Anderson, Stephen Roche, Robert Millar, Graham Jones and then me.

"The other Peugeot riders were mostly French, and although there was a little bit of a 'what are they doing in our team' attitude from them the atmosphere was really quite friendly," says Yates. "The British riders weren't allowed to speak English at the meal table, but that's understandable, it was a French team. It's not very polite if everyone sits down together and a group of British riders are down one end of the table speaking English. It's the same in Team Sky now; it's a British team so everybody speaks English when they are together. At least you learn a foreign language quickly when you are immersed in it like that."

Yates had a reasonable first pro year, with a couple of wins in France and four in Britain, although his closest friend Herety had the better results. He took the British professional road race title, partly thanks to some hard work from Yates, who finished second. Herety also won the prologue of the Tour de l'Indre et Loire, had two second places in stages of the Tour of the Mediterranean, and he would have won a big Belgian race, the Grand Prix Pino Cerami, but for an outrageous home town decision by the judges.

"I caught a two-man breakaway right under the one kilometre to go banner, with the whole of the peloton just behind me. There was no time to plan a sprint, so I just went straight past the two and held on to the finish, winning by about three bike lengths. One of the two-man break was caught by the rest, but the other, Ronny Van Holen, sprinted after me and got nowhere near. That was it, I put both hands in the air – I'd won. It was only April and I'd won a big race in my first year as a pro. It was incredible, or it was for a few minutes. Van Holen protested, saying I'd veered off line to prevent him coming past me. I hadn't, and anyway he was trying to get by on the inside where there was no room. But Van Holen was Belgian, so the Belgian judges reversed the order," says

Herety, who today is one of the most experienced and successful pro team managers in Britain.

Despite his promising start Herety didn't thrive in the European pro world. "There was so much racing, and they came one after the other. It was too much for me, and nobody took time out then. I couldn't seem to recover like the others did. The British pro scene was getting good by then, so I came back here in 1985 and did three years racing for the Percy Bilton team," he says.

Herety and Yates's first professional season coincided with the return of the World Championships to Britain. The track events were held in Leicester again, on the Saffron Lane track, which now had a much better wooden board surface and was more like a modern velodrome than the bumpy cement track it used to be. Nevertheless it wasn't a good track series for Britain. Tony Doyle had been world pro pursuit champion in 1980, but he dropped to fourth at Leicester, and there were no other medallists, although some young riders, such as the sprinter Mark Barry, showed potential.

But there was very little investment in the British track cycling effort back then. Even tracks were scarce, with Leicester and maybe Meadowbank in Edinburgh the only ones that came to anywhere near international standard. But since both were open-air tracks, training and racing on them was only possible in good weather and largely impossible during the winter.

Road racing too was suffering from a lack of investment. However, roads are at least more or less the same the world over, and individual talent has a chance to shine through. The individual talent that shone through for Great Britain at Goodwood in 1982 was Mandy Jones.

Jones comes from Lancashire, where she joined the long-established West Pennine road club as a teenager with her sister Carol. She made her world championship debut in 1980, and at the age of 18 she took a bronze medal on the gruelling Sallanches circuit behind Beth Heiden. It was a remarkable result and it made her a hot favourite in front of a home crowd in 1982.

The circuit was based on Goodwood's motor racing circuit, as Leicester was on Mallory Park, but Goodwood is in the heart of the South Downs, a much hillier area than rural Leicestershire. Goodwood suited a girl raised on long hilly rides in the Pennines. Jones was active all day at the front, trying to get in a good move. And when she did so, her rivals made a fatal error. "They let me get a gap on a descent," she recalls. "I don't know what happened but I had just freewheeled though to the front and when I looked round there was gap behind. I put my head down and went for it. I only looked round again at the beginning of the last time up the finishing hill, and there was nobody there."

Yates raced in the 5,000 metres pro pursuit in Leicester, and was the second British finisher a few days later in the 274-kilometre pro road race at Goodwood. He had good powers of recovery and adjusted well to European pro road racing. Big and strong, he soaked up races and he had his time trial talent to fall back on. And Yates loved time trialling on both sides of the Channel. He set a competition record for ten miles of 19 minutes 44 seconds, was the national 25-mile champion in 1980, and never lost his fascination with this side of cycling.

The simple joy of competing against the clock, a joy that British cyclists have shared for well over a century, has been a constant with Yates. After his pro career was over he won the national 50-mile time trial title, and he still turns out when the feeling takes him, despite having suffered a stroke, had several ablations and had a pacemaker fitted. In fact when I spoke to him recently he was wondering what the fastest ten miles ever done with a pacemaker was.

For Yates in the 1980s even short trips home would include a time trial, and it was quite common to see his black-and-white chequered Peugeot skinsuit blasting up and down a Kent or Sussex dual carriageway. Yates's team-mate in Peugeot from 1983 onwards, Allan Peiper, an Australian who came to Europe to race when he was just 16, remembers Yates talking about the time trial courses he raced on in the UK, which are still denoted by codes, just as they were when time trialling was the only road racing in Britain back in the 1890s. "He was always raving about the Q10/19 course, where he wanted to set the ten-mile record, and used to get quite excited about going home to ride a race on it," Peiper remembers.

But fascination with time trialling was something Peiper and Yates shared, and it made them stand out in the Peugeot team. "Allan and I were quite competitive with each other in time trials," says Yates, "especially in prologues, which we were both good at. We took time trials seriously, doing research to try to get the best equipment for them. We both had our own special time trial wheels, where the French riders never did that, and we warmed up properly for them, practising on the course and studying the best lines through all the corners. We always performed well in an individual time trial, and we hurt our team-mates' legs when we raced in team time trials. We both enjoyed doing that."

At first Peiper was the more successful of the two. He was more driven, more organized, but they were close, as Peiper recalls: "We did our first Tour de France together in 1984, and we dragged Peugeot to fourth in the team time trial, then spent the rest of the Tour doing anything we could for Robert Millar. After the Tour we did 25 straight days of criterium racing, travelling all over France,

Belgium and Holland together. It didn't seem like work, we were two young men on an adventure really. It was an incredibly free time; we had nothing, so we had nothing to lose."

The free and easy approach caught up with Yates eventually, but it proved to be the making of him. "It's no secret that towards the end of my Peugeot days I got done for tax evasion, so I couldn't live in the UK any more. I got in my car and drove to Nice, looked for somewhere I liked and decided to live there. It was the first time I had lived alone, so I almost always ate out and didn't need to keep food in the house. Then, with nobody to talk to and nothing to do when I wasn't racing, I rode my bike a lot. I loved it, though. I still love riding my bike today. And Nice is so good for cycling, I spent endless hours riding the back roads and the hills behind the coast. Then when I got back home I couldn't eat because I'd no food in, so I had to shower and go out to a restaurant or café.

"Eventually all this riding and much less eating added up and I lost weight. It wasn't a constant decision, there was nobody back then who'd say to you, look, you're 10 kilograms over weight, if you lose that weight your power output will go from 4.7 watts per kilo to 5.7. Nobody knew what watts per kilo were. Anyway, I lost weight, I got fitter and in 1987 when I rode for the Fagor team I started riding a lot better."

Yates had already built a formidable reputation as a domestique in the Peugeot team. He was able to ride kilometre after kilometre at the front of a group to peg back breakaways or close gaps, and he was always on hand to drop back to the team car to fetch drinks bottles to be shared around the team or, if a team-mate had punctured, pace him back to the peloton. He continued doing it with the Fagor team, then with the pioneer American teams 7-Eleven and Motorola. It was a role he chose rather than settled for, and domestiques like Yates are rare and highly prized. Being one of the best kept him in work much longer than winning a few more races might have.

"I was happier in that role than being a leader," he says. "Leaders are under constant pressure to deliver results, which is hard, whereas a rider who is there to help knows what's expected of him all the time and although it's physically harder it's mentally easier to deliver. I made a decent niche for myself by performing that role, although I still won 30 pro races, and I got my chance in races that suited me, like Paris–Roubaix."

*   *   *   *   *

By 1987 British pro road racers were a force in world cycling, but two Irishmen were even better. Sean Kelly was a multiple winner of Classics, he had won the green jersey in the Tour de France three times and would win it again. He had high overall placings in the Tour de France, he won Paris–Nice with clockwork regularity, and he would win the 1988 Tour of Spain. However, the year to end all years for Irish cycling was 1987 – the year of Stephen Roche.

Roche was class on a bike. He pedalled with a fluidity and ease that science would probably explain but looked like a gift from God. However, he was a huge talent in a fragile box. Roche's career was marked by feast and famine, good years followed by bad, when injury or illness or some other problem contrived to push him down. In 1987 everything went right for Roche and he did what only Eddy Merckx has done – he won cycling's triple crown: the Giro d'Italia, the Tour de France and the world road race title. But, in Roche's own opinion, he wouldn't have been able to do it without Robert Millar.

"Robert helped me so much on the stage when I took the lead in the Giro, I don't think I would have got through it without him," says Roche today. "It was the day to Sapadda and the Italian fans believed I betrayed the race leader, Roberto Visentini, who was my team-mate. But things weren't good between Visentini and me. The team wanted him to win, and he told me that if I helped him too he would ride for me in that year's Tour de France, but I knew he'd already booked a holiday for when the Tour was on.

"I felt I owed Visentini nothing and I was strong and I could win the Giro, but my team didn't see it like that, and neither did the fans. While the whole of my team chased the breakaway I was in, I had one team-mate with me, Eddy Schpers, who worked hard at setting the pace. Then when the fans changed from screaming abuse to spitting wine and some kind of grain at me, Robert Millar rode up and took my other side, so Eddy and Robert were a little in front and I rode protected between them. Robert was the mountains leader, he was third overall and in a rival team. He didn't have to do what he did, and it was brave because a fan could have taken his rage out on him and pushed him off his bike."

It was a brave thing to do, and puzzling really when you consider Millar's independent often isolated character, but above all it was a good thing to do, and the right thing. Luckily it didn't affect Millar's overall position, or who knows what height Peter Post would have jumped on him from, and on the penultimate stage Roche was able to pay him back a bit by working in a breakaway that saw Millar move up to second overall. And that's how the 1987 Giro stayed. Millar added the Giro climber's title to the ones he'd won in Vuelta and the Tour de France, making a full house; and by coming second overall he achieved his third Grand Tour podium place, adding to the two he'd had in the Vuelta.

The 1987 Tour de France is famous in the rest of the world for Stephen Roche's victory, but it's famous in Britain for the participation of ANC-Halfords, a British team created to ride the Tour de France with British riders in it. The transport company ANC was then owned by Tony Capper, who had linked up with former international road racer Phil Griffiths to set up the ANC-Freight-Rover team in 1985. The plan that Griffiths came up with was for the team to ride mainly British races and make forays into Europe at first, steadily building up their participation in European races until they were strong enough and had the riders to take on the Tour.

Griffiths is one of those people who don't see obstacles and will not take no for an answer. An initial barrier he faced was a rule that only allowed six-man teams in the UK whereas he needed ten men for European races. He got round that by splitting the team in two; half raced under the ANC name in the UK, and half under Halfords-Lycra, then they joined up as one team to race in Europe. Two years later it would be Griffiths's determination, and his credit card, that got ANC-Halfords around France, albeit with only three riders getting to Paris.

At first things went well. Joey McGloughlin, a really talented rider from Liverpool, scored an amazing fourth place in the 1986 Amstel Gold Race. He and other team members did well in other races, and the team was strengthened for 1987 when its two wings merged to form ANC-Halfords. It was time to take on the Tour.

There's a tendency to put ANC's efforts in the category of "nice try but no cigar". The team didn't fare well, but a lot of that was due to its money supply being cut off just as the Tour started. The riders have been portrayed as plucky lads playing outside their league, but the characterization jars with them, as one team member, Sheffield's Malcolm Elliott explains: "It's a misconception that ANC was a ramshackle assortment who were just getting through, which isn't really true. OK, in the end the money ran out, but there was a good few in the team who knew what they were doing.

"I'd put us on a par with the 2012 Endura team. We'd already done some of the Classics and ridden Paris–Nice, with some good results too. Having said that, when we got to the Tour it was like a lot of the other riders we'd been competing with had found another two gears. The race was brutal. The heat and humidity were oppressive, and when you are taking a kicking on day two or three and there's another two and a half weeks to go, that's hard on the head. Plus we lost Patrice Thévenard, Paul Watson and Graham Jones after four days, and Graham was no novice to the Tour either. I got involved in the sprints as much as possible, and got up there in Bordeaux with a third place, but prior to the Tour my only experience of sprinting was with everybody going for it. Superconfex were doing lead-outs for Van Poppel back in 1987; it was one of the first years it happened. Now it's all lead-outs, like arm wrestling for teams until the final bend, then the spearhead forms and it's a street-fight behind."

Elliott is right. He finished third in the Amstel Gold Race earlier in 1987, and he went on to have a great pro career in Europe. He was a very good sprinter and he won stages in the Vuelta and the points jersey in that race in 1989, becoming the second British rider to win a Grand Tour jersey outright after Robert Millar, and the only one until Mark Cavendish repeated his Vuelta points win in 2010. There were other riders in the team who knew what they were doing too, although some of the married ones with responsibilities were certainly affected by the money situation. It's hard enough to suffer through a Tour de France without knowing that while you are doing so the mortgage isn't getting paid.

For the 1988 season Robert Millar and Stephen Roche joined forces with Sean Yates in the Fagor team. The British presence was boosted by Malcolm Elliott, and although the team was famously disorganized and Roche had probably the worst year of his career, the British riders did well. Yates won the first stage of Paris–Nice and wore the leader's white jersey for a while; Malcolm Elliott won the Tour of Britain; and Robert Millar finished third in Liège–Bastogne–Liège, the best result for a British rider since Barry Hoban did the same in 1969.

The Tour de France was good too. Yates was the first British rider ever to win a Tour de France time trial at Wasquehal. Millar was dreadfully unlucky at Guzet-Neige, where he'd won before of course, when he and his breakaway companion Philippe Bouvatier mistook a French policeman's directions and went off course in the last few hundred metres, allowing Italy's Massimo Ghirotto to sneak by. Millar sprinted after him, only to lose by two seconds. Malcolm Elliott finished fourth in the big sprint on the Champs-Elysées at the end. Then Yates won again in the Vuelta, taking the stage to Jaca after a long two-man breakaway with fellow Brit Deno Davie, who by then was a pro with Stephen Roche's old team, Carrera.

*   *   *   *   *

No look at British cycling up to this point would be complete without mentioning Tony Doyle. He was world professional pursuit champion in 1980 and 1986, but above all he was the best six-day racer this country has ever produced. Before Doyle only Tom Simpson had won a big modern six-day. Tony Gowland had flair and was fast, and he won a six-day in Montreal, but it wasn't one of the big events. Hugh Porter was strong and dependable.

They both earned a place on the winter six-day circuit, but they didn't break into the Blue Train – the name given to the elite group of six-day racers from each generation.

Six-day races are nothing like as big as they once were. They used to be a world within professional cycling, and a very lucrative one it was too. Modern six-days revolve around the Madison race, the two-man constant relay where one rider races while the other circles more slowly around the top of the track. Then, as his partner catches him up, the slower rider swoops down alongside him and is relayed into the race with a hefty handsling. It's complicated both to explain and to watch, but it's fast, spectacular and fascinating for aficionados, and Europe was full of them.

Modern six-days are basically six-day Madisons. These are interspersed with other races, like motor-paced races and sprints, but the core of a six-day is the Madison, and the most effective Madison team is always one that pairs a sprinter with someone who has a longer lasting and slower burning power – a stayer, as this kind of track racer used to be described. The only other complication is that the sprinter needs to have a fair amount of staying power, and the stayer needs to be quite fast.

Who rides with whom in a six-day is decided by each event's promoter, but in Doyle's day and before, team pairings were only made after consultation with the riders in the Blue Train. Whereas Gowland and Porter didn't break into the Blue Train, Tom Simpson did, shortly before he died, and the only other Brit to do it was Tony Doyle. It allowed him to build a six-day partnership with Australia's Danny Clark, and for a while they were the best in the business.

Gary Wiggins, Bradley's father, was a six-day racer at that time. Bradley rode a few himself when he was younger and won the Ghent six-day, which meant a lot to him because he was born there. Wiggins senior was a tough Australian, and a good track rider. He and Doyle were the European Madison champions in 1984, and as there was no world Madison title back then, six-day riders regarded the European title as the unofficial world title.

Six-day riders are contracted and paid a fee on an event-to-event basis, and the European title brought Wiggins and Doyle regular contracts together. In 1985 they won the Bremen six-day, which was Doyle's first and Gary Wiggins's first and only six-day victory.

Wiggins had a reputation for liking a drink and being a lot less disciplined than his son, which became a problem. Although six-day racing has a party atmosphere – spectators in Europe go to the six-days for a night out where they drink and eat and listen to live music as well as watch the racing – the racers must be dedicated. There aren't as many six-days now, but in the mid eighties there were a lot, and they were concentrated into a short time period. After one event finished, riders would fly somewhere else and start a race there the next night. With that brutal kind of schedule, burning the candle at both ends had consequences.

It certainly had for Wiggins, who slipped down the rankings. He was no longer good enough to be paired with Tony Doyle, who graduated to partner Australia's Danny Clark, one of the best six-day riders of all time. Clark won 74 six-days, second only to the 88 of the accepted master, Patrick Sercu of Belgium. Seventeen of Clark's victories were with Tony Doyle, who won 20 during a career that was interrupted by a terrible crash in 1988 during the Munich six-day, which left him in a coma for ten days. Fortunately Doyle recovered, and he even raced again, winning a silver medal in the 1994 Commonwealth Games. Later he was president of the British Cycling Federation for a short while, playing an important role in changes that led to the creation of British Cycling, the sport's governing body in the UK today.

CHAPTER 5

FLAT 'BARS AND KNOBBLY TYRES

The mountain bike as we know it was invented in the late 1970s. Mountain bike competition grew through the eighties, and the bike itself probably saved a large part of the cycle industry during the nineties. However, the spirit of mountain biking came into being long before that. It was born when the first person, maybe even somebody riding a safety cycle in the late nineteenth century, looked down a farm track or a green lane and thought, I wonder where that goes.

British cycling clubs have a long tradition of riding off-road, especially during the winter. Ron Kitching, who played such an important part in developing road racing in the UK, often talked about the off-road cycling he did in the 1920s and 30s. He even adapted a road bike with flat handlebars and big tyres so he could ride motorcycle trials courses on it. And he competed in an off-road time trial held in northern Nottinghamshire each year.

The sport of cyclo-cross, which started as something road racers did to keep fit during the winter, developed through the forties and had its first World Championships in Paris in 1950. The first world title was won by Jean Robic, a Tour de France winner, but as time went on, a growing number of racers became cyclo-cross specialists, who focused on winter racing. Meanwhile special bikes began to be developed for off-road racing but they were still essentially road bikes, just with off-road adaptations.

In the UK the Rough Stuff Fellowship started in 1955 as a direct response to the development of road racing. The founding members were avid off-road riders who feared that some cycling clubs were so focused on road riding that new members might never experience the fun of tackling rough terrain on two wheels and under pedal power. Just as important, the Fellowship wanted to promote riding where the growing numbers of noisy motor vehicles couldn't go.

Off-road riding also had articulate advocates in the cycling press, notably W. M. Robinson, who wrote under the pen name "Wayfairer", and Rex Coley, who was "Ragged Staff" in *Cycling*, the predecessor of today's *Cycling Weekly*. It was Coley who thought up the Cape Wrath Challenge. Cape Wrath is at the far north-west tip of Britain, and to receive a certificate from Coley's magazine a cyclist had to supply a photograph taken at the rowing boat ferry at the start of the 11-mile ride to the Cape Wrath lighthouse, and one taken at the lighthouse. It sounds easy but it's not, even today. The ride there and back is as remote as you can get in this country, and the weather can be treacherous.

The Rough Stuff Fellowship is still going strong today, and it's hard to distinguish between what they do and what is mountain biking. In fact many mountain bikers are members. The main emphasis of the Fellowship, though, is on leisurely adventure, and adventure was uppermost in the mind of the next maker of British cycling history, although it wasn't at all leisurely. His name is John Rawnsley and he invented the Three Peaks Cyclo Cross.

The Three Peaks are Ingleborough, Whernside and Pen y Ghent, three hills of over 2,000 feet in the Yorkshire Dales. Crossing them all in a single day in an approximately 25-mile loop had been a fell runner and fell walker's challenge for a long time. Then in 1959 a Skipton schoolboy called Kevin Watson rode the Three Peaks route on his bike, or he rode the bits he could ride – he carried it over the rest, as competitors still have to, especially up the fearsome slopes of Ingleborough. Watson's time for his pioneering ride was 6 hours 45 minutes.

Rawnsley, by then a first-category amateur road racer, read about Watson's exploit in the local paper and was inspired. He decided to get some mates together and have a go at the challenge. "It was a sort of hard riding club run that first time," Rawnsley explains. "We tried it one Sunday in 1960. The group started in Ribblehead. There was me, Harry Bond, Geoff Whittam, Ron Bows and Pete O'Neil, and we climbed Whernside first, then Ingleborough, then Pen y Ghent. I made a record of all the intermediate times, the punctures and the falls, and our final time was 4 hours 31 minutes and 31 seconds.

"We did it again in May 1961 and lowered the time to 3 hours 54 minutes. So I decided to organize the first official Three Peaks cyclo-cross on October 1, 1961. There were 35 starters, including a world championship cyclo-cross rider, Bill Radford from the Midlands. We went the same way as the fell race does, Pen y

Ghent first, then Whernside and finally Ingleborough, starting and finishing at Horton-in-Ribblesdale. I won the race from Harry Bond."

Since then Rawnsley has organized 49 more Three Peaks, stepping down after the 50th in 2012 at the age of 75. As well as organizing it, he was a top finisher throughout the sixties and seventies. After that Rawnsley focused on winning his age group, and he also took up running, so he could do the Three Peaks fell race each year as well. He jointly holds the Three Peaks cyclo-cross participation record with Neil Orrell. They have both done it 45 times, but Rawnsley also completed the Three Peaks fell race 30 times. He walks it too, and still guides people on their first Three Peaks. By 2011 John Rawnsley had completed 152 rounds altogether, either walking, running or riding. He's certainly done more by now.

While Rawnsley is happy to admit that the Three Peaks are his obsession, he was also a supreme endurance athlete who was fascinated by off-road challenges. He's done the famous Bob Graham round, crossing 42 Lake District peaks on foot, a distance of 74 miles, within 24 hours. And in 1974 he set an extraordinary record when he rode the Pennine Way, 268 miles up the spine of Northern England and into Scotland, in two days 23 hours and 27 minutes. It's a ride that's strictly illegal now because it includes using footpaths where bikes aren't allowed. Rawnsley would be horrified if anyone went for it today, but back then he did it. If anyone has the spirit of mountain biking, John Rawnsley has.

In its early days mountain biking was adventure first and racing second. By the mid eighties, however, mountain bike racing in cross-country and downhill was a big thing in America, and had started to catch on in Europe too. The Grundig Mountain Bike Series billed itself as the Mountain Bike World Cup with events throughout Europe, although it wasn't an official world cup run by the UCI. Cycling's international governing body didn't become involved with mountain biking until 1990. It was the same in Britain, where a body called the Mountain Bike Club (MBC) run by Tom Sillis promoted a national series and loosely watched over several regional series.

Although the first mountain bikes were created in the USA, Britain was not far behind. A motorbike trials rider, Geoff Apps, is thought by most to have been the first in the UK to develop and produce what was recognizably a mountain bike. His were sold under the Cleland brand name until 1984.

By then David Harmon, who is known to thousands of cycling fans today as the voice of British Eurosport, commentating on big road races, was an enthusiastic young mountain biker. He formed a mountain bike club while at university in Sheffield, took part in many of the early races, and he witnessed the rapid development of the sport in the UK first hand, as well as the clash of two cultures when cyclists from a more traditional background became involved in this rapidly growing sport.

"Mountain biking was slower to start here than it had been in the USA," says Harmon. "American mountain bikes were already being mass-produced early on in Taiwan when the trend caught on here. The first mountain bike that we were really aware of was the Specialized Stumpjumper, but that was soon followed in the UK by domestic manufacturers like Muddy Fox and Saracen.

"We were a little bit behind the curve, but we soon started to catch up. Most of the high-end bikes fell into two camps: TIG-welded Taiwanese frames or, if they were built by more established British builders like Dawes, they were usually made from Reynolds tubing by highly trained craftsmen who had previously hand-built tandems or similar. Also, there were a number of hand-built mountain bikes about from small manufacturers, real artisan bikes, which were what we all coveted. Things like Overburys, Dave Yates and Chaz Roberts. When the Brits caught up we caught up pretty quickly.

"Of the early mountain bike equipment, the best was SunTour at the start, and because they were used so much on US-produced bikes we had wheels built with Araya rims, and bought Sakae chainsets. But then Shimano got into the act and started producing fantastic components. It all advanced so quickly it was ridiculous," Harmon remembers.

"By the late eighties, early nineties we also got a whole raft of specialist builders who had not been producing bikes come directly into building mountain bikes. They weren't just adapting themselves like Chaz Roberts was. Those builders included Overburys, Pace, Zinn and Orange. Some of them tended to copy the American bikes, but Overburys and Pace tried to buck the trend. They understood that we do not have the same terrain as the Americans, and their bikes were designed to cope with British muddy trails rather than American dry rocky ones. Overall, though, the pace of development was rapid and it was fascinating for real tech-heads like me; it was the biggest movement in cycling in the last 40 years. It was a time of huge experimentation, and lots of fads came and went very quickly."

When racing began in Britain, that too was based on mountain bike racing in America, but Harmon saw it change when established British pro racers became involved: "The racing tended to copy what was happening in America, so we had things like the MTB Club and NORBA UK, where NORBA was an American race series, so that was just the UK version. The races tended to be all over the place and very varied, but not often very mountainous. Most races were long and hilly, though, and the longer races in Wales, the Lake District and Yorkshire were the best in my opinion. There were some good regional series in places like the South East, the Mendips and the Quantock Hills. I never raced in Scotland so cannot comment on the scene there.

"The national championship races originally had three separate competitions: downhill and cross country, which they still have but they are vastly different nowadays, and an uphill race which doesn't exist any more. The biggest races at that time were held in Beddgelert, North Wales, and Eastnoor Park in the Malverns, which became the 'Malvern Hills Classic' after a while. Then you had some very interesting types of races like Man v Bike v Horse in Wales.

"There was a party atmosphere about those first races, with other events thrown in, like a bike limbo event I remember once. There were real parties after the races too. Most of us in the early days didn't even wear cycling-specific clothes, and I didn't even wear a helmet. Early on I remember riding back into Sheffield on my Saracen Conquest in combat trousers, walking boots and a woolly hat when some club road riders coming the other way saw me and were jeering and laughing at me.

"And then, in about 1989 or 1990, we started to get more professional riders entering races, including some who had ridden the Tour de France and won national titles at other disciplines like cyclo-cross. It began to get more organized at a national level; it was inevitable that it would happen eventually, especially as more established names came into the sport. The prevailing culture of mountain biking when it started in the UK was a sort of surfer-dude culture. But that was completely alien to the established pros, and there was a feeling that they didn't agree with it and couldn't adapt to it, so the organizers just adapted racing to them instead.

"Races were still extremely varied," Harmon remembers. "Personally, I preferred the longer, rockier races, but there were some real classic courses that everybody loved: Eastnoor, Margam Park, Newnham Park and Eastway's cyclo-cross circuit, which was the number-one place for racing in London. Then at the other end of the spectrum there were races like the Southern MTB Series, which was just mud and leaves and nothing else. And even, bizarrely, the totally flat course in Thetford Forest in Norfolk, where they used to build obstacles out of logs just to break the monotony."

The first two British mountain bike stars were David Baker and Tim Gould. Both were good cyclo-cross riders who could look after themselves in a road race, and if anyone is a link between the Three Peaks and the spirit of mountain biking, it's Tim Gould. He won the Three Peaks six times, and most early mountain bike races had a big "ride what nature presents you with" ethos.

Cross-country racing has changed a lot since then, mostly in response to television coverage and its inclusion in the Olympics, but one man who has been with the sport since the beginning is Britain's Simon Burney. He's seen, and driven, many of its changes, and he now works for the UCI as the co-ordinator for the cross-country and endurance side of mountain biking.

Burney was close to Gould and Baker, travelling to their early races as team manager, and is well qualified to describe their first races. "Tim Gould and David Baker's first mountain bike race was in Peebles, Scotland, in 1988. They were both amateur riders at the time, racing for a team I ran called Ace Racing Team, which was sponsored by Peugeot. They were first and second at Peebles by quite a few minutes, so we decided to have a go at the World Championships. It was an unofficial championships back then, and the 1988 event was in Crans Montana, in Switzerland. Two

Americans, Mike Kloser and John Tomac, were first and second, with David third and Tim in fifth.

"Kloser and Tomac were mountain bike specialists, but most Europeans were cyclo-cross riders like Tim and David, although there were a few British riders like Mike Newton and Paul Hinton, who got into cycling through mountain biking.

"Then Tim and David did the worlds again the following year, which were in America, in a race that had been calling itself the world mountain bike championships for a while. Tim and David rode the finals of the NORBA series in Big Bear before it, and Tim won. But Big Bear is 6,000 feet high, and Mammoth, where the worlds were, was up at 9,000 feet. As well as the cross-country there was a long-standing downhill race there called the Kamikaze. David set the speed trap record in it, and it stood for years. The only concession he made to it being a downhill was to wear leg warmers and pump his tyres up a bit harder; he still used his rigid cross-country bike. Tim won the Ezakimak, which is Kamikaze spelt backwards, an uphill race on the same course. He finished in the top ten in the cross-country race too, but David was affected quite badly by the altitude."

On a mountain bike Gould was just that bit better than Baker, and anyone else in Britain really. As the nineties began, the other leading mountain bike exponents in Britain were Nick Craig, who's still a formidable competitor today off-road and is well into his forties, and Tim Davis, a former motocross racer. In downhill it was Rob Warner and Steve Peat, who was 16 in 1990 and at the age of 38 is still a big player at world level today.

"That's the thing with British downhill, though, and it's something I can't really explain," says Burney. "We've got a national downhill series in Britain, but there's not the greatest race scene here really. We've very few ski centres and even fewer downhill courses where British racers can train to world cup level, but we have consistently had British men and women's downhill world champions ever since the early nineties, and if you look at a round of the downhill World Cup today there will be 25 or so Brits in the top 60. It started with Jason McRory and hasn't really stopped through Steve Peat and Rob Warner to Tracy Moseley and the Athertons today."

In cross-country, by contrast, the British started well but then suffered a slump that is only now showing signs of a reversal. Tim Gould won the first-ever round of the UCI mountain bike cross-country World Cup in Bassano del Grappa; then he finished third in the first official cross-country World Championships, held in Durango, where he won the hill climb title, a title that's no longer given out.

The year before Gould became the first man to beat a horse in the Man v Horse race held on a cross-country route in the hills around Llantrwyd Wells in Wales. Man v Horse is one of those things the British do best, an eccentric and eclectic sports event that's oddball enough to attract attention and hard enough to be a true challenge. Britain's first Man v Horse race was held in June 1980, the idea of Gordon Green, the landlord of the Neuadd Arms Hotel in Llantrwyd Wells. It was runners versus horses at first, and it still is now; but for a while, and to give a man a chance to win, mountain bikers were allowed to take part. Gould quickly became the first man to beat the first horse home, and the invitation to mountain bikers was just as quickly withdrawn. It took until 1997 for a runner to do it, and international marathon runner Huw Lobb is still the only one to succeed.

Mountain bike racing grew throughout the 1990s, and as well as providing another horizon for established pro road racers such as Adrian Timmis and Jonny Clay, who like Gould and Baker would flip with apparent ease between city centre racing, long road races and mountain bike events, it pulled people into cycling from lots of other sports too.

Good examples were Britain's top two women cross-country mountain bikers in the early part of this period, Sian Roberts and Deb Murrell. Murrell had formerly been a rock climber, and Roberts was a runner. Murrell finished sixth in May 1989 when Crystal Place in London hosted the Grundig World Cup, the biggest mountain bike event there'd ever been in the UK up to then. David Baker won the men's race on a very fast course.

Mountain bikes were still very basic, and quite heavy. The sport had few rules back then. One was about the size of tyres, which had to be at least 1.5 inches wide. The other was that no assistance was allowed, so if a rider punctured or their bike broke, they had to fix it themselves. That meant equipment had to be really reliable, so things like Shimano's U-Brake and SunTour's Rollercam brakes were really bulky. Wheel rims were extra strong, as were handlebars and handlebar stems. Frames were still made of steel, although some top riders had frames made from the lighter steel tube sets like Reynolds 753, and the American company Cannondale were experimenting with a part aluminium, part steel mountain bike frame.

The Specialized Rockhopper Comp was a typical bike of the period. It had a steel frame with a unicrown fork, which was a bike design step introduced on American-made mountain bikes. The 1989 Rockhopper had cantilever brakes with Shimano equipment and 21 gears; a triple chainset with 28, 38 and 48-tooth chainrings and seven sprockets ranging from 13 to 30.

The chainrings, Shimano's Biopace brand, were elliptical, in an attempt to make best use of the power phase of each pedal revolution. However, although they were on the right lines theoretically, Biopace was soon abandoned. Round chainrings prevailed for the next 25 years, just as they always had, until a French company developed Osymetric chainrings, which are oval shaped but non-symmetrical. These really do make best use of the power phase while reducing the non power phase of each pedal revolution. There is a particular reason for mentioning this French invention in a book about British cycling: as well as being a first for Britain, Bradley Wiggins's 2012 Tour win was a first for Osymetric chainrings. Chris Froome also used them in 2013.

Mountain bikes of the late eighties and early nineties were a world away from the super-light sophisticated machines the top riders use today, but if anyone is a link between those two eras it's Gary Foord. He's younger than Gould and Baker, and was mentored by Gould on the World Cup circuit. Foord was also more of a mountain bike specialist than Gould and Baker were, and unlike them he has stayed in the sport. Foord coached Liam Killeen, who is still one of Britain's best male cross-country mountain bikers today.

Foord won the Mammoth Mountain round of the 1994 UCI World Cup, and was on the podium again the following year. He had 15 top-ten World Cup places by the time he stopped competing at that level in 1998. "But after Gary we lost some momentum," says Burney. "A lot of that first generation retired from racing at the same time, and those who carried on, like Nick Craig, and others coming up after him, like Oli Beckinsale, found it harder to compete and Britain dropped down the ranks. We had an idea what was happening: EPO had got into road racing in the 1990s and it was maybe inevitable that some mountain bikers would be tempted try it. Then Filip Meirhaeghe got busted."

Meirhaeghe is a Belgian, the world mountain bike champion in 2003, and after he was caught he admitted using the performance-enhancing drug EPO, a red blood cell booster. It confirmed what Burney and others thought, that EPO and perhaps other drugs were being used in mountain biking, although he believes the situation didn't last long, certainly not as long as it did in the road side of the sport. "At first all the UCI could do was a blood test to get a rider's haematocrit level, and if it was over 50 per cent the rider would be made to rest. It couldn't be proved if the reading was natural or if it was caused by drugs. It's only a personal theory, but once a test came in that detected EPO I think it scared off anyone who might have been tempted to use it. There isn't the money in mountain biking that there is on the road; riders couldn't afford to employ doctors or techniques that we now know some road riders used to get around the tests. So British riders' results are slowly coming back now," he says.

Burney thinks that Oli Beckinsale's career, which is not over – the 37-year-old is still racing and is still winning – could have been adversely affected by other riders using drugs. He raced in the 2000, 2004 and 2008 Olympics and became a regular in World Cup races and at World Championships after his debut in the late nineties.

Beckinsale isn't from a cycling family, as many champions are; instead he was inspired to take up cycling after watching one of the Kellogg's city centre races. "There were no cyclists in my family, but my dad started riding his bike a couple of nights a week with some mates and he took me to the Bristol city centre professional criterium, where I saw Allan Peiper win. I thought it was pretty cool, and right then and there I knew I wanted to be a cyclist. Dad promised to buy me a bike. It was a choice between a Raleigh Mustang mountain bike or a road bike. It was a real sleep-losing decision, but I went for the mountain bike and eventually started racing on it, basically because there were a lot of mountain bike races around then.

"Eventually I got a road bike as well and joined the Clevedon club. I started road racing, but it wasn't to improve as a mountain biker. I raced because it was racing. Even now, mountain biking pays the bills, and everything has to fit around it, but first of all I'm a cyclist. I like road racing, I like razzing around the streets in criteriums, and I really like cyclo-cross, as well as mountain biking."

One of the differences between road racing and mountain bike racing is the damage the latter does to your body. "Cross-country mountain biking is full on," Beckinsale explains. "It used to be at least two hours at your threshold and dipping just above it every few minutes. Enduro races are easier than World Cup cross-countries. You are racing for maybe four hours but you are near threshold or on it, you don't keep dipping over the red line, which is the killer. I am wasted for a few days after a World Cup level cross-country race.

"You can't race like that every weekend. If you did, all you would do is recover and race, you wouldn't train. In the end you would get less fit. What I do is block off a period for racing. I train up for it, riding some road races to get form, and maybe one or two mountain bike races to find out where I am. Then all I think about for a few weeks is racing and recovering, no training."

This may help to explain why British cyclists haven't had the level of success in cross-country mountain biking that they've had in other areas of the sport. Mountain biking requires a big budget because riders have to specialize in it. But because mountain biking only has two sets of medals at Olympic level, and after Beijing its presence in the Games went on probation over the way it was televised, it didn't get the budget within British Cycling that other branches of the sport get.

That could change, because mountain biking's Olympic status was confirmed after London, as Simon Burney explains. "The first Olympic mountain bike race was in Atlanta. There was a cross-country event in Sydney in 2000 and Athens in 2004, but then the course in Beijing wasn't great, and when the numbers all came in the IOC saw that it was the most expensive sport to cover on TV in the whole Games. The UCI were told to make mountain biking cheaper and easier to film.

"So the first thing they did was cut the length of the races, which had an immediate effect on TV costs, from two hours to 90 minutes. They also made the courses shorter and decided to make them 100 per cent rideable. That made them less of a technical challenge at first, but bikes improved so much in the last two to three years that course designers could safely bring in technical sections because the best full-suspension cross-country mountain bikes can cope with anything and are really light.

"They made courses technical again, with drop-offs, berms, rutted descents and even man-made rock gardens. The London Olympic course at Hadley Farm in Essex was a real technical challenge. The men's and women's races were both exciting, they both produced worthy champions and medallists and they were easy to film. The IOC were over the moon with how the events were presented, and the probation thing was lifted. Mountain bike cross-country is a strong part of the Games now."

The two British selections for the mountain bike race in London were Liam Killeen and Annie Last. Killeen is 31 and Annie Last is 22, so they are at different ends of their career. Killeen took the cross-country bronze medal at the 2002 Commonwealth Games and he won the under-23 World Cup in 2003. Since then he's won the British national title several times and has come very close at world and Olympic level. He won the Olympic test event on the Athens course but finished fifth in the Games race. He won the 2006 Commonwealth gold medal, but had almost the whole of 2007 out of competition suffering from chronic fatigue. It was a major setback.

"Doctors thought I had glandular fever, and maybe it was originally," he says. "Eventually, though, everyone came around to thinking I had blitzed my immune system, probably by taking too little notice of a virus picked up at the 2006 World Championships in New Zealand, maybe during the travel to get there."

It took a long time before Killeen could start training, and even longer before he could race, and it took its toll on him mentally. "You know when you are looking forward to something and the event keeps getting postponed, then it's postponed indefinitely? Well I was looking forward to the 2007 season and I had really high expectations of myself, then suddenly my mind and body were out of step. All my racing previous to being ill, all the improvements I made led me to feel confident, not just in my physical ability but in my mental strength. You know, mind over matter when the chips are down. Then suddenly the mind was there but not much matter.

"What added to the problem was that I was pretty resistant to changing my behaviour. It took a long time for me to stop beating myself up, feeling guilty about letting people down, and it was difficult to lay off the bike. You try to stick to habits, routines you know, like getting out on the bike every day. But when they don't work, then you are disorientated and a bit lost. I learned from the experience, though. I guess it's true that you learn from everything.

"When I got the all clear to start training it was a matter of building up and feeling the way. There were some false starts because of overdoing it without realizing it – because I would feel OK. I took the approach of riding one day on, one day off for at least the first couple of weeks. It took about four to five months of 2008, including some races, before I felt right. I knew things were really coming better around the time of the World Cup race in Fort William, which was in June."

With his strength finally back, Killeen finished fourth in the 2008 World Championships, and because he was improving and most of his competitors were at their peak, he became one of the hottest favourites for the gold medal at the Beijing Olympics. But fairytale endings are few and far between in sport and Killeen crashed inside the first few hundred metres. It left him in last place, and although his fight back to seventh was an amazing performance, he still hadn't got the Olympic medal he deserves.

Almost unbelievably, Killeen crashed again in the London Olympic race, breaking his ankle. It took a long time for Killeen to get going again, understandably, but he's back in training and looking forward to Rio 2014. He's still the number-one British men's mountain biker and is very much part of British Cycling's plans, even though there are youngsters coming through with real potential. "The young riders need Liam in the national series races. He's still the best and he's who they should be measuring themselves against. They will develop quicker with Liam racing," says one of British Cycling's top coaches, Matt Parker.

Annie Last will have a big role to play too. She's so determined that she put a place in medical school on hold so she could do the 18 months of World Cup racing she needed to qualify for the London Games – there wasn't an automatic place for Team GB because none of the women had enough World Cup points. She finished eighth and is very much part of Britain's continuing Olympic effort.

THE BATTLE OF BOARDMAN AND OBREE

Towards the end of the 1980s there were more European teams employing British professional riders than ever. In 1988 the Fagor team with Malcolm Elliott, Sean Yates and Robert Millar disbanded, so Millar went to Z-Peugeot, Yates to the American team 7-Eleven, and Elliott joined Teka in Spain for 1989.

Joey McGloughlin was already riding for Z-Peugeot, and confirmed his promise with a win and a second place in two stages of the Tour du Limousin, but was plagued with ligament injuries and returned to race in the UK in 1990. McGloughlin had joined Z-Peugeot with another British rider, Adrian Timmis, but he went home earlier, in 1988. Timmis had been one of the four ANC riders who battled through to the finish of the

1987 Tour de France, but it cost him. Finishing that Tour helped Timmis get a contract with Z-Peugeot. It was common knowledge within pro cycling that the ANC riders weren't getting paid, yet the four of them, Timmis, Elliott, a Czech with an Australian passport, Kvetoslav Palov, and Frenchman Guy Gallopin, battled through. Timmis had a lot of ability, and maybe could have developed into a really good climber. Just before the 1987 Tour he won a stage of the Midi Libre race.

Timmis now looks back on his time as a pro in Europe with mixed feelings. He's proud to have finished the Tour de France, as it's something that not many British riders have done, even now, but he feels he pushed himself too far to do it. He thinks that maybe if he'd pulled out he might have been better able to prove himself with Z-Peugeot. As it was he was tired and ill for most of 1988.

"The Tour was so hard, unbelievable at times," Timmis recalls, "but there was only one day when I thought I might not make it to Paris. It was the day we went over the Galibier. As soon as we started there was a long rise up a valley before the first mountain, and the speed everyone rode up there was incredible. I kept thinking it would ease, that the back group with the sprinters in, the grupetto, would form soon.

"I even tried to make it happen by swinging out of the line. But then Paul Kimmage told me not to do it. He shouted, 'Get back in, it's too early.' Eventually a group did form, but the pace at the front was so high that we had to really chase in the valleys. And when we finished at La Plagne we were nearly 40 minutes down.

"Paris was an experience too. Everybody said that the final stage would be a relaxed promenade to the Champs-Elysées, but the Panasonic team attacked from the gun. I found out later that they attacked because their big rivals, Superconfex, had come to an arrangement with race leader Stephen Roche that Van Poppel would win the green jersey. Roche led Van Poppel narrowly but the two teams agreed not to contest the intermediate sprints, and because he was a better sprinter Van Poppel would take the green jersey in Paris. Panasonic found out and caused havoc, because there was a big rivalry between the two. We were lined out in the gutter almost from the start. I asked Robert Millar, who rode for Panasonic then, what was happening, but he just shrugged. I'll never forget coming over the brow of the hill, though, and seeing the Champs-Elysées and thinking I'd made it.

"The thing is, I was exhausted, and I'd been exhausted during the Tour. When I got a place in Z-Peugeot I lived with Joey McGloughlin in Charleroi, and if you aren't going well, and I wasn't, then living on your own abroad like that feels isolated. It wasn't the best place to be based either. There weren't many other cyclists there, so hardly anybody to ride with even. And the feeling of tiredness never left me; nobody could put their finger on what it was, but I suppose it might have been diagnosed as chronic fatigue now," Timmis says.

Sean Yates and Malcolm Elliott were both older than Timmis, and perhaps more durable athletes. Each had a brilliant year in 1989. Elliott won a stage and the points jersey in the Vuelta a Espana, becoming the second British rider after Robert Millar to win a Grand Tour classification. He also won two stages in the Semana Catalana, two stages in the Trofeo Castilla y Leon and one in the Tour of Galicia to establish himself as one of the best road sprinters in the world.

Elliott was a classy cyclist, so classy that he didn't always have to train as hard as others did and could live a less than monk-like existence. It may also have been a mistake to stay so long in the UK, where he was an undoubted star. His career was good, but there are those who believe that it could have been better with a bit more application. Elliott has almost admitted as much, both in his comeback to cycling as a pro at nearly 40, and in the way he trained and some of the things he did and said during that time.

Elliott's return was unprecedented. He seemed to improve year on year, winning more and more British pro races. Then he won the Rutland CiCLE International Classic, a UCI 1.2 ranked race, against European pro opposition at the age of 47. He also raced in the Tour of Britain against World Tour opposition before stopping for good at nearly 50. But to achieve those results and the level of fitness he did, Elliott trained as never before. He seemed to rediscover the joy of cycling that made him take it up in the first place as a kid.

His experiences then also made him think about his first pro career. This is what he said during an interview in 2008 when asked if there was anything he wished he'd known or done during that time: "I wish I'd had the general accumulation of experience that makes you realize that although you thought you knew everything at 25, there was so much you had to learn. And I wish I'd known how to focus and work really hard, and suffer, which I didn't know and didn't have the application to do the first time around."

Sean Yates too was on great form in 1989. He won the Grand Prix Eddy Merckx, two stages of the Tour of Belgium and the prologue time trial of the Tour of Holland. He was also beginning to establish himself as the best team worker in the business. By 1989 Yates understood how pro cycling worked. He recognized chances and knew how to take them, but at the same time he recognized that a team is only as good as the sum of its parts.

He was also coming to his peak physically. Yates could and maybe should have won Ghent–Wevelgem in 1989. He was in a breakaway for 246 of the 270 kilometres in freezing rain. "There were four of us at first: me, Gerrit Solleveld, Bruno Cenghialta and another rider. We lost Cenghialta and the other guy first time up the Kemmelberg, but we kept on going. Solleveld was strong, he certainly didn't shirk his turn, but looking back now I think I made a mistake by not attacking him last time up the Kemmelberg. I really thought I'd beat him in the sprint, but instead he whopped me," Yates says now.

Robert Millar was the star of the 1989 Z-Peugeot team, and it was a bit like coming home for him, except this was a new and improved version of the Peugeot team Millar joined in 1980. It was backed by the forward-thinking French businessman Robert Zannier, whose Z children's clothing chain was the headline sponsor, and an equally modern team manager in Roger Legeay, who would go on to play a big role in the British cycling story over the coming years.

Millar went well, winning a stage in the Tour of Romandie, where he finished third overall, and taking another in the Critérium du Dauphiné on his way to second place there. Millar was in good shape for the Tour de France and he won stage 10 from Cauterets to Superbagnères, outsprinting Pedro Delgado in an uphill finish after leading over every one of the climbs. He finished tenth overall.

Later in 1989 Millar was a popular winner of the Tour of Britain. Kellogg's had switched their sponsorship from city centre racing to an international stage race, something the organizer of both, Alan Rushton, thought might have been a mistake. "It was maybe too early. The one-hour city centre format was easier for non bike fans to understand than a stage race. City centre is also a much easier racing format to put on," he said soon after the Tour of Britain's run ended in 1999.

He might have been right at the time. There were some city centre pro races and even series after Kellogg's, such as the Provident Series of the early nineties, but the British-based pros more or less lost their best shop window until the Tour Series televised races started in 2009. And after a promising start the Kellogg's Tour of Britain became the Kellogg's Tour and then the Pru Tour before stopping in 1999. Unlike city centre racing, it's debatable how many new bike fans the stage race attracted. Luckily Britain's cycling success from 2000 onwards has made all arguments academic, and now both the Tour Series and the Tour of Britain, which returned in 2004, are looking strong.

Millar took his 1989 form into 1990, when he had an amazing run of results: second in the Tour of Romandie, first in the Critérium du Dauphiné, and second in the Tour of Switzerland. It was as if he was trying to make hay while the sun shone before the Tour de France, because the Z team – Peugeot had dropped out of top level cycling sponsorship after nearly 100 years – had brought in the 1989 Tour winner, Greg Lemond.

In the 1990 Tour de France Millar played the role of a team man in what was a magnificent team performance. Z took the yellow jersey early in the race, not through Lemond, but through a younger team-mate, Ronan Pensec, who explains: "I got in a break with Frans Maassen, Steve Bauer and Claudio Chiappucci. I stopped working when we had a good gap to protect Greg Lemond. Bauer took the yellow jersey but I was a climber, so on the stage from Geneva to St Gervais, Bauer finished behind me and I took over the race lead."

Pensec turned professional for Peugeot in 1985, when Millar, Sean Yates and Allan Peiper were in the team, and being a big anglophile the young Frenchman loved it. "I liked the music and fashions from England. When I was still a teenager I came alone to London and went to a number of concerts. I visited Portobello Road market, and the Kings Road to buy clothes as well. I loved the music of the Sex Pistols and everything about the Punk Rock movement. It was a big influence, so in my last amateur season I had pink and green hair," he says.

Pensec defended the jersey next day on the legendary Alpe d'Huez climb with some terrific support from Robert Millar. "Millar was a rider I aspired to be like, so it was a great honour to have him help me. He was a climber, but also a true professional, very correct. I hope he knows what his support meant to me," Pensec says.

With Millar's help Pensec saved the jersey on Alpe d'Huez, but he lost it soon after in a mostly uphill time trial to Villard de Lans, where Claudio Chiappucci took over the lead. So why did Millar work so hard for Pensec, when you might have thought all the team's effort would have been going into getting Lemond up the overall standings?

"Because it was part of our overall team strategy," says Pensec. "As long as I was near the top overall, Chiappucci and Greg's other rivals would have to chase me. Millar didn't help me so I could keep the jersey, he helped me so I could stay a threat. It worked perfectly, because next day I made a big attack very early on. It was crazy, but Chiappucci couldn't ignore me, he had to chase. I went very hard, so he had to chase hard too, which tired him and our other rivals and Lemond was able to gain some time. Chiappucci held on to the lead through the Pyrenees, but Lemond destroyed him in the final time trial, winning for the Z team."

That story demonstrates something else about Robert Millar: he was the perfect pro rider. He won big races, he knew his worth, but could put personal ambition aside if it was best for his team. In this he was very different from Tom Simpson, for example, who always insisted – in a short career, admittedly – on being number one. Simpson left St Raphael in 1961 when Jacques Anquetil joined, taking a wage cut to do it. He would even attack a team-mate if it suited his ambition. He attacked in the 1966 Tour de France on a stage when his team-mate Karl-Heinz Kunde had the yellow jersey, causing him to lose it; and then Simpson crashed, which meant the attack didn't work. Simpson did the same to Eddy Merckx in the 1967 Paris–Nice, but at least that time he won the race.

If Millar, Yates and Elliott were among the world's best pro road racers as the eighties ticked into the nineties, Colin Sturgess was another rider who had the potential to become a contender in the Classics. The son of two British international track riders, Sturgess showed so much promise when he started cycling that the family left their home in South Africa and moved to Leicester to be near the Saffron Lane track. The move allowed Sturgess to train and race in front of the British team selectors for the World Championships and the Olympics, and it worked.

Sturgess rode the 1988 Olympics in Seoul and finished fourth in the track pursuit, when he was just 19 years old. It was a sensational debut and boded well for the next Olympics, but Sturgess wanted to be a pro road racer. Maybe he was a bit too impatient, because his first team wasn't the best place for a young rider who still had plenty to learn, as he explains.

"I signed for the ADR team in Belgium, which was a big team with a lot of big riders. I chose Belgium because I'd done plenty of amateur racing there, so I was known there, but when I look back now I realize the manager, Jose De Cauwer, had so many egos to manage that he couldn't work with a young rider. There was Greg

Lemond, Eddy Planckaert, Ronny van Holen, Fons De Wolf and Johan Museeuw."

There was no planning or structure in pro teams back in 1989, especially not in Belgian pro teams. Nowadays the best World Tour teams run several different programmes, and where they have very young riders they will try to work out a development programme for them. They might even assign one of the team's *directeurs sportifs* to be responsible for the younger and more inexperienced riders. Back then Belgian teams like ADR expected their younger riders to keep fit by riding kermesse races in Flanders, while standing by for the call if one of the established riders in the first team had to drop out of a race through illness or injury.

That's what happened to Sturgess. His first race in 1989 was Paris–Nice. "I was the best ADR rider with 17th in the prologue, but the stages after that were all pure pain, and I dropped out on the same day that Eddy Planckaert did. I didn't do many big races after that," he says.

Feeling ignored, Sturgess left his Belgian base to train in Leicester for the World Professional Pursuit Championships in Lyons. ADR didn't even know what he was doing until the night before the pursuit series began, but Sturgess didn't feel much loyalty to them as they were relaxed about when and what they paid him, and would end up owing him money. He had no team track bike or team staff to help him, so he used his own Harry Quinn pursuit bike, the one he'd used in Seoul, and he was looked after at the worlds by his mum and dad. It was no handicap, though; Sturgess was the best all through the pro pursuit series and he beat Australia's Dean Woods in a thrilling final.

The following year wasn't much better for Sturgess as far as his team were concerned, but he won the British pro road race title, which helped him get a place in what could have been a better team for him in 1991. It was sponsored by Tulip Computers, and Allan Peiper, Peter Peters and Adrie Van der Poel were among his team-mates.

"It was a good team but there was a lot else going on in cycling. It was the start of the nineties, and we all know what happened then. It was the start of the EPO years. I remember the World Track Championships that year. A soigneur came up to me after I'd broken the world record and said, 'You won't win.' I said, 'Why not? I'm the fastest,' but he just grinned. And I didn't win, and that cracked me," says Sturgess.

Sturgess left European pro cycling, raced in South Africa for a while, and then after completing his degree he worked as a journalist in Australia. He would eventually come back to the sport and rejoin the British cycling story in the late nineties. Meanwhile another potential big race winner, Chris Walker, was trying to step up to the big time.

Walker is from Sheffield, where he lived in the shadow of Malcolm Elliott a bit. He also suffered from the same inferiority complex that a lot of good British riders had, which basically stemmed from the way the amateur side of cycling was run and funded in the UK. It was the amateurs who did the Olympics – the first open Games weren't until 1996 – and amateurs had their own world titles to race for. Eastern European amateurs were state funded, but in many cases so were the best from the West. Many French riders worked for the state or in local government. The best Belgian amateur teams were funded by businesses, and promising riders also had big supporters' clubs who would organize money-raising initiatives for them. Italian amateur racing teams were well supported too, and the national squads of all these countries, as well as Spain and Holland, received state support.

British amateurs got nothing. When they were racing for their country, their transport and hotels would be paid for by the British Cycling Federation (BCF), but that was it; the BCF had little funding to use apart from its members' fees. Race kit was terrible, coaches were mainly well-meaning amateurs – although some were quite good – and there wasn't much of a development system. Things were basically done as they always had been done, the BCF survived on a race-to-race basis, and if a world champion or an Olympic medallist came along it was great.

Walker's teenage son Joey and daughter Jessie are both good riders now. Jessie won her first Great Britain selection in 2012, riding as part of the GB team that saw Lucy Garner win her second junior world road race title. They are products of a completely different British Cycling system: a well-funded, well-staffed system that is the envy not just of the cycling world but of the whole of sport.

When the Walkers were interviewed for a cycling magazine recently, Joey was asked what race he most wanted to win. Without hesitation he said, "The elite world road race championships." Chris Walker was surprised, but only for a moment. "That's the difference," he said. "Jess and Joey have seen Mark Cavendish win, they've seen British Olympic success and they've seen Bradley Wiggins win the Tour de France. Now they are in the same system they see no reason why they can't do things we never dared think about. My generation never saw any British riders win those races. And when we went abroad to race, the other riders didn't expect us to win like they do now. They expected us to lose."

Walker turned pro for a British team, Watertech-Dawes, in 1987, and he won the sprints jersey in the first Kellogg's Tour. It was a good start, but Walker's confidence took a knock when he raced for the late 1980s incarnation of the Raleigh team. The bike brand had won the 1980 Tour de France and almost everything else as TI Raleigh, then won some more and came close in the Tour when it co-sponsored Laurent Fignon's System U and Castorama teams in the late eighties. It also sponsored a British-based team, but for some inexplicable reason in 1988 the team started doing what hadn't worked back in the early days of TI Raleigh: they started riding big European races without proper preparation.

"Paul Sherwen took us to Ghent–Wevelgem and we all got our heads kicked in," Walker recalls. "It was terrible, a real eye-opener, and my confidence took a hammering. After that I began to think being a British-based pro was fine. The money wasn't bad, and you were with your mates and living in familiar surroundings. Then you go over there and see how hard it is."

Walker was content for a while, but he also kept improving. He moved to another British-based team, Falcon-Banana, and won 16 races in the UK in 1990. Then they started going abroad in 1991. But it was a stronger and older Chris Walker who went this time. He won four stages and took second overall to Lance Armstrong in the Settimana Bergamsca. Then he won the final stage of the Tour of Vaucluse, where the overall winner was Miguel Indurain. He also won the 1991 Milk Race.

Chris Walker certainly had potential. If he'd also had more self-belief earlier, or if he'd been part of the system British Cycling has now, who knows what he would have won. The same can be said of several others from his era; John Tanner, Wayne Randle and Chris Lillywhite, for example, all had what it takes physically. They just didn't have the self-belief of riders like Brian Robinson, Tom Simpson, Barry Hoban, Robert Millar and Sean Yates.

But there was one man who had the belief, who was in the right place with the right talent at the right time, and who met the right person to help him. The man was Chris Boardman, the person he met was Peter Keen, and together they dug the foundation that underpins the success of British cycling today.

They were introduced by Doug Dailey, an unsung hero in the British cycling success story. Dailey was the British Cycling Federation's national coach during the eighties and into the nineties. He's an Olympian, the national amateur road race champion in 1972, and he was perfect for the job, which was all-encompassing. Dailey was responsible for everything on a day-to-day basis, but he still looked for talent and backed it. He put Boardman with the best man to help develop him, and he also backed and stuck with Graeme Obree no matter what.

After his stint as national coach – a job nobody could have done indefinitely at that time – Dailey continued to work with British Cycling in a number of roles until he retired in 2012. Dailey was awarded an MBE for his services to cycling, and those who worked with him have nothing but praise. Olympic bronze medallist and 2000 world pursuit champion Yvonne McGregor says, "If you cut Doug in half he'd have cycling written right through him."

The British cycling scene Boardman found when he took up the sport was the same one that Walker experienced. "British cycling was an amateur set-up when I started racing," says Boardman. "People got jobs or went away with teams as coaches or managers just because they could get time off work. Everybody did the best they could; then the lottery changed everything," he says.

But lottery money didn't fund Boardman. His first international triumphs were a long time before lottery cash funded British Cycling's performance effort. He had an innate ability, he had it in spades, and Peter Keen knew how to exploit it. But it should not be forgotten that Boardman's ability had already been fully recognized by his first coach, Eddie Soens, who had also encouraged his rider with a remarkable prediction.

Eddie Soens was from a different, older school. Whereas Keen is a scientist who worked out formulae for success, Soens worked in inspiration. He knew how to get cyclists fit, but he also had the gift of getting them to own their talent, which in fact is quite a modern coaching concept. Right from the start of his career Boardman was a brilliant time triallist, so good that he hardly did any road races. But after his first real road race success, the Onchan Cup, which was part of the Isle of Man cycling week, Soens told Boardman that he would be the best road racer this country had ever seen and that he could win Classics and stages in the Tour de France. The prophecy didn't come true exactly as Soens saw it, but it shows that some of the old school knew their stuff; a fact that is often overlooked.

Peter Keen was a champion cyclist as a kid, winning the schools 10-mile time trial championships in 1980. He studied sports science, and towards the end of the eighties started working with Chris Boardman – but in his own way. This is how Boardman summarizes their relationship: "Peter wasn't interested in the history or mystique of cycling, but just in looking at the demands of the event, breaking it down into its unique pieces then doing the training to meet the demands. I'm fascinated by how things work, including how I work. My background is in wood, so I'm into how things are made, and into measuring. Peter Keen gave me something I didn't have when I was younger; he gave me process and I became fascinated by it. I probably became more interested in the journey than getting there, to be honest.

"Peter lit a spark in me. He told me there's evidence that if you do this then this will happen, and that was wonderful. From then it ended up not about winning or losing, instead it was about why we got this or that result. We would unpick everything, a training session, a race, and even a whole season, take it to bits and see how to build it better. From the moment I started working with Peter that process drove me until one afternoon in 1997. We were having a meeting to see how we could get something more out of me, and I lost interest. I drifted off and that was it. I'd got everything out by then, we were looking for stones to turn over but they'd all been turned, there were no stones left, there was no more left, and I suddenly realized it then."

Boardman always had a good sense of his destiny. In 1988, after he won his first national titles in the pursuit and the senior national 25-mile time trial, he was interviewed by Les Woodland for *Winning* magazine. Among other things he spoke about his talent and where it could take him. He was barely 20, and this is what he said: "If you are a pursuiter you are good at five minutes. If you can be the best at five minutes, you can be the best at an hour. That's a fact, a physical fact. If you are fast, you're fast. I mean up to one hour, endurance really doesn't come into it. It's not a case of how long you can last."

Up until then Boardman was a track racer and a time triallist. He started doing more road races in 1990, but solving the riddle of how to cover a distance in the shortest possible time fascinated him. It always would. He was the national hill climb champion four times from 1988 to 1991, and the 25-mile champion five times from 1989 to 1993. He set new competition records for 25 miles in 1992 and '93, recording a blistering time of 45 minutes 57 seconds on a course near Oxford on a fixed gear, although by then he was in search of a much bigger cycling record. "The 25 came from the preparation for the hour record really. It was a good test, a similar demand, which is why I used the fixed gear. I almost wished I hadn't on one corner, though. I still don't know how I got round it without grounding a pedal. I was going so fast I needed to lean the bike, but I had to take the widest line through this particular bend to do it," he says today.

If Boardman started to dominate short-distance time trialling in Britain toward the end of the eighties, Ian Cammish dominated longer time trials for the whole decade. He was the British Best All-Rounder from 1980 to 1985, a title he won again in 1987, '88 and '89. His favourite distance, though, was 100 miles, where he won nine national titles, and in 1983 he broke his own national record by seven minutes with an astonishing time of 3 hours 31 minutes.

Cammish's 100 record stood for years, and was only beaten when riders started using the aerodynamic bike adaptations that began in the mid eighties and advanced in big jumps until the point when Greg Lemond used tri-bars to win the 1989 Tour de France. Tri-bars gave a revolutionary and much faster riding position, similar to the one used by cyclists in time trials today. However, there are two faster riding positions, both invented by a maverick Scotsman and both subsequently banned by the UCI.

Graeme Obree began racing in Scotland towards the end of the 1980s. He rode time trials, and was soon questioning the very fundamentals of what he was doing. The position he used on a standard bike, the same one that all his competitors used, just seemed wrong, or at least wrong for riding alone as fast as possible, which is what a time trial is.

Obree began experimenting. He liked riding on a fixed gear, even on the road; its direct drive simplicity appealed to his engineer's mind. But then he looked at the aerodynamics of cycling. The two keys are frontal area and air flow over the bike and body. To go fast, the former needs to be as small as possible and the latter as smooth as possible. He also realized that because the rider is by far the bigger part of the bike–rider combination, he should focus on rider position more than bike shape.

Frontal area is reduced by crouching low over the bike, which is something that was addressed by the low profile bikes introduced in the mid eighties. Next comes the question of a cyclist's arms: once the rider is up to speed all they do really is support the upper body, but while they perform that function they are creating drag, because they are in the air flow. Tri-bars reduced the amount of drag a cyclist's arms create because, among other things, they bring the arms together and place them within the frontal area of the rider's upper body. But Obree set about seeing whether his arms could be taken out of the drag equation altogether.

Obree's first solution was to invert a pair of dropped handlebars. When you do that, the flat bottom bits are at the top, so Obree could hold them and lay his upper body on them for support. His arms were then tucked underneath him and he was leaning forward. This meant he was low, his arms were out of the air flow, and he had come forward on the saddle, rotating his hips, which meant he could apply more power to the pedals. Obree had taken his first step towards cycling greatness.

Meanwhile in Norfolk another inventor was developing a quite different kind of bike. Mike Burrows saw carbon fibre as the best material to make racing bikes, but he knew that the best way to use the material was to produce a monocoque (one-piece) frame in a mould rather than gluing sections of carbon fibre tubes together, mimicking the way a steel frame is brazed or an aluminium one welded. Also, given the inherent strength of carbon fibre and the ability with monocoque design to use shapes different from those previously used on bikes, Burrows questioned the need for two fork blades and two chain- and seatstays.

The resulting design had a low frontal area and great air-flow properties. Burrows produced a time trial bike, and tried to sell the idea as a design principle that could be rolled out across a whole range of bikes to the British cycle industry. They weren't interested, but Peter Keen and British Cycling were.

Keen began working with Boardman in the run-up to the Barcelona Olympics, where he felt that Britain's number-one pursuit rider had the chance to win. Burrows had a friend who worked for the sports car manufacturer Lotus, and when he saw the design, he got Lotus to make a bike for Boardman. The UCI decided to allow monocoque frames in competition in 1990, which gave Keen and Boardman the green light to use the Lotus.

It was an aerodynamicist's delight. Helped by Boardman's innate ability to achieve a very low riding position, the designers kept the frontal area of the bike to a minimum, and they were able to fit special all-in-one tri-bars to what was effectively the fork crown. The bike had a one-fork blade, which not only reduced frontal area but helped the air to flow smoothly around the front wheel. The frame's shape did the same by leaving a large space behind the front wheel, while its overall shape and the lack of seatstays, and only a single chainstay to hold the rear wheel on its drive side, helped smooth air flow too. The bike didn't win Britain's first cycling Olympic gold in 72 years – Boardman did that – but it helped.

With that box ticked, Boardman and Keen began looking at another objective, Francesco Moser's 1984 world hour record of 51.51 kilometres. It was ambitious, but as Boardman said three years before, "If you can be the best at five minutes you can be the best at an hour." But somebody else was looking at the hour, and he was looking at it out of necessity.

Graeme Obree's bike shop had gone bust and he needed money. Talking about the hour record in 2008, Obree explained why he chose "The Hour", and how his situation motivated him: "The record has fascinated me since Moser broke it. It's the ultimate test, one man in a velodrome against the clock, with no traffic. I didn't tell myself I will attempt the record, I said I would break it. When your back is against the wall, you can say it's bad or you can say I'll go for it. When I decided that's it, I'd as good as broken the record."

As Boardman prepared for Barcelona, Obree had been a thorn in his side, occasionally even beating him, which made him uncomfortable. There he was, the sponsored golden boy, with British Cycling's Olympic hopes riding on him, trained by one of the best coaches in the world, and getting beaten by a self-sponsored inventor of weird bikes who lived on jam sandwiches and Weetabix – it was enough to keep anybody awake at night.

Wih hindsight, though, Boardman sees things differently. He now knows that Obree did him a lot of good and is lavish with his praise. "As an amateur I was a big fish in a small pond, and I could have languished there if it wasn't for Graeme. He pushed me. He also changed the approach to pursuit cycling, not once but twice. He was like me in that he didn't look at the sport's history, he only looked at its demands. He saw aerodynamics were crucial in the pursuit, so he thought let's get these two huge cylinders, your arms, out of the air flow, and it worked. I didn't want to go that way at first, because to me it was getting into the world of Human Powered Vehicles, but the second riding position Graeme came up with after the UCI banned his first – the Superman position – was so much faster. Ironically I think that because of my body shape I got more from it than Graeme did."

Obree now applied his mind to the hour record. He kept refining his bikes until he built the one on which he attacked the record, the bike that has become known since as Old Faithful. It had flat handlebars, and Obree rested his upper chest on these while holding mountain bike bar-ends. He wanted his legs closer together when he pedalled, which would reduce frontal area even more, and he felt he'd get more power, so the bike had to have a narrow, custom-made bottom bracket. Obree made it himself, using bearings from a washing machine, thinking logically that since they were designed to spin at 1,200 revs per minute they would be good quality. He also made the frame, which had one sloping cross tube that continued down into the chainstays, elevating them and removing the need for a top tube, to facilitate his narrow pedal action.

Very few people could have ridden that bike, and those who tried said it hurt their arms after a few minutes, but Obree would ride it for an hour. To do it he applied his logic to training, which Obree always believed should be absolutely specific. For example, when training for pursuit championships Obree would ride flat out for five minutes in the morning, then flat out for five minutes in the afternoon, which exactly matches the heats and rounds of a pursuit series. So for the hour record one of Obree's key sessions was riding one hour as hard as he could on a home-made turbo trainer.

While this was going on, Boardman and Keen were working together on "their" hour record attempt. They started training for it using specific doses of effort that Keen calculated would bring Boardman into the shape he needed to break Moser's record. They chose Bordeaux as the track to do it on, worked out a pace schedule and chose a date. Then, two weeks before the attempt, they travelled to the venue to test their kit. They had to leave it until Boardman had the form, because it was the only way to know that what they had chosen worked at record pace.

"We tested five bikes under controlled conditions," Boardman recalls. "After a warm-up for each bike I'd start riding at 45 kph, then ramp it up by one kph per lap until I hit hour record pace, 51.1 kph. Then I held it for five minutes, with Peter Keen blowing a whistle to show me where I should be each lap. It wasn't too hard holding that for five minutes, because 51.1 kph is about 4 minute 45 second 4,000-metre pursuit, and I could do 4-22 flat out for that distance by then. My pulse was logged for each five-minute effort, and basically the lowest pulse reading must correlate to the bike that requires least power to ride at record pace," he says.

Unfortunately the Lotus bike wasn't one of the five tested, because Lotus said they wouldn't release a bike unless they sent an engineer. But the French manufacturers Corima were very helpful, and in the end that was the bike Boardman and Keen decided he should ride on July 23, the day of the record attempt.

But then Obree went for it on July 16 in Norway, and failed by nearly a kilometre. Anybody else would have been crushed. Obree was exhausted but he was also desperate. He'd booked the track for 24 hours, so he decided to go again early next morning. The intervening night was torture. Obree drank loads of water, so he'd wake up every hour to go to the toilet. After doing that he stretched his legs, drank some more water and nodded off, only to have to get up again an hour later. That's how he spent the whole night: drinking water, sleeping, then waking up and stretching over and over again, so his legs didn't seize up from the huge effort he'd already made. Next day Obree broke the record, riding 51.596 kilometres in the hour. It was unprecedented, in terms of both human performance and sheer guts.

Boardman didn't let it get to him. He started fast on July 23, getting well ahead of his schedule by 20 kilometres, before dropping his pace slightly and then picking it up towards the end, when he was doing laps at 54 kph, to reach 52.270 kilometres. It was very cool, very professional, but coming so soon after Obree's record it left traditional European cycling stunned.

The pair captured the interest of the European press, who were astounded by the fact that two British riders had broken a record seen as being the province of the truly great. Fausto Coppi had held the hour record, as had Jacques Anquetil and Eddy Merckx. They were the kind of cyclists who you'd expect to do it, not two British time triallists hardly anyone had ever heard of. "The European press lumped Graeme and me together at first, although we were worlds apart. We were both painted as eccentric and a bit of a novelty," Boardman says.

Maybe so, but the European press saw Obree as the more eccentric of the two. They knew Boardman from the Barcelona Olympics anyway. But then Obree won the World Pursuit Championships held on the same Hamar track in Norway where he'd set his hour record. And to do it he beat Boardman and another great pursuit rider, the former world champion Philippe Ermenault of France.

To one German journalist Old Faithful was "The Devil-Bike". A Norwegian paper said the world title had been won "by an eccentric Scotsman from a nation of inventors and explorers". Another compared Obree to Jan Boklov, who revolutionized ski jumping by turning his skis outwards. The French sports newspaper *L'Equipe* sent a photographer and a reporter to The Ards Cycling Club's 25-mile time trial in Northern Ireland because Boardman and Obree were riding against each other.

Unfortunately Obree was never quite able to harness his talent to make money in cycling. He raced in the GP Eddy Merckx in the autumn of 1993, but his bike didn't work so well on the twisting road circuit near Brussels. A spell with a French pro team in 1995 came to nothing, and later on the UCI would ban Obree's riding position for a second time. Cycling wasn't ready for Obree, but it was for Boardman, and Roger Legeay saw the difference.

He offered Boardman a place in his team, which was sponsored by French insurance company Gan – the same company who had sponsored the team Barry Hoban raced for during his best years. It was the first time a British rider had entered a top European pro team like that, but Boardman says it's the only way he could have done it. "It had to be that way for me. I would not have survived going abroad as an amateur and living there for two years. It's such a dangerous path to follow and so many things can go wrong. I didn't even want to turn pro originally, but I thought I may as well try to move forward because at least I could come back to where I was."

He was lucky to have an enlightened team manager like Roger Legeay, who saw Boardman's potential and helped him to realize it. "It was good to have Roger Legeay," Boardman agrees. "I went in not knowing what to expect, but when we had our first meeting Roger asked me, 'What do you want to do?' I said that in 1994 I wanted to ride this and that, then the Dauphiné, then the Tour de France. But I only wanted to ride the Tour for ten days, then do a hot weather camp, because I wanted to win the time trial and pursuit at the World Championships in Sicily that year.

"Roger said we'd see about the Tour because not many first-year pros get to ride it, but he was relaxed about everything else, and he signed off on it, and that became our process for each year. Luckily I'd won the GP Eddy Merckx GP at the end of 1993, because I struggled for a few months at the start of 1994 due to the fact that I had so little road race experience and suddenly I was mixing with the most skilful cyclists in the world. But then I delivered in the Dauphiné, and we went to the Tour for eight minutes where everybody else had gone for three weeks. Later I won both world titles and Legeay's gamble with me paid off. He didn't pay me much; more than a new pro's salary normally was, but nowhere near a star's wage, so he could afford to gamble."

When he says he delivered in the Dauphiné, Boardman means he won the prologue time trial, then a longer time trial a bit further into the eight-day race. That gave him the overall lead, but he lost it when he was dropped on a stage with a mountain-top finish. But then he won the final road stage with a tremendous lone breakaway. His performance was a marker of Boardman's Tour de France potential, or at least it was thought so at the time. The significance of him being dropped on the uphill finish was missed; at that stage in his career it could be put down to him just having a bad day.

The eight minutes Boardman refers to was the 1994 Tour de France prologue time trial held on the streets of Lille in northern France. Boardman had targeted it, trained specifically for it, and he won it in grand style, rocketing around the 7.2 kilometres at 55.152 kph. It's still the record average speed for a Tour de France time trial. Boardman had the yellow jersey, the first Brit to wear it since Tom Simpson 22 years before, and the Tour de France was coming to Britain.

It would have been amazing if Boardman could have worn the yellow jersey on the two British stages in 1994, its second visit to the country, but although the Gan team defended his lead for two days across northern France they lost it with a ragged team time trial performance around the windswept headlands near Boulogne-sur-Mer on a route that went in a wide loop from Calais to the Eurotunnel.

Massive crowds turned out to watch the Tour between Dover and Brighton, and then on a big circuit around the back of Portsmouth. Well over a million people turned out to cheer on the riders, but this wasn't the Britain we live in today; the British public were interested in the race but some elements of the press were quite negative. It would be very different when the Tour returned in 2007, and it will be unrecognizable when it comes in 2014.

The European press were positive, even if they and the European riders didn't always know what to make of the country. The Belgian journalist Noël Truyers did a straw poll of opinion, asking riders and managers on the Tour what they knew about Britain.

Frans Van Looy of Telkom told him that one of their team mechanics thought that the race was going through the Channel Tunnel.

Jan Raas, by then the manager of the Wordperfect team, said he'd heard that Allan Rushton, who did all the organizing on the British side for the Tour de France, had asked the mayor of a town on the route if they could have a feed station there, and the mayor replied, "We'd rather not. I don't think we have enough tables and chairs."

One rider, Rudy Verdonk, said, "I know about the British fairy tale, King Arthur and the Seven Dwarves." Marc Sergeant said he was looking forward to the British stages because he played Ivanhoe with his friends using wooden swords when he was a kid. And Hennie Kuiper said, "I love the country and its people. The pubs are nice, and the houses are dinky. They always drive on the left just to show they are different, but I like that."

A British yellow jersey in Britain would have been great, but it wasn't to be. As soon as the Tour returned to France, however, Sean Yates did ride into the iconic jersey. His team, Motorola, were second in the team time trial, so when Yates profited in a breakaway on the stage to Rennes, he gained enough time to take the lead. There was some unforgettable TV as he freewheeled to a stop and was told he had the jersey. A team-mate came in behind Yates, and in passing turned to ask him what he'd got out of the break. Yates punched the air, smiled broadly and shouted, "Yellow!"

Yates lost the jersey next day. Motorola had a race favourite in Alvaro Mejia, so they couldn't waste energy defending Yates's lead, and he returned to his day job as a team rider. Boardman battled on to stage 9, a 64-kilometre time trial, but was getting increasingly tired as he did so. He placed fifth in the time trial, and with that his first Tour was over.

Boardman had his wish, he went back home to the Wirral and started to prepare for the World Time Trial Championships and the pursuit in Italy, where he would have to beat Graeme Obree, and that could be a problem. Or at least it could have been if the UCI hadn't banned Obree's riding position.

They'd been after him since he broke the hour record. The UCI seemed to regard Obree as an inventor first and an athlete second. His case wasn't helped by Francesco Moser coming out of retirement in his forties and using a version of Old Faithful to get very close to the record. You could see the UCI thinking that if a veteran can just rock up and get close, then it must be the bike. They took no account of Moser's class, or the fact that he prepared very seriously for the record with sponsors who spent a fortune on it.

Old Faithful was faster than a regular pursuit bike. Boardman tested a version with Peter Keen the previous winter and reached that conclusion; but it wasn't that much faster. There was far more of Obree in his hour record and world title than there was of his bike, but the UCI couldn't or wouldn't see it. So in a quite ham-fisted way they brought in a succession of regulations that made it impossible for Obree to ride Old Faithful in any effective way.

But while they were working out ways to ban it, Obree scheduled a crafty go at the hour record again, achieving a new mark of 52.713 kilometres on the Bordeaux track in April 1994 in front of a packed crowd. The UCI's new regulations came in almost immediately after. Obree tried to adapt the bike for the World Pursuit Championships, but was disqualified because he breached a rule that the UCI had only brought in that morning. Boardman had no such trouble. He was in outstanding form and won the pursuit title; then a week later he won the time trial. It had been a very successful first year.

Naturally Boardman wanted more, and naturally more meant the Tour de France. But Boardman was still essentially training like a track rider; he needed to train the way road riders do, or at least did then. He needed to get some miles in, but he didn't like it. "One year I had to do a week of back-to-back eight-hour rides. I turned some of them into little adventures and would ride to new places and meet my wife in a hotel at the end. One of those started where I live in the Wirral, went into Lancashire, over the Nick O'Pendle, and ended in North Yorkshire. It was winter, it rained all day, there was a headwind and because there was no such thing as sat-nav, just some notes I made on a scrap of paper, I got lost. It was horrible," he says.

There was still some science behind those rides. Long rides help cyclists become more efficient, which means they can make the same effort for less physical cost. This spares fuel reserves, and in a race like the Tour de France fuel is a crucial factor. Long rides also give cyclists deep strength, which scientists still can't explain. And they would help Boardman lose weight, although when asked a few years ago if there was anything he'd seen while working as part of British Cycling's more recent Olympic effort that could have helped him, he said that a better understanding of nutrition now could have saved him some long, cold and very hungry rides. He also said something else quite revealing.

"I would have benefited from the psychological help that's available to athletes now. I was always a glass-half-empty sort of person. That meant I tried not to fail, rather than tried to succeed. It also meant that I tended to avoid situations where I could lose, things like the national road race championships. I think my approach, my nature if you like, could have cost me some chances of success, and I think some psychological work could have helped me with that."

Unfortunately Boardman's new long-distance training regime didn't bring immediate success. He crashed a few minutes into the 1995 Tour de France prologue, run on wet roads in St Brieuc, Brittany, and sustained a shattered ankle and a broken wrist. His ankle still isn't right today and it prevents him running.

The year was one of change for Graeme Obree too. He signed a contract to race for a new French team called Le Groupement, where he'd be joined by a fellow Scot, Robert Millar. Millar had raced with the Dutch team TVM, but he was well into his thirties and wasn't getting the results he used to get. But cycling was also well into the early EPO years, which would put anyone trying to ride clean behind the performance curve they had been on.

Le Groupement was a disaster. Obree was fired for missing the team's first organized get-together on January 1 because he was ill with flu. However, he has said that a team member told him he'd have to pay a sum of money for medicines, which he took to mean doping, which he refused to do. He thinks that was more likely to be the reason he was fired.

The team was launched with lots of razzamatazz, but it didn't last long. Le Groupement was essentially a pyramid sales set-up and the company went bust in 1995, the team folding in June that year. There were warning signs before that, with unreliable payments and low morale among riders and staff, a situation that brought a memorable quote from Robert Millar. Asked by a journalist shortly before the team's demise how things were going, Millar said, "Great, we don't hold team meetings any more, we hold séances." Ironically Millar won the 1995 British road race championships, but he couldn't show off the jersey in the Tour de France as he'd have liked. With no team he had to stop racing instead.

While all that was happening, Graeme Obree fought back. If the UCI banned his bike position he'd develop another. Arms were still the problem. His first solution had been to tuck them underneath him to get them out of the air flow; his second was to stick his arms out in front of him. Superman was born.

He began training and racing on Old Faithful with a new front end. Obree used a long, upwards-sloping mountain bike stem with flat handlebars that had mountain bike bar-ends turned backwards to pull on when he started. Clip-on tri-bars were also attached to the flat handlebars, but extended to their maximum. This set-up gave Obree a flat-backed, stretched position with his arms out in front, fists almost together, like the comic-book hero Superman in flight. It was a very aerodynamic position, but because his arms were fully stretched they locked the rest of his body in place.

Four times world track cycling champion Marion Clignet of France, who used the Superman position to set a world record for the 3,000 metres pursuit, recalls how she once got a personal demonstration from Obree of Superman's locked-in effect.

"We were at the worlds and I just happened to get in the lift with Graeme. There was a few of us, but as a pursuiter I was interested in the new position he'd developed and was doing amazing times with, so I asked him about it. He explained that opposing forces were at the heart of it, and I'll never forget how he demonstrated what he meant by climbing up the lift by walking up the walls with his hands on one side and feet on the other.

"He ended up stretched out across the ceiling, with his butt touching it, and said, 'See, I can stay here all day because my hands are pushing on one side of the lift and my feet are on the other, and both push my backside against the ceiling. They're opposing forces, and it takes hardly any effort to stay here like this.' Graeme said that it was basic mechanics, and he rode all the way to the top floor like that.

"Anyway, when I got the chance I tried the new position and by seeing it demonstrated like Graeme had, I understood it. Your hands push forwards against the handlebars, and because they are straight your arms push your butt back against the saddle, and your legs push down on the pedals opposing the push of your arms. That's how Superman works, it's very aerodynamic too, and I set a world record using it," she explains.

Obree won the pursuit at the Athens and Australian rounds of the 1995 track cycling World Cup. Then he got close to his own world record, set on Old Faithful, at the national track championships in the newly opened velodrome in Manchester. It confirmed his selection for the World Championships in Bogota, where after a slow start in the final he just beat Italy's

Andrea Colinelli. Recovering at home, Boardman watched this with interest, as did other track racers like Marion Clignet, and copies of Obree's handlebars started appearing on many pursuit specialists' bikes.

Boardman won the Critérium International early in 1996, then survived a brutal Tour de France. This one was hard not just because of the uncharacteristic cold weather, but because of what was going on within the peloton. The winner Bjarne Riis later admitted using EPO to boost his performance. Looking back, though, it was obvious that something funny was happening, especially on the day that Riis attacked on a Pyrenean mountain climb called Hautacam, using his big chainring, and left everybody for dead. It was unreal, literally unreal.

Jan Ulrich, who was runner-up that year, recently admitted being involved in the Eufamiano Fuentes doping ring. Third-placed Richard Virenque and fourth man Laurent Dufaux were part of the 1998 Festina scandal. Battling through to 39th place overall in that Tour de France did a clean rider like Boardman credit; and looked at in the longer term the 1996 Tour was a bout of really deep overload training.

Boardman had a good second half to his season, with a time trial bronze medal in the Atlanta Olympics, when he was probably still tired from the Tour. He later won several time trials, and took an astounding world pursuit title when he set a world record of 4 minutes 11 seconds.

Obree's 1994 hour record was beaten later the same year by Miguel Indurain, and then Indurain's was beaten by Tony Rominger. Neither had used the Superman position, but by now Boardman knew it suited him perfectly. He isn't as tall as Obree, and right from his early days of riding time trials, Boardman had the significant natural advantage of being able to get extremely low on his bike, thus vastly reducing his frontal area. It was time for him to put Superman to the test.

The Manchester track was probably faster in 1996 than it is now. The temperature was perfect on September 6, 1996, and the track was full of supporters who were willing Boardman to break the record. It was a rare combination. Nick Rosenthal, a Manchester cyclist and regular photographer at the track, was there that day, and this is what he heard and saw.

"A roar of applause came from a sell-out crowd of 3,300. Chris spent the first lap and a quarter out of the saddle, getting on top of his gear before adopting the Superman position that he was to hold for the next 60 minutes. It was the first time anyone had taken this extreme position over this distance. Could Boardman do it?

"The first kilometre was covered in 1:2.829, and Chris then settled into a pretty steady rhythm of covering the kilometres between 1 minute 3 seconds and 1 minute 4. Our first real check was at the 5km point. The big electronic scoreboard showed Rominger's time of 5:30.25, and we all held our breath until Boardman passed it in a faster time. The only anxious moments came in the second half. Chris eased himself out of the saddle a couple of times on the north banking, before settling back down and getting on with the job in hand. He soon had his rhythm back.

"At the 50km mark, Rominger's time was 54:18.73. Boardman hit his 50km mark in 53:21.752, almost a minute faster. Right in front of me, his trainer Peter Keen held up a board with the number 875 on it, which I assume was telling Chris how many metres he would beat the record by. Chris responded by easing himself out of the saddle again, causing flashes of concern to cross many faces in the crowd. We needn't have worried. As Chris approached the end of the 221st lap, a huge roar broke out. Somebody had marked the track just into the first banking at the point where, on his 222nd lap, Chris would take Tony Rominger's record of 55.291 km, and he passed it with a full minute in hand.

"Peter Keen was now holding up cards showing the minutes then the seconds to go. Boardman was lapping at about 15 to 16 seconds per lap, and he gave it all he had in the last half dozen laps. Then it was over. Boardman wound down for a couple of laps, Peter Keen held out his arms in an expression of admiration, and Chris handed him his helmet. He, they, had done it."

Boardman would go on to win the prologue time trial in the 1998 Tour de France, and set the new hour record after the UCI's banning of the Superman position. Then, when his racing career was over, Boardman played a huge part in the British cycling success to come.

Obree won more British titles, but missed his chance of becoming a professional. He was never able to find a place where he could fit into cycling in a way that gave him the financial reward his tremendous talent deserved. Obree is a great engineer and a profound thinker. He has the intellectual gift of being able to see solutions that others can't, and he has the curiosity and intellectual confidence to question things that others accept. While Boardman clearly played a continuing part in the British cycling success story, Obree's spirit is in there too. He showed just what can be achieved by questioning the norms, and that as much as anything is the blueprint for the next part of this story.

CHAPTER 7

FACTORY RECORDS

Factory Records was a label that fizzed and popped and brought Manchester back into the centre of the music world during the 1980s, 90s and early 2000s. At the very same time another kind of factory was being established in Manchester – but this one produced world and Olympic cycling champions, and it's still going strong today.

In 1994 Peter Keen wrote an article in *Cycle Sport* magazine called 'The truth behind the race of truth', in which he stripped cycling bare of myths and reduced it to what it is: physiology and physics. In it he plots the relationship between speed and power, and air and rolling resistance. He plots power against oxygen uptake and explains what the limits are on human performance.

He also introduces a new piece of kit that helped him in his work, the SRM power measuring system that quantifies the amount of power a cyclist puts into the bike through the cranks. "At last I could go and measure directly the power Chris [Boardman] had to produce during the hour record," he said.

Keen had already developed a training system based on heart rate. It involved identifying four levels of training intensity, where each one was a zone determined by upper and lower percentages of an individual's maximum heart rate (MHR).

Maximum heart rate is individual to everybody, and back then British Cycling Federation coaches used to establish a rider's MHR during what they called a Performance Potential Test using a scientific version of a stationary bike called a Kingcycle. The protocol for doing the test was called a Ramp Test, and tests were done on a regular basis at what were called Centres of Excellence.

In Keen's system, training level 1 meant riding at a heart rate of 45 to 50 beats per minute (BPM) or more below the measured maximum heart rate. If that was 200, then level 1 training effects would take place at below 150 to 155 BPM. Level 1 was used mainly to recover on days between harder training sessions.

There were actually five training levels because level 2 was divided into lower level 2 and upper level 2. Lower level 2 was performed at around 45 BPM below MHR for between three and five hours, and it was used to boost stamina. Riding at this intensity for long periods forced the continuous recruitment of a great number of slow-twitch muscle fibres. The main fuel for this level of effort was dietary and body fat, and it was aimed at improving muscular efficiency.

The next level was called upper level 2. It is the training intensity at which the major biological mechanisms which determine performance as a cyclist start to become taxed. For most riders this level equates to a heartbeat in the range of 35 to 45 BPM below measured maximum heart rate. Training at upper level 2 brings on a number of important physiological changes. These include an improvement in the supply of oxygen to the working muscles by an increase in the heart's capacity to pump blood; a rise in the total volume of blood; the growth of small blood vessels within the muscles called the capillary bed; and the fine tuning of controlled blood flow in the body. The ability of the muscles to use oxygen also improves through changes in the biochemistry of the muscle fibres, enabling a rider to work more efficiently, and at higher work intensities, without the onset of fatigue. A further effect is to encourage the body to use fat as a fuel source in preference to the all-important carbohydrate stores. Upper level 2 is very powerful training.

Level 3 was based on the anaerobic threshold principle that holds there is a critical level of effort, beyond which an athlete is incapable of maintaining a steady pace without rapidly fatiguing. The Kingcycle Performance Potential Test gave an indication where this was for each individual in terms of heart rate, but a good approximation was to work in the range of 15 to 25 BPM below MHR.

It was thought that level 3 training stresses the mechanisms that control fatigue-causing processes occurring in the muscles at higher work rates. Training at this intensity ensures a heavy aerobic stress and should improve the power output a cyclist can maintain before the onset of fatigue.

Level 4 training was based on repetitions of intervals of hard effort and recovery, with the work efforts near to or at maximum heart rate. The primary objective was load the cardiovascular system almost to its maximum by repeatedly pushing almost to the point of exhaustion, and the major benefit of this training is resistance to short-term fatigue. There are training effects throughout all muscle fibres, and maximum power is developed by increasing the rate at which carbohydrate can be broken down to lactate in the muscles. Therefore, specific skills such as sprinting and climbing are enhanced.

This is a bit of a long-winded sports science lecture, but it's important. The four levels of training could be handed out by the BCF to all their coaches in their regional Centres of Excellence. The levels facilitated a coaching structure and system that for the first time could be taught and rolled out all around the UK. Instead of relying on gut feeling or an innate understanding of how training worked, which good coaches like Harold Nelson, Eddie Soens and others had, it provided numbers to work to. And with numbers you have control, you have something you can work with, and cyclists didn't have to depend on what today's popular press are fond of calling a postcode lottery, or have to try to live near a Nelson or a Soens.

But even heart rate isn't as accurate as coaches need it to be. For a variety of reasons the heart rate a specific effort elicits can vary from day to day. Heart rate is a good way to quantify training effort, but it is a long way from being perfect. Something more accurate was needed to refine the numbers coaches and athletes worked with, and bring greater accuracy to their training.

Power output, measured in watts, quantifies the "work" done by any machine. Static bikes called ergometers that measured power output had been around for a while and had been used by coaches, sports scientists and by racers who were curious about human power output. Scientists at Loughborough University used ergometers during the 1960s to help them measure the power output of athletes they studied. Later, links were made between power output and anaerobic threshold by a number of scientists, including Dr Andrew Coggan.

Once mobile power meters were invented that could be fitted to normal bikes, Dr Coggan's work, and that of other scientists, continued outdoors in real-life studies with cyclists. Power meters not only quantified the demands of racing accurately; they also made it possible for training designed to meet those demands to be prescribed accurately.

Hunter Allan, an American coach and former pro racer, collaborated with Dr Coggan to write the definitive *Training and Racing with a Power Meter*, which is considered to be the power training Bible. This is what he says about why power meters are the definitive training tool. "The power meter has been the greatest change in how coaches work with athletes. We can absolutely quantify the actual training being done, understand how training load impacts fitness changes for each athlete, ensure that the athlete is improving in the correct physiological zone, and plan, predict and create 'form' for the athlete instead of just guessing at what will get them there.

"Power meters also create an added sense of responsibility to and from the athlete, along with clearly improving the lines of communication. Before power meters, so much was guesswork and trial and error because we didn't have a way to understand what and how much training 'dose' created a training 'response' in the body. By using a power meter and analysing the data it produces, the relationship between workload and physical improvement is very clear."

There's no doubt that training with heart rate helped Chris Boardman win an Olympic gold medal and set his first world hour record. But once Keen established that the SRM Training System measured power accurately by comparing it in an experiment with the Monark Ergometer, which was a sports science gold standard static machine for measuring cycling power output, Boardman benefited from using SRM. So did the next player in the British cycling story and then all the ones who followed.

Yvonne McGregor was a fell runner who then dabbled in triathlon and found that her true talent was as a cyclist. "I did what many runners do," she says. "I ruptured my Achilles tendon. I stopped running for six months, rode my bike more, and was talked into riding a time trial in October 1990. I raced the following year, then in 1992 I won the bronze medal in the national 10- and 25-mile time trials. I improved in 1993 and was selected for England for the 1994 Commonwealth Games, where I won the points race."

If there was a marker of McGregor's potential it was that points race gold medal. She explains: "I had never ridden a bunched race on the track before, actually I never rode another points race after it either. I was on my pursuit bike, so I just rode around the bottom of the track until the rider in front of me swung up and I went for it. I rode the rest of the race on my own like a time trial and led for enough laps to collect enough points to win."

The performance led to an invitation from Chris Boardman's personal manager, Peter Woodworth, to join Boardman's cycling club, North Wirral Velo, which was sponsored by Kodak. That brought her into contact with Peter Keen, who in December 1994 suggested she should have a go at breaking the women's hour record.

"If there was anything I shone at, it was the hour record," says McGregor. "It's the thing that suited me most. Internationally there was the pursuit on the track, which is what I focused on later, but I felt I was better over the hour. I'm just better at keeping going – they used to call me the Duracell Bunny at home when I was a kid."

She's probably right, because the 47.411 kilometres she rode in June 1995 on the Manchester Velodrome was an incredible performance, especially since she was then only halfway through her third season of racing, and she wasn't yet even a full-time athlete. But if Obree found it hard to turn his hour record into money, the women's world record had no currency value at all.

"It was very hard back then," McGregor recalls. "I remember standing in a shop one day and counting up pennies to see how many carrots I could buy. I went full-time racing and training in 1997 because I'd hit a plateau and I needed to do that to get to the next level, but it was really hand-to-mouth stuff. I was on the verge of quitting several times, and the only thing that kept me going was that I knew I hadn't got the best out of myself. Then I finally got some direct personal funding in 1998."

That was when some lottery funding came in, and it changed the game. When Peter Keen was the BCF's national coach from 1989 until 1992, it was an unpaid post. He still worked full time as a teacher, at Chichester College and then the University of Brighton. When Dave Le Grys was national sprint coach in the run-up to the Barcelona Olympics in 1992, it was also on a voluntary basis, and he recalls: "My budget for the year was about £2,500. What is it now, millions? I even had to do sponsored runs to raise money for basic things like a training camp."

Peter Keen became the BCF's first-ever performance director in 1997. He had a budget, and certain national squad riders were lottery funded. But funding was £10,000 per rider per year at the most, and they had to pay for a lot of things out of their own pocket first, and get reimbursed later. He also instituted a plan, the World Class Performance Plan (WCPP), which plotted a course towards long-term success. For this Keen drew on his work with Chris Boardman, and when he stopped racing Boardman helped him.

"When lottery money came, Peter implemented what he'd done with me on a wider scale by introducing the concept of the business plan for sport," says Boardman. "It was called the performance plan, and in it we looked at a rider's performance, then looked what they did the day before, then the day before that and so on, changing things, until by unpicking 12 months of training we could make a 12-month plan that would reach a goal. And because they help create them, athletes will buy into plans like that."

At first, though, the little money Keen had wouldn't stretch as far as some people wanted, and that caused friction. Maybe because he knew about pursuit racing, having coached one of the greatest pursuiters ever, and maybe because Great Britain had been able to hold their own at the pursuit in world competition even without funding over the years, Keen focused his resources on the individual and team pursuit events in the run-up to the 2000 Sydney Olympic Games. It caused a lot of resentment in the sprint camp – and sprinters tend to be quite fiery characters anyway.

The sprinters didn't have a national coach when WCPP started, although an Australian, Martin Barras, was quickly appointed and proved a success. They were promised special sprint bikes, but these didn't materialize for quite some time. They also felt that Keen was putting up barriers between him and them. Sir Chris Hoy remembers in his autobiography what Keen said when sprint squad member Jason Queally took him to task about the bikes that were promised but never came.

"He pointed out that Yvonne McGregor made do with the same old bike, while we were demanding this and that, but there was a crucial difference between Yvonne and us. At about 60 kilos Yvonne was generating up to about 800 watts, while we 90-kilogram sprinters were, briefly, kicking out a couple of thousand."

It's not surprising that Keen felt on safer ground with the track endurance riders. It was where he could use the numbers his power meter work with Chris Boardman provided. Power numbers are transferable between riders and distances; so if Chris Boardman did 409 watts to ride 52.27 kilometres in one hour, and if you divide his power output in watts by his weight in kilograms, which was around 70 at the time, you get 5.84 watts per kilo.

Given the watts per kilo figure, you can work out that if Chris Boardman needs to produce 5.84 watts per kilo to go at 52.27 kph, and you take, say, the world record for the women's 3,000 metres pursuit and work out the average speed of it, then you can work out how many watts Yvonne McGregor at 60 kilograms needs to produce to get near to it or beat it.

Once there is a figure to work towards, all the coach needs to do then is prescribe training sessions at certain power outputs that will get the rider into the condition to put out the watts, while the rider works, perhaps with a nutritionist, on controlling their weight. It's a system British Cycling uses today to brilliant effect, and it was even adapted to help Bradley Wiggins win the Tour de France.

Boardman used power meters in the latter part of his career, but knowing what power he was capable of putting out seemed curiously to create a puzzle. If Boardman averaged 409 watts during his 1993 hour record, he probably had a much higher average during his 1996 hour record. The Superman position was faster than the one he rode on his Corima bike in Bordeaux, but it wasn't four kilometres per hour faster. Also Boardman's weight in his Tour de France days was probably a bit less than 70 kilograms. That means he was probably capable of getting into the six watts per kilogram area for a sustained effort on a mountain climb.

Six watts per kilogram is around the required figure for winning a Tour de France mountain stage. Later on in Tour de France history Lance Armstrong was winning Tours, and riders like Tyler Hamilton were challenging him, with figures of around 6.7 watts per kilogram, but they were doping to do it.

The intention in quoting these numbers is not to suggest that Chris Boardman was doping; quite the opposite. He's always been held to be a clean rider, not just by British bike fans but by fellow pro riders in Europe. The reason for quoting them is that Boardman was *not* winning mountain stages in the Tour de France. If anything he was getting worse at climbing, when his hour record power and his weight suggested he should be flying uphill.

It was a puzzle, and Boardman and Keen tried everything to think of a way to train around it. Then in 1998, when he won the Tour de France prologue again, Boardman was diagnosed with an illness that's similar to osteoporosis. It was caused by his body producing less testosterone than it should have, and that was the reason he couldn't climb as well as his numbers suggested he should.

"The low testosterone was there throughout my career. I was bemused, I kept being presented with the fact that I should have been able to climb, but I couldn't. Why, because I wasn't recovering, and if you don't recover, it shows most in the hills. The low testosterone level was picked up in a routine blood test, maybe the first I had to do with the biological passport. When they saw the results, somebody suggested that I get a bone scan, and they found my bone density was low," Boardman says.

Testosterone does many things, but above all for athletes it helps them recover from training and racing. It's so potent that it's been used as a drug. If you can boost your recovery rate you can do more hard training sessions and therefore get fitter, and speedy recovery is a key to winning stage races. All through his career Boardman was capable of big one-off efforts, like setting the Hour Record or winning a world title or winning a time trial, but in a stage race he would start strong then get weaker every day. It was because he wasn't recovering.

By the time he got the diagnosis, Boardman's racing career looked to be nearing its end anyway. As he said about training with Keen, he had turned over all the stones and there were none left to turn. However, he had one last hurrah when he set the Athlete's Hour Record in Manchester in 2000.

The Athlete's Hour Record was basically the UCI's response to Graeme Obree. It's since been officially called the UCI Hour Record, and the record Boardman set in 1996 is now called the Best Human Effort. The idea behind the Athlete's Hour was to standardize bikes and so take advances in design out of the equation. The bike the UCI chose as its standard was basically one similar to the sort Eddy Merckx rode when he set his hour record in Mexico City in 1972. Aerodynamic helmets weren't allowed either.

Boardman trained specifically for the record and rode ten metres further than Merckx to set the first Athlete's Hour at 49.441. His cycling career was over, and he reckons he'd been running on fumes for the previous two years. "At times I only kept going because of the infectious enthusiasm of Jen Voigt. He joined our team in 1998 and I've never known anybody more positive or upbeat no matter what the circumstances. You'd wake up on a stage race and it'd be pouring down with rain and freezing cold outside and I'd look through the window and think, 'Nah, I don't fancy that at all.' But Jens would be, 'Oh Chris, look, it's raining. We are going to smash them today.' He was, he still is, incredible."

Sprinters use power, but not in the same way that endurance riders do. Sprinters are looking for maximums all the time. Power to them is like doing a one-lift weight training test; they are looking at how much power they can produce in one short burst. The power meter is an important tool in that it shows where they produce their peak, which is something they work on by analysing their power outputs per pedal revolution. One world-class sprinter's powerfile showed that he achieved peak power on the second pedal revolution after he jumped in a sprint. (Their "jump" is what track sprinters call the sudden acceleration they make during a match sprint to try to gain distance over a rival.)

Track sprinting is all about putting every calorie of energy and every watt of power into a short space of time. Dave Le Grys, the former national sprint coach and Commonwealth Games sprint silver medallist, has a good way of explaining the difference between sprinters and endurance riders. "Sprinters have the ability to put everything they've got into a few seconds, and if you aren't a sprinter you can't really appreciate it. When I was the national coach I used to get it all the time from the road coaches that sprinters were lazy because they don't ride for hours on end. But a sprinter can put 80 miles of effort into one sprint. Think of your energy on an 80-mile bike ride as being like water in a bath. An endurance rider empties the bath by letting the water go down the plug-hole over the duration of the ride. A sprinter just rips off the bottom of the bath and the water is gone – bam! Gone."

A sprinter's world is still hard for those of us outside it to appreciate. Shane Sutton, the former British Cycling head coach and one-time sprint team manager, explains it by referring to a sprinter's weight training. "Weights are crucial to a sprinter now.

Half their training time is spent in the weights room and half on the track. Sprinting is that specialized, it's that much different to the rest of cycling. But you should see how much effort they put into their training.

"Sir Chris Hoy works towards doing maximum squat lift at the end of each training cycle, and there comes a day before a World Championships or an Olympic or Commonwealth Games when he does a one repetition maximum lift, and it's a big day. It's crucial that he at least equals his personal best, but it's better if he beats it. He warms up, does the lift, and after it, after that one maximum lift, you can feel the heat come off him like a radiator. Why? Because he's put in the same energy, the same effort, that you or I would put into an 80-mile bike ride."

Sprinters train with the same intensity on the track. Barney Storey is a Paralympic coach and a Paralympic champion as a tandem pilot for visually impaired riders. "As coaches we instil in the sprinters that every effort they make on the track from January to December must be a dress rehearsal for the World Championships. If they are doing a flying 200 metres, they've got to imagine it's the world championship 200-metre qualifying time trial. Anything less is just going through a training process," he says.

Given that the British sprinters felt a bit like poor relations, it's ironic that they were the more successful of the two sides of track racing at the first Olympic Games since Keen's WCPP was instituted. The team pursuit squad of Bryan Steel, Paul Manning, Chris Newton and a 21-year-old Bradley Wiggins, making his Olympic debut, took the bronze medal in Sydney, while Yvonne McGregor did the same in the women's pursuit. Rob Hayles had near misses in the individual pursuit and in the Madison with Wiggins, scoring two fourths.

The sprinters did considerably better. First they won a silver medal in the team sprint, and then Jason Queally delivered a gold medal in the 1,000 metres time trial. Queally had been a water polo player who took up triathlon and found he had the blend of fast twitch muscle, anaerobic power and endurance that perfectly suited the longest sprint event.

*   *   *   *   *

The 1,000 metres time trial is extremely hard. To get a feel for its demands think about the 400 metres if you ran one at school. You get up to speed quickly, then cruise along at a high pace, one that you think will take you all the way to the finish. At 250 metres everything feels good, then at 300 it's like you hit a wall. Some sort of brake comes on, and you have to grit your teeth, pushing limbs that don't want to work any more for the final 100. You've gone anaerobic.

That's what the 1,000 metres is like, except that when top sprinters do it, it hurts a great deal more. This is partly due to their muscle mass: sprinters don't look like other cyclists, they look a bit like body-builders, so they just have more muscle to hurt. And it's partly due to their ability to give everything they've got in a very short space of time. The 1,000 metres time trial is the longest continuous effort they make, and at world-class level it takes just over one minute.

A sprinter riding the 1,000 metres gets up to speed quickly with an explosive burst out of the starting gate that has metabolic costs of its own, which bites later. Then they drive hard through the middle bit, but in doing so they use up all the oxygen they had in their body at the start, and their lungs cannot suck in anywhere near enough to keep up with their muscles' oxygen demand.

That's when they go anaerobic – it's a word that means without oxygen, but in the track sprint world it stands for pain. Muscles can work without oxygen, but they produce waste products that build up inside them, and it used to be thought that this was the source of the pain experienced from this point to the end, and for a good while after.

Now, though, many exercise scientists believe in something called the "central governor theory", which holds that the brain controls muscles in a way that keeps them from going to the point of exhaustion – a protective mechanism that looks after the body's continued wellbeing. Classical exercise theory was that muscles tire because they run out of fuel or they are swamped by the toxic by-products of exercise. Central governor theory says that the brain starts limiting the amount of muscle fibres being contracted at any one time in order to protect the body from damage. Whatever the reason, a sprinter has to drive through a solid wall of pain in the last lap of what on standard 250-metre tracks is a four-lap race.

Training for the event is grim. On top of the weights work that all sprinters do, and short race intensity efforts on the track to build leg speed, sprinters have to do their static bike work. There's a room deep in the bowels of Manchester velodrome where they do this. The room is very well lit, but the sprinters drive themselves into a very dark place there.

One of the most effective sessions they do in the room is seven times 20 seconds flat out with 20 seconds rest between each flat-out effort. Twenty seconds flat out doesn't sound much, but we are talking sprinter's flat out, which means ripping the bottom out of the bath – every time. They hit these efforts so hard, and the 20 seconds rest between each one isn't enough time to recover. They do them so their muscles get used to working in a bath of lactic acid, or maybe even start to override the central governor. Whatever, there's a pile of exercise mats and a bucket in the room, and it's not unusual for a rider to collapse on to the mats and be sick in the bucket. In fact if they don't, their coaches want to know why.

There were four sprint events in the 2000 Olympic track cycling programme: the match sprint, the Keirin, the team sprint and the 1,000 metres time trial. The match sprint starts with everybody doing a flying 200-metre time trial, after which the fastest in that is matched against the slowest, the next fastest against the next slowest and so on. Then the winner from each of those matches goes into the next round. A series of rounds follow, leading up to a best-of-three final between the two riders who came through the semi-finals.

In the Keirin the sprinters line up behind a pacing motorbike, which slowly increases speed; then at a given point it gets out of the way and there's a free-for-all sprint between the sprinters. With maybe six riders fighting for very little space, body contact is part of the game, and crashes are frequent.

The team sprint sees three riders from each country ride in heats of two teams, one team on either side of the track. Rider one – let's call him man one, as track racers do, whether man one is male or female – from each team sets off as fast as he or she can, while man two and man three follow as close as they can. Man one peels off the front at the end of the first lap, and man two sets the pace for man three. Man two's effort ends at the end of the second lap, leaving man three to do the last lap on his own. First man three over the line wins. There are heats, rounds and then a final.

*　　*　　*　　*　　*

At Sydney 2000, as soon as the dust settled on Queally's victory in the 1,000 metres time trial, he was up again in the team sprint. Man one was Chris Hoy, making his Olympic debut; man two was Hoy's training partner and fellow Scott, Craig MacLean; Jason Queally was man three. They got through to the final against France, who had the best sprinters at the time, and Team GB got a silver medal.

It was a much better performance than Atlanta, when the British cycling team came home with two bronze medals. Chris Boardman got one in the time trial, and the modern equivalent of Michael Wright, Max Sciandri, an Italian who just happened to be born in Derby, took another in the road race.

Great Britain's overall performance in the 2000 Olympics justified the lottery funding. What a difference there was: Britain had come away from Atlanta with one gold medal; in Sydney the team haul was 11 golds, as well as ten silvers and seven bronze medals, giving Team GB tenth place in the medals table. It was good going, and because cycling contributed a gold, a silver and two bronze medals, they got some more lottery cash.

British cycling was changing, in more ways than one. The British Cycling Federation rebranded itself as British Cycling (BC) after absorbing most of the various bodies in the country that looked after other branches of the sport, such as the British Cyclo-Cross Association and the Mountain Bike Club. David Brailsford, who'd been involved on the performance side since lottery cash came on stream, now got more involved, effectively becoming Keen's second-in-command, and after Keen left in 2003, he took over as performance director. Meanwhile Shane Sutton took over as the sprint team manager in 2002, working in conjunction with sprint coach Ian Dwyer, who was appointed when Martin Barras left.

Brailsford and Sutton had slowly spread their influence, and unlike Keen they were steeped in the history and mystique of cycling. Brailsford and Sutton have always been very practical and level-headed in driving things along, but they also have a passion for cycling. And passion, as much as numbers and knowledge of physiology and aerodynamics, was needed to meet the challenges that lay ahead.

Bryan Steel, one of the four who got the team pursuit bronze medal in Sydney, remembers Brailsford's early days on the scene. "Dave started working with the track team in 1998, I think, and he immediately made an impact. He asked about everything, about why we did things a certain way. The first thing he asked about with the team pursuit was, 'Why do you swing up so high in the changes?' We thought about it, and there was no real reason; it was because we'd always done it that way. It was how every team changed. So Dave suggested we try staying lower down in the changes. So we did, and we went faster.

"Then he said, 'Why do you always change after each lap?' Again, it was basically because we always had; but you lose half a bike length when you change, so Dave suggested some riders doing two laps. Man three was the first position we tried it on; he did two laps and that saved a half bike length, but it also gave man one longer to recover from the big effort he makes to get the team up to speed. We tried it and we went faster. Then we started trying other combinations with other riders.

"We worked on other things too," Steel recalls. "We tried them and timed them, and if they worked, if we were faster, we did them. If they didn't work we left them out. The whole team pursuit process was the definition of Dave's marginal gains thing. Each one was a small thing, but when you added them all together we went fast enough to get fifth in the 1999 worlds, then silver at the 2000 worlds and bronze at the Olympics."

World titles were won on the track during the next Olympic cycle, the one leading to Athens in 2004, when David Brailsford fully took over from Keen as performance director. In 2000 Yvonne McGregor won the women's pursuit; in 2002 Chris Hoy won the 1,000 metres time trial, Great Britain won the team sprint and Chris Newton the points race; and in 2003 Bradley Wiggins won the individual pursuit; while other British riders took medals in other events.

Medals, especially gold ones, mean money in British sport now, so more lottery funding came on stream for cycling. As well as funding the efforts of the established WCPP riders, the money was invested in the future. A plan to go into schools to search for talent was rolled out, and so were different levels of coaching so that the talent could be developed. The last stage of that was an under-23 academy, where the best riders from the age of 18 would be selected for a limited number of places as full-time academy members.

It was the brainchild of a former international and pro rider who became a coach, Rod Ellingworth, and the regime he created was tough. The academy members spent the winter in Manchester, where twice-daily training sessions on the track, practising team pursuit and Madison skills over and over again at race pace, were interspersed with long road rides in the Peak District.

They also had language lessons and cookery tuition. The former British pro road race champion John Herety, who is a fully trained chef, taught the riders how to shop and cook nutritious food for themselves. "I still use John's recipe and remember to cook the meat for 90 minutes so it's easier to digest," says academy alumnus Matt Brammeier. They lived in a Manchester flat, where they had to cook and clean for themselves. They also had to find their own way to the track or wherever that day's training rendezvous was, and they weren't allowed motor vehicles. They rode there, night or day, whatever the weather. You'll still see young riders in British team kit, slipping lights on to their bikes and pedalling off into the dark after a late session at the velodrome.

A typical week is described by a current academy member, John Mould: "We get Mondays off. Tuesdays we are at the track at 8 a.m. for a session, then after that we get changed and do two hours on the road. That's followed by French lessons and the Manchester track league races in the evening. Wednesday is two track sessions, Thursday a good long road ride, and we do three hours on the road followed by another track session on Friday. We do a long road ride in the Peak District on Saturday and the same again on Sunday."

In the early days the riders moved to a house in the Tuscan town of Quaratta from spring until autumn each year. They either trained in the hills or raced in the tough dilettante road races in Italy, where every rider is desperate to be a pro. Nowadays academy members spend most of the summer doing various stage races in Europe.

Mark Cavendish, Geraint Thomas and Ben Swift are all graduates of the academy, and it's still producing some great riders, but the academy isn't for everyone. Adam Blythe didn't like it at all, but went on to build a good pro career and races with one of the top World Tour teams, BMC. "I didn't hit it off with some of the coaches. I didn't like it being 24/7 cycling either. And they put us in Fallowfield, where all the students live. You'd be looking out of the window on a nice summer evening at people your own age enjoying themselves. I cracked a couple of times and went out, but that got me hauled in front of the bosses for a telling

ABOVE: Chris Hoy wins gold in the 1,000 metres time trial at the 2004 Athens Olympics. This was his first gold in an Olympic career that began in Sydney in 2000 and ended in London in 2012 and which saw him become Britain's greatest-ever Olympian.

ABOVE: Mark Cavendish celebrates his first stage win in the Tour de France, in 2008. He went on to win three more stages in the race that year, establishing himself as one of the greatest sprinters in the history of road racing.

BELOW: Victoria Pendleton in the women's sprint at the 2008 Beijing Olympics. She went on to win gold, repeating that winning performance in the keirin in London in 2012, where she also took sprint silver.

ABOVE: Mark Cavendish becomes only the second British rider to wear the rainbow jersey of the road race World Champion. He beat Australia's Matthew Goss into a close second place at the event in Copenhagen in 2011.

LEFT: Bradley Wiggins (left) looks apprehensive at the Team Sky launch in 2010. No one could have predicted that he would take the top spot in the Tour de France just two years later.

BELOW: The final time trial of the 2012 Tour de France is over, Bradley Wiggins has won the race and David Brailsford has fulfilled his promise to deliver a British winner of the Tour de France.

ABOVE: Bradley Wiggins stands on the top step of the podium in Paris having just won the 2012 Tour de France, earning his place in the record books. Wiggins was the first British rider to win the Tour, 109 years after the first edition.

Barely ten days after winning the Tour de France, Bradley Wiggins sets off towards Olympic gold in the road time trial at the 2012 London Games, to the delight of an ecstatic British public.

Dani King leads Laura Trott and Joanna Rowsell to women's team pursuit gold in the London 2012 Olympics. Many thought that the British track peformance at Beijing in 2008 could not be more spectacular – but it was in London.

ABOVE: Chris Froome wins stage 15 at the top of Mont Ventoux in the 2013 Tour de France after a stunning solo breakaway. British cycling fans now have something happy and glorious to connect to the place where Tom Simpson died in 1967.

off. Eventually I left and went to Belgium. It was freer, I felt more independent and I raced better because of it," says Blythe.

With the track riders training hard, the WCPP widening its remit to look at road racing as well, and the academy set up, the wheels were in motion for the Athens Olympics in 2004 and beyond. First, however, there's another story to tell.

*   *   *   *   *

David Millar was born in Malta in 1977. His parents are Scottish and his father was doing a tour of duty in the RAF at the time. After the family's return to the UK his parents divorced, and Millar lived with his father in Hong Kong, which is where he started cycling. More than that, Millar seemed to fall in love with the sport. Like Brian Robinson and Tom Simpson before him, he read magazines, in which he saw pictures of great riders in the Tour de France, and they sparked something in him.

Millar started road racing on a holiday to visit his mother in the UK, and he soon started winning. He became part of the British junior road team in 1994, raced in the Junior World Championships in 1995 and won the junior national 25-mile time trial title. In 1996, at the age of 18, he moved to France. He raced for a club based in St Quentin in northern France, won eight races and was offered places by five pro teams. He chose Cofidis because he knew their team manager, Cyrile Guimard, had a flair for developing talent. Guimard suggested that even though Cofidis would pay him, Millar should spend another year as an amateur with a big team in Brittany. He didn't, Millar couldn't wait that long, and in 1997 he was a fully fledged pro.

The next years were a whirlwind. Millar wrote a column in the magazine *Cycle Sport* and it reads like a breathless travelogue of getting hammered in races, then rushing somewhere else to get hammered again. Or he'd stay in one place and get hammered on long training rides instead. In between he would try to recover but never quite succeed.

In an interview in the same magazine in 1997 Millar said: "Racing as a pro isn't as hard as you think it's going to be, it's harder. I didn't really struggle much as an amateur in France. Even if you weren't going very well you could do OK, but that's not the way it is as a pro. I've got to start every climb at the front of the bunch and ride flat out, 100 per cent, if I still want to be on the back of the bunch going over the other side."

He was also learning why. The first Cofidis rider Millar roomed with on his first professional training camp was taking the banned substance cortisone, because he felt pressured to do so. Race speeds were insanely fast and stories of EPO use were rife in the pro peloton. Millar heard them, and he saw evidence of EPO use in his own team during that first year: ice bags being delivered to riders' rooms, surreptitious behaviour from team-mates, and their body language when they came out of the bathroom clutching little toilet or shoe bags that they always stuffed deep into their suitcases.

As one of Millar's team-mates, Bobby Jullich, explained to him, the ice was for storing EPO, and the bags contained syringes and other medical equipment. He asked if EPO made a difference, and was told it turned donkeys into racehorses. Then he began to hear the word "preparation". Riders would ask each other if they were prepared; it was a euphemism for doping. "Recovery", or recovery products, was another; and "good vitamins" was a popular one in Belgium.

You could ride clean. Millar was told by a very good rider from his generation that it was possible to ride well in single days races without "preparing". In his own team David Moncoutié was renowned as a clean rider, and he won stages in the Tour de France, occasionally. Millar wanted to race clean, as he says in his candid autobiography *Racing Through the Dark*. He was clean when he won the opening time trial of the 2000 Tour de France, but after that he was slowly drawn towards the side of the dopers.

Millar won the final long time trial of the 2003 Tour de France, and he won the world time trial title that year too. During this time he became an increasingly important part of David Brailsford's plans to expand British Cycling's performance effort. Then, on June 23, 2004, his world collapsed.

Millar was having a meal with Brailsford in a restaurant in Biarritz, where Millar lived, when he was arrested by the police. They were conducting an inquiry into possible doping within the Cofidis team, and Millar had been implicated. They not only wanted to question him but searched his house, where they found two used syringes Millar had hidden in books. The syringes were found to have once contained Eprex, a brand of EPO. Millar says he'd decided to stop doping by then, and his increasing desire, some might say desperate desire, to work with Brailsford and British Cycling could be evidence of that; but there it was – he'd been caught.

Millar was stripped of his 2003 world title, and he was banned from cycling for two years. And due to legal ramifications from the doping enquiry he lost nearly every penny he'd made, but Brailsford kept his faith in him. As a convicted doper Millar can't be picked for Team GB in the Olympics, but he can be and is part of Britain's world championship effort, where he has played a very important role. Since returning to the sport, Millar has been an outspoken and articulate critic of the drugs culture in top-level men's pro road racing. As a result he's listened to, and he's admired and respected. If he was indeed going straight, then maybe, just maybe, it's a shame he was caught, considering what else was going on at the time. However, if he wasn't, then it was a good job he was caught. If Millar had been caught doping while riding for Great Britain, it could have damaged more than him.

*　　*　　*　　*　　*

There is another important character to introduce before moving on to the 2004 Olympic Games in Athens: Dr Steve Peters. He's a consultant psychiatrist who began working with British Cycling on a part-time basis early in the 2000s. Steve Peters has been responsible for training the riders to remove emotion and think logically when they go into any competition, as he explains: "Emotions are counter-productive, they can erode self-confidence and even the most driven athlete can lack self-confidence. There are two sides to anyone's brain; one is emotional and irrational, the other works purely on logic. Going into a competition the logical side must be in charge."

Peters has drills to help athletes arrive at this logical state of mind, and works closely with individuals, as everyone is different. "What I'm aiming for is for them to be aroused but to be logical, almost cold, about what they are doing," he says.

Peters stresses that while all top athletes are physically gifted and have similar, exceptional physiological traits, their minds vary greatly. In fact, there's very much the spread of mind-sets you would find in the general public. "Everyone is an individual. There are athletes in the BC system who deal with pressure, for example, by saying 'bring it on' and others who end up thinking they just don't want to be there. And it doesn't matter what event they do, they are still very different within the same event.

"I sit down with each one and we work together to discover what their mental processes are, basically how they think and how they view things in their mind. We all do those things differently. I work on 30 parameters with each individual to establish how they operate. Then we work on numbers. You know where you are with a number, you can add to it or subtract from it to arrive at an ideal.

"I might ask somebody to put a number on their anxiety state, picking from 0, for comatose, to 100, where if someone in the room was to sneeze they would jump in the air and scream. They might say 70, so then we have something to work on. I'll work out what the ideal anxiety state would be for that person going into a race and give them strategies to bring them up or lower them down to that ideal number."

A number of top British riders speak highly of Peters, but none more so than Victoria Pendleton. She was in a dark place in the run-up to the Athens Games, and she didn't perform as she should have done. As she reveals in her autobiography, *Between the Lines*, she had big confidence issues and low self-esteem. David Brailsford was so worried about her at the time that he sent Peters to meet her at the UCI cycling school in Aigle, Switzerland, where she was training. Peters was able to identify her problems, but together they needed more time to fix them, time that stretched beyond Athens.

The value of his work cannot be overestimated. Peters was to work full time for British Cycling as part of the Performance Plan and is still available as a consultant to Performance riders and to Team Sky. His influence is all over both.

Sir Chris Hoy calls Peters "the glue that holds the British cycling team together". And he should know, because Peters had a direct hand in Hoy winning his first gold medal in Athens.

As Peters says, he gives riders drills to help them focus on what has to be done, breaking everything down into what will make the perfect ride. In 2004, as the reigning world champion, Hoy was the last starter in the 1,000 metres time trial. Then, with another three riders to go before Hoy, Australia's Shane Kelly broke the Olympic record with 1 minute 1.224 seconds. Next up was Stefan Nimke with 1 minute 1.186 seconds. Dutch rider Theo Bos made a bit of a mess of his turn and couldn't challenge Nimke, but then Arnaud Tournant of France did 1 minute 0.896 seconds, becoming the only man ever to go under 1 minute 1 at sea level.

Effectively that was the new world record. Riding at altitude really benefits sprinters. Air resistance increases exponentially with speed, but at high altitude the air is thinner, so the exponential curve drops down by a significant factor. Having less oxygen to breathe has less of an effect in a sprint event, because sprinters do not use much of the oxygen they inhale anyway.

All Hoy had to do was become the fastest man ever at sea level, break the world record, and he would become Olympic champion. It was enough to make anyone panic, but not an athlete with a mind trained by Peters. Hoy went through the processes of getting ready, of starting, of holding his line around the bottom of the track, of driving through the pain and pushing all the way to the line no matter how much his body cried out for him to back off, and he won.

Bradley Wiggins was the other big British success story in Athens. He won a gold medal in the individual pursuit and a silver medal in the team pursuit along with Steve Cummings, Rob Hayles and Paul Manning. Then he paired up with Hayles to take a full set of medals from one Games with a bronze in the Madison.

Wiggins had come of age. He was racing in Europe with a pro team, something he'd always wanted to do, and his natural speed had been refined by working with Chris Boardman. Not that it was always an easy relationship. It couldn't be, between two such different people.

"I worked one to one with a number of riders," Boardman says, "but it was mainly Bradley when he joined Cofidis. I asked him what he wanted to do, and he was always brave enough to answer and state his aims. Then I'd ask, what will you do to get there? And when he came up with something, I'd ask, how is that going to work? So by a process of getting him to suggest things, then seeing why they wouldn't work, but then me and him suggesting alternatives, we created a path for Brad."

Wiggins confirms the value of working with Boardman: "Chris got me organized really. I'm not very academic. At the start of working with Chris I'd write stuff down and he just said 'No, that won't work.' He wouldn't let me off with anything and it got quite frustrating at times. I felt like he was always on at me, but it worked. Chris got me thinking straight, not just about what I wanted to do, but how to go about doing it."

Wiggins wanted success on the road as well as the track, but his early years were very frustrating on that front. In a magazine feature shortly after the controversial 2006 Tour de France, when the winner Floyd Landis was thrown out for doping, he showed his bitter disappointment: "The way pro road racing has gone it has no credibility. If I won something big there would just be nods and winks, and outside the sport people would think I was doped. Everything everyone does now is under suspicion. No one knows what to believe. I'll keep racing. I love doing the big races. This year, riding the Tour, I just had goose bumps all the time just because I was actually in the Tour de France," he said.

Since he was young Wiggins had hankered after excelling in races like the Tour of Flanders, as well as on the track. He hadn't yet been able to do that, and since he was now saying, "I'd rather stop than take that stuff," it looked as if he would have to give up on those dreams. He also said, "I've given up worrying about it. I'm not bitter, I just accept it," but he couldn't disguise the anger welling up inside him at the way road cycling was going.

For the time being Wiggins would have to use road cycling as a tool. That's how the Tour de France and other big road races were seen by British Cycling then. As a tool to help their top endurance track riders get the depth of strength they could build on to achieve great rides on the track. Straight after he finished his first Tour de France in 2007, Geraint Thomas said: "I'm stronger, I know it. I've lost some top end now, but I feel very strong and the top end will come back when I start doing track training in the winter. My attitude to distances and to what tough really means has changed too. Bradley Wiggins told me they would. He said that four kilometres in a pursuit on the track would never be the same for me after the Tour."

*   *   *   *   *

Athens was good, but David Brailsford knew Beijing had to be better. There's something relentless about Brailsford's pursuit of perfection. The expression "marginal gains" became a buzz phrase after the Beijing Olympics. It's attributed to Brailsford, who is great at giving good soundbites to the media. That's one of the things he does best, packaging a pyramid of painstaking effort into media-friendly chunks. "The full phrase is 'performance by the aggregation of marginal gains'," Brailsford explains, "and we were using it for ages before Beijing brought it to everyone's attention. It means taking the one per cent from everything you do, and finding a one per cent margin for improvement in everything you do."

Chris Boardman says that Brailsford was exactly the right person to take over at the point he did. "David Brailsford is the common denominator in all the success, certainly post 2000, so the credit can be laid at his door. He took what Peter Keen did and added passion. David is above all a total fan of cycling. He went out to get the best of everything, and he's not risk averse, which me and Peter are. Call it courage or call him a gambler, but David is one of those two. He's also very good at having and pursuing a gut feeling. And he's not afraid to announce things publicly; it's like doing so means he has to achieve them. Take his statement that a British rider in Team Sky would win the Tour de France within five years. But what he does after he's announced something is throw his heart and soul into achieving it."

British Cycling's performance effort received even more lottery money after 2004, so it let Brailsford start looking beyond the fairly straightforward demands of the track. One of the riders his eye fell on was Nicole Cooke, who dominated women's road racing, and had done since 2002, when she won the Commonwealth Games road race gold medal at 19. She was racing in Europe that year, winning big races in Italy and Holland.

She won the UCI road World Cup in 2003, plus Classics like the Amstel Gold Race and the GP Plouay, and she was third in the World Championships in Hamilton. She won the biggest stage race for a woman in the world in 2004, the Giro Donne, and she was fifth in the Olympic road race. She won the Flèche Wallonne three times in 2005, 2006 and 2007. She was second in the World Road Race Championships in 2005 and won the World Cup again in 2006. And that's just skimming the surface of her career.

Cooke's record in the run-up to Beijing was incredible. Brailsford backed her to win and got to work on his marginal gains. She wore a one-piece skinsuit, like a time triallist, to gain a slight aerodynamic advantage, and she also used lighter tyres than conventional wisdom said were best for such a race. Little things, but they added up. But the win wasn't about marginal gains, it was about Cooke. She made the race her own and opened the flood barriers of Olympic success for Team GB cycling that was unprecedented – not just within cycling or within the various British teams there, but really for any team from any country in any sport.

Emma Poolley took the silver medal in the time trial. Bradley Wiggins won the individual pursuit, with Steven Burke in third. The men's team pursuit squad of Wiggins, Paul Manning, Ed Clancy and Geraint Thomas took gold in their event. Rebecca Romero and Wendy Houvenaghel were first and second in the individual pursuit. Chris Newton took the bronze medal in the points race, and Victoria Pendleton took gold in the sprint.

Pendleton was amazing. After taking three world titles in 2007 she was overwhelming favourite to win. This got to her at times, but Peters was there to help, telling her, as he told all the riders, never to imagine the moment when they win, but only focus on the process. It's a British Cycling principle: focus on process, because you can control that, whereas you can't control how fast the opposition go. But of course if riders train correctly, and if they focus on getting everything right in the process of riding and racing, then winning can be a consequence.

And Pendleton had trained properly. She lifted heavier weights than before, and for longer than before, because it had been identified that her slender physique needed strength training right up to an event. She was doing the times in training, and her legs felt good. When she qualified fastest, inside 11 seconds, she says that she hardly felt them.

In the final she faced Australia's Anna Mears – with whom she had history – and blitzed her. Mears, much stockier, more an obvious sprinter type, had tried to ride Pendleton rough to take advantage of what Mears sensed was Pendleton's fragility. But it hadn't worked in their recent meetings, and she got nowhere near to Pendleton in Beijing.

Then there was Chris Hoy. He won the sprint gold, with Jason Kenny in second place; he won the team sprint gold with Kenny and Jamie Staff; and although the IOC had removed the 1,000 metres time trial from their cycling programme, Hoy's answer was to win the Keirin. It was incredible: three gold medals in one Olympic Games and four in his career to date. That winter Chris Hoy became the second cyclist (following Tom Simpson) to win the BBC Sports Personality of the Year award, and the first ever cycling knight.

Could anything surpass Beijing? It was a remarkable team performance. Not just the team of riders, but the coaches and back-up staff. There is a big "be the best you can be" ethos in British Cycling nowadays. Everybody is appreciated, encouraged to do the best they can and treated as an equal part of the whole. Steve Cummings, who won a gold medal in the Athens Games, sums the BC spirit up best when he says: "Everybody has to be a fanatic to get in. For example if BC set on a new bike mechanic they have to be a bike pervert."

So could anything surpass Beijing? The answer, it turned out, was yes.

CHAPTER 8

PROJECT RAINBOW JERSEY

Rod Ellingworth first met Mark Cavendish when Cavendish was 16 years old, and he says two things stood out about him: "How unfit he was but also how fast he was." But Ellingworth soon found out that there was a third remarkable thing about the teenager from the Isle of Man, and that was the way he processed the world going on around him.

Ellingworth guided Cavendish from a raw talent to an accomplished track and road racer, and on from there almost to where he is today. Cavendish is the only British rider other than Tom Simpson to have won a monument of road cycling, the only British rider other than Simpson to have won the elite world road race title, and he has set a record all of his own.

As of 2013, Cavendish has won 25 stages in the Tour de France, 15 in the Giro d'Italia and three in the Vuelta a Espana. He has also won the points jerseys in all three Grand Tours as well. In terms of victories he is by far the most successful British cyclist ever. He's also homing in on a record set by the great Eddy Merckx of 34 Tour de France stage wins. Not that Cavendish is motivated by records.

"I don't think about them," he says. "I only think about winning stages, and that means winning the stages I can win. I focus on each one of those in turn. It's the same as winning the green jersey; winning stages is the only way for me to do that. Different riders might go on the attack to try for the green jersey, but for me it's a question of winning enough stages to get enough points."

Ellingworth is a Team Sky directeur sportif today, and Cavendish rides for the Belgian team, Omega Pharma-Quick Step. The two are still close, but Cavendish knows all he needs to know about how to get into shape mentally and physically now, so they are friends rather than athlete and coach. However, there is still nobody better qualified to talk about Cavendish than Ellingworth, who's been there with him right from the start.

"There are lots of reasons why Cavendish is special; some of them are down to facts and figures and natural ability, and some of them are down to who Mark is. Mark stood out as different right from the first day I met him, and I've met a lot of very talented young bike riders. I invited him to some coach-led racing sessions at the Manchester track along with some of the best juniors and under-23 riders in the country. It was our policy in British Cycling at the time to get together the best two development riders from each region and really put them through it.

"The sessions were intense, race scenario followed race scenario, but after each one we would sit down and analyse it. It went on all day, a 15-minute race followed by half an hour of analysis, then repeating it again and again. I deliberately tried to make things difficult. I tried to take away the protective coaching they were used to and to put them into situations where they were stressed. I split them into teams and gave them different jobs to do for their team in each race. After it was all over, Mark was the only one who came up to me and thanked me for the day. That took me by surprise," says Ellingworth.

After that first track session Ellingworth and Cavendish went their separate ways, and the next time they met was when Cavendish applied to become a member of British Cycling's under-23 academy, which Ellingworth ran at the time. "I knew a bit more about him by then. I knew he was fast, I knew he was prepared to work hard, but during the interview he surprised me again.

"I ask all the applicants to describe their journey to Manchester. I do that to see how aware they are of their surroundings, which I think is very important. Mark described exactly how he got there, what the road numbers were, the places he went through and at what time. The detail was unusual."

That awareness is a big piece in Cavendish's jig-saw of talent, and as Ellingworth grew to know him he began to understand the importance of it. "The question is designed to test how aware applicants are, which I think is a measure of how self-sufficient they will be, which is important in any sport. But Mark's awareness is something more, something deeper. His judgement of speed and distance borders on the uncanny. It was first brought home to me when he won the Bob Chicken Grand Prix, which in 2004 was run in the centre of London and was the prelude to the last stage of the Tour of Britain. Mark won, but afterwards he told me how he memorized where all the drain covers on the circuit were, and how he used them as markers so he knew when to move up in the bunch. He also rehearsed the sprint and used marks in the road to judge how far he was from the line and to measure his speed.

"Later, when we would talk about a sprint, Mark would say things like 'I moved a metre this way, or half a metre that way.' Or he'd say that something happened 125 metres from the line. And when you played the sprint back on a video and measured what happened, he did move one metre, or whatever he said happened did happen exactly where he said it did.

"And the other thing I think is a crucial factor with Mark is that he says that for him a sprint happens in slow motion. It's like he can slow down what's happening around him and run it inside his brain at half speed. It gives him the time to make good decisions. It helps him map a way through, measure distances, and do what he needs to do. Everybody is sprinting at 70 kph plus, but what is happening in split seconds in real time gets stretched out inside Mark's head."

That's a remarkable gift, but it's something we all have. You'll recognize it if you've ever fallen off something, or seen something remarkable or shocking happen, or even had a minor road accident. Such things always seem to happen in slow motion to the person involved. The reason they do is due to the heightened awareness the incident brings. For most of us this heightened awareness is an involuntary reaction to stress, but some people can switch it on when they want. Mark Cavendish is one of them.

Top racing drivers, cricketers and baseball players have a similar ability, and it's so prized in sport that some athletes try hypnosis to help them switch on this state of heightened awareness. It's the state that sports people and writers are referring to when they talk about being "in the zone".

In addition to his ability to focus and zone in totally on what he's doing, Cavendish also studies sprinting. "I watch them on TV, recording everything and playing the sprints back. If I've won I look at what I did right, and if I lose I look at what I did wrong. I also look at what other teams did right or what they did wrong. I look at the tactics of all the teams, and it helps me understand in race situations what they are likely to do. If I can, I get others from the team to watch them. When we were in the same teams I watched loads of finishes with Bernie Eisel," he says.

He's built up a vast knowledge of sprinting over the years, which helps him time his moves, because there is no coaching manual written on how to win a Tour de France bunched sprint. "You get a feeling for when it's right to start your sprint. You have a lot of variables: the wind direction, the gradient, the speed I'm travelling at, and how I feel. A lot of it is gut feeling, but there are elements of calculation," Cavendish says.

Bunch sprints in Grand Tours are dominated by lead-out trains. This is where the sprinter's teams get into a straight line with each rider going as fast as he can for a pre-determined distance until their sprinter is just far enough from the finish line to make his move count. It's not quite like the track sprinter's jump, because the line will be moving in excess of 60 kph on a flat finish, but it is a marked acceleration. The whole lead-out procedure requires exact timing, so everybody in it must know what they are doing, because as Cavendish points out, it's almost impossible to communicate in the line: "You can sometimes in smaller races with a smaller crowd, but in the Tour with massive crowds and all the noise it's impossible."

His ability to see sprints in slow motion while they are taking place is a key factor in Cavendish's success; so is the deep knowledge of sprinting he's gained from watching countless replays, but weapon number one in Cavendish's sprint arsenal is his blistering natural speed. Ellingworth has seen it so many times he knows exactly where it comes from.

"It is natural. Mark has never worked on his sprint. Well, to say he never works on it is a bit misleading. He probably sprints every day, unless he's on a real easy recovery ride, and has done so since he was a kid. When he trained with the academy when they were in Tuscany, which he used to do even when he turned pro, they always used to sprint, and the young ones always tried to beat Mark. He loved that.

"He's naturally fast and he probably has lots of fast twitch muscle, although we have never done tests to find out, but the other key thing is that he is so small when he sprints. He isn't very tall anyway, but he has the knack of getting so low and narrow when he sprints, so he just causes a lot less drag. Mark's frontal area when he's sprinting is tiny compared to the other sprinters. That means he creates less drag, so where Cav is producing maybe 1,500 watts to go 75 kph, someone like André Greipel needs at least 1,700 watts and he still goes slightly slower because he's so much bigger."

Numbers are a great training tool, and a cornerstone of British Cycling success, but they must be interpreted correctly and put in the right context. Numbers misled T-Mobile when Cavendish first joined them as a new pro in 2006. They put their faith in Greipel or Gerald Ciolek because they were knocking out 1,600 watts in sprints and Cavendish was doing less. But when they started racing Cavendish was faster because the other two are so much bigger. Cavendish's sprint power output grew over the years until, the last time Ellingworth saw any data, it was also around 1,600 watts; but the key to his speed is the watts he puts out per square metre of his frontal area.

Numbers also misled British Cycling coaches when they first tested Cavendish. He hates tests and couldn't hit the watts target that the coaches needed to let him on their programme. At that point Shane Sutton and Rod Ellingworth had to go in to bat for him, arguing that his race results and how he performed in training, both on the track and on the road, made a nonsense of his test figures.

When he began coaching him, Ellingworth worked a lot on Cavendish's sprint technique. "We didn't do much about getting him low, that's natural. We worked on keeping his elbows and knees in so they don't cause extra drag, but another natural advantage Cav has is that he isn't a stiff sprinter. What I mean by that is he doesn't hold his arms rigidly and lock out. Track sprinters do that, they lock out their arms so that all their leg power goes into the pedals. But although locking out makes a sprinter faster, it makes them unstable if they get a knock. In fact if Cav is up against a stiff, straight-armed sprinter I used to get him to give him a bit of a nudge because they can't handle that. They can't handle the contact."

Cavendish can handle it, and if he's leaned on in a sprint, he says, "I try to keep myself upright, not lean any way. Often, though, the other riders are bigger than me, so I have to brace myself or I'll come off. It's something you get used to a bit."

Cavendish might not lock his arms out straight like a track sprinter, but the other technique he worked on with Ellingworth was a straight lift from something track sprinters do. "It was grabbing the handlebars and really pumping them all the way to the line," says the coach. "That sounds a bit stupid, a bit

221

obvious, but when I ask riders to remember the last time they grabbed the bars, headed for the line and held it, going really hard all the way there, they begin to understand what I'm talking about. Most racers never do that, but track sprinters do it all the time. Track sprinters have a mantra: 'pump for it'. Their coaches shout it at them all the time in training. Mark does that every time he sprints. He gets it all out in 200 metres if you like. Only real sprinters can do it."

There are other tools in Cavendish's box, according to Ellingworth: "Great recovery, a big capacity for hard work, and he can sprint when he's on his knees, but all sprinters can do that." But Ellingworth reckons the most important, after his power to frontal area ratio and spatial awareness, is the ability to accelerate quickly then appear to go again later in the sprint. "His acceleration is phenomenal, nobody can jump from 60 to 75 kph quicker than Cav, but the jump and go again is something we worked on, something I coached," says Ellingworth.

Pundits talk about Cavendish's second kick, comparing him with some of the great track sprinters who possessed the same quality, but Ellingworth says it's an illusion. "What Cav does is jump, recover, then jump again. He goes 100 per cent, backs off to 80 then goes back to 100. Tactically it's great, because his rivals respond to the first jump, but while they are flat out to close on him Cav is recovering slightly. At the same time they think they are catching him, but then he goes away again, and that does their heads in."

Cavendish hit the big time in 2007 winning the Grote Scheldeprijs in Belgium, which almost has Classic status. He rode the Tour de France that year but crashed out. One of his team managers at the time, Allan Peiper, thinks that his disappointment in 2007 made Cavendish train even harder for the 2008 race, and he took the Tour de France by storm, winning four stages.

Cavendish does that; he comes back stronger from setbacks, and much stronger from defeats. He hates losing: "I almost have a self-loathing when I get beaten, but it's not just because I let myself down. I let the team down if I lose," he says.

Road sprinters are under a lot of pressure. The way road racing is these days means that sprints are a team effort, not just in the lead-out during the final kilometres, but if a sprinter is feeling good he might ask his team to ride all day on the front of a race to control it. They are asking a lot of sets of legs to endure a lot of pain, as well as ride out of their socks and risk their necks in the final dash to the line. If Cavendish loses, he feels his team-mates' pain, and if he wins they are the first people he credits. Being prepared to shoulder the responsibility of going for the win is the mark of a great sprinter, and Cavendish does it as a matter of course.

Cavendish suffered a bitter disappointment in Beijing. He cut his Tour de France short to go to China, where he wanted to win the gold medal in the Madison with Bradley Wiggins. They were the world champions, so they were favourites, but two things happened that worked against them. The first – and the biggest because the other is only a suspicion – was that the whole field seemed to ride to make Cavendish and Wiggins lose rather than go for the win themselves. It's fair enough; it's a race, and competitors choose their tactics, but it did look very negative on TV and it stifled what could have been a great race. The other factor was that Bradley Wiggins had already won two gold medals by the time he got to the Madison and there's just a suggestion that he was tired. However, as Wiggins pointed out later, everybody concerned, including Cavendish presumably, signed off on Wiggins going for the three gold medals in Beijing. He'd done so successfully at the World Championships earlier that year.

But Cavendish and Wiggins didn't get a medal, and that hurt Cavendish. It hurt even more when all the British medallists were upgraded to first class for the trip home. Cavendish was the only member of the British track cycling team who hadn't won one. He didn't speak to Wiggins for two months after that.

Cavendish's next big project with Ellingworth was to try to win Milan–San Remo. It had increasingly been won by sprinters over the years, but it's a very long race with significant climbs, so any sprinter who has won has had to adapt their training to its demands.

But that's where a good coach comes in. "Mark never really needed coaching to win sprints, all I did with him really was refine his technique. It's getting him to the sprints, training him to cope well with the rest of the race where I've done my work, and it's where Mark has worked hardest too," Ellingworth says.

"We always look at races and say, what does it take to be in with a chance of winning? We identify the factors involved and work on them. It's the basic BC way really. For example, we have worked for hours on Mark's climbing, but he rarely did regular uphill intervals once he progressed. Instead we worked on re-creating what happens on a climb in a race, and we tried to do it at race speed. Mark isn't going to win a race on a hill, he just has to be still with the group at the top, or not far off. So with me in front on a little motorbike and him behind, we'd practise hitting a climb hard, or picking up the speed on it. We practised answering attacks or accelerating over the top. We would try to re-create everything that could happen in a race, and we practised it at race speed."

That's the sort of training Cavendish did with Ellingworth before the 2009 Milan–San Remo. He worked so hard at cruising over a succession of climbs, just like the ones along the coast road to San Remo, that his body got used to doing it at race speed. "As well as getting fitter it's to do with perception," says Ellingworth. "If you do something a lot you become more comfortable with it. Because of the track work he's done, Mark's dead comfortable riding at 50 kph; it isn't a problem because he's used to extended periods at 55 kph on the track. So just sitting in the peloton takes very little out of Mark, no matter how fast they go.

"But shortly before San Remo, Mark still did an hour on the track behind a motorbike at 54 to 55 kph. That was good for his cadence, but the real reason was to work on his perception of speed. In the end the first two hours of Milan–San Remo were done at 50 kilometres per hour, and I bet there were some riders in the middle of the group thinking, 'This is a bit fast,' but not Mark. It's all to do with perception," says Ellingworth.

Being able to cruise economically in the peloton is a crucial skill in road races. Cavendish sums it up by saying, "You have to conserve as much energy as possible, stay out of the wind, and do the least amount of work possible."

But it's an added bonus if you can play mind games and trick the opposition. Cavendish played a blinder in the run-up to the Milan–San Remo. A stage race, Tirreno–Adriatico, always precedes the Classic, but Cavendish cunningly hid his climbing form during the 2009 race. That it was a ploy was clear to see a few days later in Milan–San Remo when one of the race favourites, the great Belgian Classics star Tom Boonen, looked around to check who was still in contention at the front when they got to the top of the final climb. When he saw Cavendish,

Boonen's body language spoke volumes. A few kilometres later Cavendish edged past Heinrich Haussler just before the line to win the race.

Cavendish marched onwards after that, continuing to collect Grand Tour stages like a kid collecting stamps, and he won the points jersey in the Vuelta in 2010, then the green jersey of the Tour de France in 2011. In three years he'd done things that only Tom Simpson, Malcolm Elliott and Robert Millar, albeit with the Tour de France polka-dot mountains jersey rather than the green one, had done before. And while he was doing so, Ellingworth was well into the planning of another prize.

Back in 2007 Ellingworth had a long talk with Cavendish about what he wanted to achieve in cycling from that point on. One of his ambitions, he said, was one day to win the elite world road race title. Only one British rider had ever won it before, so it was ambitious, but Ellingworth looked at it from his coaching viewpoint, which meant asking, as always: what does it take to achieve it?

"For Mark to win he had to have a sprinter's course, which was outside of our control, but we decided that he also had to win the sprinter's Classic, Milan–San Remo before even thinking about the worlds," Ellingworth says.

So with the Milan–San Remo box ticked in 2009, Ellingworth began looking at the courses of the upcoming World Road Race Championships. The 2010 course in Australia was a bit hilly, but the course chosen for Copenhagen to host the title races on in 2011 was much flatter. There was every chance of a bunch sprint on that course, including in the elite race, especially if Ellingworth could stack the odds and get a Great Britain team to commit to making sure it happened and commit to setting up Cavendish to win. He started a plan which he named Project

Rainbow Jersey, after the rainbow jersey that every world champion is entitled to wear for a year in the type of event they won it in.

The title had previously been won by Tom Simpson in 1965, and knowing that I am Simpson's nephew and that I had one of his original rainbow jerseys, Ellingworth contacted me. He'd arranged a meeting of the squad of riders from which he would pick his Copenhagen team, but wanted something inspiring to show them to start it off. I had some film on a video of Tom winning in San Sebastian, so I let him borrow that and the jersey, which is framed in a glass case.

"We put the jersey up at the front of the room and we ran the film, and you could see it made an impression. Everyone in the room felt something. They wanted to be involved in the project, and from that single meeting it was something we all believed we could do," said Ellingworth later when handing the stuff back. Project Rainbow Jersey was on its way.

There was a slight glitch when Cavendish pulled out of the Vuelta, which he was going to ride through as his final preparation for Copenhagen. Cavendish suddenly felt he had no energy, and his room-mate had been ill, so he decided to drop out of the race to have a short rest. Then he would see if he could recover in the controlled environment of training, where how hard you ride is decided by you and not the race.

After taking three or four days off, Cavendish went to Girona in Spain, where he started doing five- or six-hour rides in the mountains. In order to keep some leg speed he also did some training behind a car, with Ellingworth driving. "We went to Essex for a week, and Mark did quality work there for leg speed, 90 to 100 kilometres behind the car every day, plus some 250-kilometre rides. Long rides are not as important physically for the worlds, because the riders are fit and strong by that time of year, but doing the distance is very important mentally.

"The weather was bad when we were in Essex, but I said it could be like that in Copenhagen, so Mark rode every day. He did some sprint sessions too, and some capacity work, like five-minute intervals riding as hard as he can. To round off his training Mark rode the Tour of Britain and did 60 to 70 kilometres behind the car after some of the stages. In Copenhagen he had four days of recovery riding, then one four-hour ride on the Friday before the Sunday race."

There was only one tactic that could be played in Copenhagen. On that course, even if Great Britain hadn't got a sprinter, the worlds would have probably ended with a big bunch sprint, so that was the Great Britain team tactic for the race; but they wanted to dictate it, so that they and nobody else was in control.

Ellingworth started his BC-trained coaching process again, asking: what does it take to achieve it? In this case that meant: what should the team do to ensure a bunch sprint? "What I came up with involved the team controlling the whole race, the pace, everything. That meant the team being on the front and riding at 45 to 48 kph for a very long time, which is why I insisted that they all raced in skinsuits. Some of the riders didn't like it, but I made them do it. Some of them, including Mark, also used helmets with filled-in vents. I don't know how many watts it is exactly but there's measurable saving from doing that, and we decided that saving any energy, no matter how little, was crucial considering the length of time our riders would be at the front," Ellingworth says.

Cavendish's skinsuit and helmet combination actually provided an energy saving of four watts, so a rider would have to put four watts less power into his pedalling to travel at 45–48 kph. Some analysts said afterwards that considering Cavendish's winning margin was just three hundredths of a second, i.e. around 0.001 per cent of the whole race time, those four watts could have clinched it, but that assessment misses the point. The sprint at the end of the Copenhagen worlds was much slower than a typical Tour de France sprint. The speed for the final kilometre was 56 kph, and for the final 400 metres it was 51.5 kph, whereas a typical Tour de France sprint will have a 60 kph final kilo, hitting 66 plus in the last 400. The aerodynamic advantage of what Cavendish and the rest of the team wore was more effective at saving energy throughout the race than on increasing his sprint speed at the end. Just as Ellingworth thought it would be.

Team selection and the decisions about who should do what were very specific too, as Ellingworth recalls. "We needed some big engines from the start of the race to control it. So we used Chris Froome as one of those, Steve Cummings too. They had to ride at their anaerobic thresholds for a long time. We had other big engines in the team, like Geraint Thomas or Ian Stannard, who can do the same as Froome and Cummings, but we saved them for later in the race because they both handle themselves well if a race gets chaotic. They keep their heads and know what to do when things get a bit crazy.

"Race experience was important too. That's where Jez Hunt came in. One way Cav saved energy was by dropping to the little chainring and spinning up the hills. They weren't steep hills, he could have managed them in the big chainring, but we reckon Cav saved 20 to 30 watts every time he did it. The thing is, though, he dropped back through the bunch every time he did it too. It was Jez's job to ride next to Cav and drop back with him on the hills, then pace him back to the front over the other side."

It was a really hard day in the saddle for Hunt, although he was a tough and experienced pro by then. As well as guiding Cavendish around for lap after lap, Hunt was given another duty. Ellingworth didn't want Cavendish picking up the little food bags that get handed to the riders from time to time in long races. The feed stations where this happens are notorious places for crashes, so Hunt was assigned to pick up any food Cavendish might need. And if Hunt wanted a bag as well, he had to take two.

The riders couldn't carry much, because skinsuits don't have pockets. So, with getting on for 5,000 calories used by every GB rider in the race, getting food from the roadside was crucial. But the way the team rode the race like a team time trial, relaying each other at the front, helped the riders collect their food bags and bottles more safely than if they had been further back in the peloton.

Food choice was left up to the individual riders, who were all very experienced and knew what suited them best. All Ellingworth told them was not to get it wrong. "It was the same with wheels," he says. "Cav had his aero frame, but he didn't go for the most aero wheels. There's a trade-off; it was no good going for every aero gadget if it compromises bike handling. Mark went for wheels he was used to riding."

Communication was another crucial factor. With no rider radios allowed in the race, and only an official clock at the finish, it might have been necessary for a rider to keep dropping back to the team car for information on time gaps etc., which would have stretched the team's high-energy-cost tactic. "So we had lap boards all round the circuit, and I kept relaying times and information I was given about the breaks, plus what I wanted the riders to do, to the people with the boards, using the radio I had. They then wrote the information down on the boards and held it up for the riders to read as they went past," Ellingworth explains.

Then, having controlled the race so well, it was left to Bradley Wiggins to play to his physiological strengths. He did an absolutely blinding last lap, never letting the pace drop below 50 kph and accelerating if any of the opposition tried to overtake him and start dictating tactics. Nobody tried, nobody could do it.

Wiggins delivered the team for the final charge, and then as Cavendish fell back it looked as if it had all gone wrong at the last minute – but even that was planned. "I didn't want us to lead Cav out," says Ellingworth. "We only had two riders left with fresh legs by then, and the worst thing on that finish would have been for Cav to be third wheel from the front. He had to come from further back, so he got shelter for longer. When he saw the finish before the race, Cav said he wanted to be eighth or ninth when the sprint started."

And that's how it worked out. Geraint Thomas added a bit of tactical genius when he backed off his place in the line through a corner because he'd realized that some riders who could have been a threat to Cavendish were behind him. That instantly left a gap that the riders behind had to waste precious energy to close.

Cavendish won the sprint without a lead-out. At one point he looked to have gone the wrong side to overtake an opponent, but he says: "You see those things before they happen. You can see where a gap will open. Cycling is a series of calculations and decisions, and sprinting is the same. You just have to make the right choices."

He was also full of praise for the British team. "I wish they could all wear a rainbow jersey. We planned for this, we took it on from start to finish and delivered." It was an amazing performance from everybody, but particularly from Cavendish. To plan for, then deliver a victory in a single-day race with so many variables takes a lot of guts, but Cavendish just seemed to absorb the pressure.

Having repeated Tom Simpson's World Championship victory, Cavendish repeated his and Sir Chris Hoy's BBC Sports Personality of the Year win, becoming the third cyclist to have his name on one of the little metal shields around the iconic trophy's base. And since that glorious year Mark Cavendish has if anything grown in stature.

He rode for Team Sky in 2012, a move that was more of a success for the team than it was for Cavendish. He didn't get the protection and help he's used to in the Tour de France, because the team was committed to helping Bradley Wiggins, and although that caused him frustration he didn't vent it in the way he might have done in the past. Indeed one picture from that Tour says a great deal about Mark Cavendish.

It's a shot of him riding back through the team cars to the peloton. His rainbow jersey is stretched to capacity by drinks bottles stuffed into every pocket, down the neck and up behind his back as well. He's taking them to hand out around the team. The world champion becomes the team water boy for the day. It's a sight seldom seen, but it speaks volumes about Cavendish's inherent humility. Yes, he's ambitious, yes, he can be outspoken, and yes, he can lose it when things go wrong – although that's a much rarer occurrence nowadays – but he's not arrogant.

Cavendish still won stages, and to round out the 2012 Tour the yellow jersey led out the rainbow jersey on to the Champs-Elysées in what really has to be the best day in British cycling history. Cavendish won the Tour's final stage for the fourth year in a row. "That's the one I want most," he says. "For me the Champs-Elysées is the best thing about the Tour de France. It's iconic, so to ride there is an incredible feeling, but to win on the Champs-Elysées, there are so many emotions ..."

And Cavendish felt plenty of those a few weeks later when the Olympic road race didn't work out for him. He could have won on that course; it could have ended in a bunch sprint. That was Team GB's plan, but it didn't happen.

Since then he's carried on winning. The Tour of Qatar, a fourth victory in the Scheldedprijs, the opening stage of the Tour of Italy and the chance to wear the pink jersey. Cavendish also won the British national road race title just before the Tour, so he lined up at the Tour team presentation in the national jersey, white with a blue and a red band, edged with the rainbow bands he's entitled to wear to mark his 2011 world title. Cavendish won two more Tour stages in 2013, taking him to equal third place with Andre Leducq of France in the all-time list of Tour stage winners.

He has plans to carry on too. An Olympic medal is missing from his CV, and he needs to change that. He's even talked about returning to track racing, where the early days of the WCPP suggest the odds are stacked more in his favour. He will go on – "He loves what he does, he loves riding his bike and racing," says Ellingworth.

"But it's hard," says Cavendish, "and I don't think people realize how hard it is. Never mind the sprints, take the mountains in the Grand Tours. They are hard for everyone, but for me they are mentally hard too because as a sprinter you are going as deep as you can go, but you are not going for a win. It's just to survive."

CHAPTER 9

MARGINAL GAINS, MAXIMUM THRUST

Team Sky was launched in January 2010 with huge razzamatazz at the Millbank Tower in London. There were lots of media people, lots of light and glitz, and lots of buzz words like marginal gains getting bandied about. But at one point in the show Bradley Wiggins found himself standing next to Russell Downing. They'd shared something else; they'd been here before.

They were there in 2001 when the Linda McCartney team was also unveiled to the media in London. It was the McCartney launch into the big time, with some big-time co-sponsors. Linda McCartney was also supposed to be Wiggins's and Downing's first pro team, but there was a problem. The big-time sponsors didn't know they were sponsors and the team launch was just smoke and mirrors. It wasn't long before the truth was found out and everybody was out of a job.

As they stood on the stage at the Team Sky launch nine years later, Wiggins leaned over to Downing and whispered out of the corner of his mouth, "Do you think they'll let us keep the bikes this time, Russ?"

It was a light moment on a serious day. Team Sky was British, it was aiming at the Tour de France, and it was already up and running. They had all the backing they needed and they were coming to pro cycling to win. However, unknown to most guests at that launch, and certainly unknown to Sky, even here there was a tiny bit of smoke and mirrors being played out behind the scenes, as Sir David Brailsford admitted to me when we spoke at a Team Sky training camp a year or so later.

"I promised Sky that the team would ride the Tour de France in its first year, in fact it was a condition of the deal with Sky that we would, but I didn't really know for definite that we would get in the Tour, it was never certain. I'd had assurances, but until the day they announced it, until they announced we had a wild card entry, I was constantly thinking, 'Is there something I don't know?' It was an anxious few months until it was confirmed." And what would have happened if they hadn't got in? "I don't know," he replied. What did Chris Boardman say about Brailsford being a gambler?

But Boardman was also right about Brailsford being the only person who could have pushed British Cycling's effort on to this stage, to the point where Sky became involved in sponsoring the national squad, then committing what is reputed to be well over £30 million on the four-year project that is Team Sky.

Boardman was also right about Brailsford's passion and love for cycling. The team's first race was the Tour Down Under, which started a few weeks after the launch. The night before the race started there was the usual serious talk about the first stage, the team's overall strategy and who was expected to do what, but at the end of it Brailsford stood up and spoke to all the riders. "Whatever happens from now on you must try to remember tomorrow, you must remember you were the riders who were there for the first race that Team Sky ever took part in. Whatever happens in the future, you were the first, and that's important," he said.

Brailsford also spoke to some individual riders as they filed out of the room. Russell Downing remembers it well. "I was still a bit jittery and still had a little bit of self-doubt right up until the night before the first race in Australia. I'd done the training, including riding in a home-made heat chamber on a turbo trainer in my bathroom, but it was still a big step. But Dave Brailsford has the knack of saying the right thing at the right time, and as I walked out of the room he grabbed my arm and said, 'Right, Russ, your career starts now.' It put it all in perspective and I settled down to doing what I do best, and that's racing."

Team Sky was Downing's big chance. While Bradley Wiggins's career had spiralled ever upwards after the McCartney presentation, Downing's had been a stop-start road to frustration. He'd won some big races but found it hard to attract a place in a big team. As he got older there appeared to be a marked resistance to taking him on, and he even had to fight hard to get into Team Sky. In the end he was one of their best riders in 2010.

Sky ended the year with 22 wins. The best was probably Bradley Wiggins's win in the prologue of the 2010 Giro d'Italia. He wore the pink jersey of race leader for a few days, but then the team made a bit of a collective mistake that compromised his Tour de France performance that year, as Wiggins explains.

"I thought I could get on the Tour podium before the Giro. We hadn't made a mistake until then. It was one of the best years of my life, and pre-Giro I felt fantastic. Then we made a mistake. I underestimated what would happen if I won the Giro prologue, which I set out to do as a target on the way to the Tour. The Italian press were never going to let us get away with that. They were totally wound up and as soon as I got off my bike it was, 'Can you win the Giro?'

"You can't say, 'No, I'm here for the training,' but that was the plan really. I was going to win the prologue then go for six days full-on to defend the lead, then slip back. It worked. I lost the lead, slipped back, but then I got in a break that gained 20 minutes and I was back in the frame, tenth overall and on paper I could finish fifth or sixth. Suddenly it was a case of what do we do now? It would disrespect the race to bow out. Also, the team had worked hard for me. But working against us was the fact that the route and the weather were both savage. I tried hard on the Monte Grappa stage and ended up seventh, which was good, but I was pretty exhausted, and we still hadn't decided what to do.

"Then we came to the Monte Zoncolan, and I cracked a bit. But the thing is I still couldn't decide what to do. Do I push as hard as I can or back off completely? In the end I did neither, and that was absolutely the wrong thing to do. After the Zoncolan I began to worry about the Tour. We still had a terrible week to do in the Giro, and I couldn't stop after all we'd shared in the team, so I saw it through and ended up a bit sick with a chest infection."

The team made another mistake in the Tour de France prologue. The previous year's top ten get the option of going off last in the reverse order of their previous finishing position, or they can choose where to start in the order. The weather forecast said Rotterdam would be hit by a storm at some time during the prologue, where the riders start individually at intervals, but most likely it would hit at the end. This presented two options. Play it safe and go at the end, so any time lost through the storm would effectively be only on your closest rivals who all chose towards the end. Or take the battle to them, go earlier and try to use the weather to steal some time from them.

Someone in Team Sky had access to a bit of state-of-the-art weather prediction, the sort used by yachtsmen in ocean racing, which said the storm would indeed hit late. So Wiggins went early and the storm hit him. The ones who went towards the end of the prologue had better weather, so Wiggins lost time to all the race favourites.

It was a possible marginal gain that turned into a big loss. Team Sky were no longer in contention, Wiggins was unable to produce a challenge in the mountains, and the damage included a loss of face. After all, they had gone into World Tour cycling amid lots of publicity about them questioning the old ways of doing things and saying that they were determined to apply some of the things that had been learned through British Cycling's experience in Olympic Games and World Championships. Now a lot of established teams were smiling.

*   *   *   *   *

The team didn't have a bad year in 2010. Far from it, as Brailsford points out: "I think for a new team, we did pretty well. Juan-Antonio Flecha won Het Nieuwsblad, we won a stage in Paris–Nice, we won one in Tirreno and in the Dauphiné and in the Giro, where Brad had the pink jersey. We were in there, even the first week of the Tour with Geraint Thomas getting second on the cobbled stage. Then we went into the mountains and it just felt like we were a bit behind there."

So they went back to the drawing board and used the old British Cycling approach to meeting the demands of a project, asking the crucial question: what does it take to win? As far as the Tour de France was concerned, the answer was that Bradley Wiggins had to be able to stay with the leaders in the mountains. So the next question was: what does it take to do that? And the answer, as it usually is with cycling, was in a number.

The number is VAM, which stands for Velocita Ascensionale Media. It means the number of vertical metres that a rider can rack up in an hour. It's a phrase coined by the infamous Italian cycling coach, the man who guided Lance Armstrong to the seven Tour wins of which he was subsequently stripped because of doping, Dr Michele Ferrari. But there's nothing dodgy about VAM, it's simply a way of quantifying climbing performance. Calculating VAM is done like this: count the metres climbed, multiply them by 60, then divide by the time it took to climb them.

There is a slight complication in that VAM is affected by gradient. Steeper hills give a higher number, and Dr Ferrari reckons that VAM increases by 50 for each one per cent increase in gradient. But this can be factored into calculations if you remember that a VAM of 1,650 vertical metres ascended per hour on an eight per cent climb is almost the same as 1,600 on a seven per cent and almost the same as 1,700 on a nine per cent climb. I say almost because the relationship between VAM and gradient isn't strictly linear, and it gets less linear on shallow and steep gradients.

"VAM is a performance measure you can work with without using power," says Team Sky's Tour de France coach Tim Kerrison. "You might not know a rival's power, but you can time how fast they climb. The times for climbs get published too. We knew what VAM was being ridden by the best guys in last year's Tour, so that gave us a figure to work with in training."

And that's what they did before the 2011 Tour, only for Wiggins to crash out of the Tour when in the form of his life. They used the training tool again in 2012. Wiggins and his Tour team spent days doing Tour de France-type climbs in 30-degree heat on Tenerife, riding them in a controlled manner and building the sustained pace until they produced VAM numbers comparable with what were achieved by the front groups during the 2011 Tour.

Just before the 2012 Tour started, Wiggins said that Team Sky had set a VAM of 1,700 on the Col de Joux Plane in the Critérium du Dauphiné, when defending his yellow jersey. He said that they had seen VAMs of 1,500 done by the front groups in the 2011 Tour and were happy about where they were. However, the Joux-Plane is very steep, so 1,700 there isn't as superior to the 1,500 average of the 2011 Tour as it looks, because of the 50-point jumps in VAM for every one per cent gradient increase. But still, Wiggins and Sky knew they were in the ball-park for winning the race.

That's why you saw Sky riders in the front group on crucial climbs looking down at their power meters when their rivals attacked. They knew from training and races what power produced what VAM for a given gradient, so they were checking their power meters to see where they stood. When attacks went over their sustainable numbers the Sky riders knew their rivals couldn't keep up that pace, and so it proved.

Training using VAM is just one of the ways in which Team Sky have revolutionized what teams do in top-level pro cycling now. Not to put too fine a point on it, a lot of them now copy the Sky team. British Cycling were the first to bring in the idea of using skinsuits in some road races; Team Sky used them, and so do other teams now. BC and Team Sky were the first to use aerodynamic road race helmets in certain races; now most of the other teams do so as well, and helmet manufacturers make them. When some riders in other teams, and some of the media, saw Sky riders warming down on rollers or turbo trainers after races or a Grand Tour stage, they laughed at them; now every team does it.

Sky rider Ian Stannard, who has been with the team since it started and witnessed the revolution first hand, recalls how attitudes changed: "We were maybe a bit in your face in the first year, probably a bit media led when we hadn't got the history to shout about, but in the second year the team became more friendly and we tried to engage with the fans and press. We also started getting better results, and that caused the other teams to respect us more. Now I think we are accepted, and the teams even copy some of the things we do. Look at doing warm-downs on the rollers after a stage. It was common sense to us, but the teams thought we were weird. Now they all do it. You get riders giving interviews on a turbo trainer, where before they were just stood or sat down."

"But why wouldn't you warm down after a race?" asks Brailsford. "It's a coaching principle, after a hard effort you ride easy to help your legs recover, so why not do it after a Tour stage, when recovery is crucial in a stage race? It made no sense to us to race hard then sit down on a bus to travel to the hotel, when for just a small investment of time the riders can spin their legs and help start the recovery process."

* * * * *

Aero helmets, skinsuits, and warming down all produce marginal gains, and Team Sky apply the same approach to every aspect of the team. Among the most important is nutrition. Team Sky's nutritionist is Nigel Mitchell, and he does the same job for British Cycling too. Like Steve Peters he's available on tap to answer any questions a rider might have or to help them address particular problems or demands they are facing. He worked with Bradley Wiggins when he lost weight, and he supervises short bouts of calorie restriction that road racers occasionally need to help them get to their best watts per kilo level. He's also worked with sprinters, who have very different requirements when they are trying to build muscle during intensive bouts of weight training.

He's even been able to redesign riders, as he did with Wiggins and Steve Cummings. When they switched from being primarily track to primarily road racers he helped them lose muscle from areas of their bodies where they didn't need it. But all the while he had an eye on their overall health; and it's the same when he's designing nutrition plans for stage races.

It is worth looking quite deeply into Team Sky's nutrition strategy, not least because it has relevance to the doping issue. When Sir David Brailsford made his famous promise at the start of the Team Sky story of delivering a British winner of the Tour de France within five years, he added a caveat. "A British winner has to be clean, otherwise it would be worthless." The promised victory was delivered in 2012, and in the light of the Tour de France's past there were questions then about Team Sky and Bradley Wiggins's anti-doping stance. And a number of people have voiced suspicions. But looking in depth at just one aspect of Team Sky's approach might help allay such suspicions.

One of the key phrases Nigel Mitchell uses when explaining his work is "a functioning stomach". He spoke interestingly about this in 2011 after the UCI announced that they were banning the use of injections in cycling, unless for a specific and documented medical need. Needles had been used in pro cycling to deliver certain nutrients, vitamins and minerals, which were taken because it was accepted wisdom within pro racing that a rider's stomach didn't function optimally when stressed by bouts of heavy training or by a Grand Tour, especially towards the end of one.

The ban came about in response to an argument put forward by David Millar, among others. Millar thinks that administering vitamins and minerals by injection makes the step up to injecting drugs just that bit easier. The UCI agreed and injections were duly banned, to break the link that Millar says helped make the step to drugs easier for him.

But Mitchell says he was shocked that needles had been used for delivering nutrients in cycling in the first place, because in his view it was totally unnecessary. "At first I didn't understand why the new rule was important. Doping is banned anyway, so I didn't get the significance of banning needles. Then I found out that there had been a perception in the past that recovery was accelerated when some nutritional needs were supplied by using needles. Well, I come from a clinical background, and even there, although some very sick people might need nutrients provided intravenously, my clinical training taught me to use the gastro-intestinal tract wherever possible. Basically, if you have a functioning stomach, use it," he says.

Mitchell says he can meet all the nutritional needs of Team Sky and British Cycling riders through "carefully prepared quality food, while at the same time maintaining gut health, which is where I think things have gone wrong in the past. If teams haven't invested in maintaining gut health, then recovery will be compromised, no matter how well an individual eats."

Mitchell's approach focuses on maintaining gut health as the front-line weapon in the war against fatigue brought on by hard training and racing. Because if the gut isn't healthy it might be able to absorb some of the fats, carbohydrates and protein the body needs for fuel and repair, but not all of the micro-nutrients that help keep the body functioning optimally.

It was the micro-nutrients, minerals like iron, which used to be injected, often in cocktails with other micro-nutrients such as vitamin B12. However, maintaining gut health, often by means that simply weren't known years ago, now allows these to be absorbed adequately through the gastro-intestinal tract.

The human digestive system works best in a quite narrow Ph range, Ph being a measure of acidity. So Mitchell ensures the team's diet helps keep their stomach Ph within the optimal range, and sometimes he uses supplements that help maintain gut Ph. Once Ph is under control, there are other factors that help digestion and absorption of food.

"The protein supplements we use are fortified with probiotics and with an amino acid called glutamine, which both help maintain gut health. I also try not to overload their bowel with fibre. Riders eat quite a lot of salad, and I'm quite keen that some of this is liquidized into a drink. Vegetable juice retains its soluble fibre, but there isn't as much insoluble fibre in juice," Mitchell says.

Probiotics are live micro-organisms that have a beneficial effect on the hosts in which they live. In human digestion probiotics feature in a number of processes, including killing harmful gut infections, and increasing lymphocytes, which also fight disease. They have an anti-inflammatory role too, which is very important because an inflamed gastro-intestinal tract won't digest and absorb nutrients as it should. Fish oils are also used by Team Sky riders for their anti-inflammatory function, as well as other effects.

The un-denatured protein in the products that Sky's nutrients supplier CNP provide may also act like Colostrum in a gut health role. Colostrum is first milk taken from lactating cows, and it contains a number of immunoglobulins specific to human pathogens, such as salmonella. It also contains several valuable antioxidents, including an important one called lactoferrin, which helps bind iron to red blood cells. These have a positive effect on recovery rate and therefore on maintaining and even improving performance. Colostrum also plays an important role in protecting gut function, especially in hot weather.

It's also interesting to look at Team Sky's nutrition strategy on a stage, because it really is a lesson in marginal gains and leaving no stone unturned in giving their rider the best chance of performing to their potential. Mitchell has developed the strategy over time and he works very closely with Team Sky's chef, Soren Kristiansen, who as well as preparing delicious food has a good grounding in sports nutrition.

"On stage races Team Sky's riders start drinking as soon as they wake up," says Mitchell. "Each rider sees the doctor first thing just to check how they are getting on, and when they do they're given a fruit juice drink. The fruit's not there for any specific reason, it's just there to make the drink taste nice so they start drinking. If you start drinking early in the day it gets you into the habit.

"If it's hot, or the previous day's stage was, we might give them an electrolyte drink before breakfast, which contains all the electrolytes they lose through sweating. They drink juice at breakfast plus anything else they want to increase their uptake of fluid. We flavour most of their drinks; not because pure water is no good, it's just they're more likely to drink more if it tastes good. We also give each rider 1.5 litres of juice drink for on the bus when they are travelling to the start, and we encourage them to drink at least half of it. We might add an electrolyte sachet to it if we have any concerns about dehydration.

"Then during a stage they should aim for drinking one bottle of water and one bottle of sports drink every hour, just standard-size race drinks bottles. They get electrolytes from their gels and we include rice in their race food, because cooked rice holds lots of water.

"After the stage they get a protein shake, which helps with fluid replacement as well as general recovery, and again, if we suspect dehydration we use the electrolyte drink. We've found that it's effective even when racing day after day in 40 degrees.

"The core thing is keeping the gut right, then everything else falls into place. It's true that riders in a stage race are placed in a situation of systemic stress, where they could lose muscle mass, but given quality nutrition, and if they have good health, they can get everything they need to remain strong and healthy without recourse to needles."

That's important. One of the arguments that used to be put forward by pro cyclists who were caught doping was that cycling was so hard that they needed to take artificial sources of things like testosterone. The methods used by Mitchell and Sky contradict that stance. It's also true that in years gone by riders used to come out of the Tour de France wrecked because in the last week their bodies were so run down they weren't absorbing the macro- and micro-nutrients they needed, so in extreme cases they were consuming their own bodies. But in those days teams didn't have access to specialists like Nigel Mitchell.

Other World Tour teams now have their own chefs working with nutritionists, and they work with sports nutrition companies, but BC and Sky are still ahead of the curve. Their nutrition supplier has a small laboratory at the Hyde factory, not far from Manchester Velodrome, where they can mix limited runs of specific products that take into account any food allergies or intolerance a team member might have.

And so it goes on. Team Sky riders have their own mattresses, pillows and bedding, and they follow them around France in the Tour, or to any race, so effectively they sleep in the same bed every night no matter where they are. They have mobile humidifiers. They have a luxury bus stuffed with mood lighting, air conditioning, sound systems, flat-screen TVs and showers.

Everything is done that can be done to underpin their riders' performance. When defining what he means by marginal gains, Brailsford says: "It means taking the one per cent from everything you do; finding a one per cent margin for improvement in everything you do. That's what we try to do, from the mechanics upwards. If a mechanic sticks a tyre on, and someone comes along and says it could be done better, it's not an insult. It's because we are always striving for improvement, for those one per cent gains, in absolutely every single thing we do. Then when you put a number of these things together they make a significant performance gain."

Team Sky weren't the first pro road team to follow the marginal gains line. That was probably HTC Columbia, whom Mark Cavendish once rode for, but who stopped racing in 2011. They were the brainchild of an American businessman, who took over the German team Telekom, where doping had been rife. But the team back then had some young staff, notably a German called Sebastian Weber, who saw that there was another way in cycling.

They had the team doing different things; small things, but things that when they were added up made a difference.

Allan Peiper, who was a directeur sportif with the team, made the case in 2008: "This team is the way to go, this is the way to change cycling. They say that the best doping products can give a ten per cent advantage, but if you take ten one per cent gains, like the guys are doing here, and roll them up, then you have your ten per cent just the same."

*   *   *   *   *

Team Sky is also very good at problem solving, and adapting and assimilating new stuff on the fly. For example, Wiggins went to train at altitude in Tenerife in 2011 after a test following the 2010 Tour showed that he tended to de-saturate quickly on climbs above 2,000 metres. This meant the oxygen saturation of his blood dropped suddenly at altitude, which in cycling terms means past the 1,800 to 2,000 metre height mark.

The 2011 Tenerife camp, just before the 2011 Critérium du Dauphiné, was meant to remedy an identified problem, so Wiggins would be better prepared for the high-altitude stages of the 2011 Tour. But when Wiggins won the Dauphiné straight after the camp he was in the form of his life, so the same high-altitude camp was chosen to prepare for Tour 2012. In fact so good was his performance after the Tenerife training camp that it must have given him more than the expected adaptation to high altitude. It therefore became part of the Sky programme, and Wiggins and his Tour team used Tenerife camps a lot in 2012.

The success of the altitude training camp can probably be explained by discoveries that sports scientists have made recently about altitude training. In the past, endurance athletes trained at altitude in order to increase the number of red blood cells in their bodies, and thus increase their oxygen-carrying capacity.

But now sports scientists regard the red blood cell boost almost as a side-effect of altitude, and a fleeting one at that.

It's fleeting because the concentration of the hormone responsible for creating red blood cells increases steadily for the first two weeks at altitude, then falls to base levels after a month. Also, the post-altitude boost to red blood cells boost only lasts for the life of the cells, about 28 days.

Wiggins and his back-up team were mindful of the temporary effect. He returned to sea level on May 26, one week before the Critérium du Dauphiné, which ran from June 3 to June 10, to allow a week for what's called the post-altitude slump, a period when the body readjusts to working at sea level. During this period Wiggins was also able to recover from the heavy workload of the training camp.

Team Sky then held an altitude camp from just after the Dauphiné until June 24, which riders could drop in and out of, and according to reports Wiggins was there some of the time, although he also did some route reconnoitring in France.

But there are other effects, some of them more lasting ones, that come from sleeping and training at altitude. A few years ago the late Aldo Sassi, a famous Italian coach and the man who guided Cadel Evans to become the formidable Grand Tour racer he is now, told me several things about altitude training.

"An increase in the number of blood capillaries in the lungs and muscles is a big and lasting adaptation. More capillaries means more oxygen can be picked up by the lungs and more delivered to working muscles. The body also becomes better at taking up, transporting and delivering oxygen. There are hormonal changes too, mostly to do with the testosterone to cortisol balance in the body, which maintain muscle. That's a very valuable thing during a hard training camp," he said.

Sassi also pointed out another advantage of training at altitude: "Athletes use their lungs fully, breathing deeper and using a greater proportion of the places in them where oxygen is absorbed by blood, which concentrate in the lower parts of the lungs. It forces them to breathe deeper and more efficiently, and it conditions the muscles involved in breathing. There are also some changes of muscle enzymes that are of lasting benefit to performance," he said. There was more, but he was getting really technical by then.

He did make one very important point. Using EPO or any red cell boosting blood manipulation could be very dangerous for an athlete training at altitude, he said, because doing so could thicken the blood to dangerous levels. Looked at in those terms, Sky's extensive use of altitude training provides even more evidence that they race clean.

In 2012 Wiggins and Team Sky followed a mixed programme in Tenerife, riding down Mount Teide to do sea-level training, mixing in quality sessions on the many other slopes the island has to offer, and climbing back up the big mountain, where the roads reach 2,100 metres plus, to get the benefits of some hypoxic training.

The sleep-high, train-low model is the best use of altitude for athletes. Athletes gain the positive benefits by sleeping at altitude, while avoiding the negatives of altitude by training at lower levels. The negatives are a loss of muscular power and increased stress on the body if it's constantly working at altitude. Doing hard training at lower levels helps preserve muscle mass.

Wiggins had begun training for the 2012 Tour de France in November 2011, when he did a lot of low-intensity work to build a base. Then he worked on his threshold by doing long climbs at a power output calculated to push him towards his optimum power at threshold, which is the factor that puts a racer in the ball-park for winning the Tour. And while this was going on, Wiggins had to become as lean as possible.

The training Wiggins did while in Tenerife in 2012 was very specific to the demands of the Tour de France. Throughout April and May he did long climbs, working at the power calculated to push him towards his optimum threshold, until he was doing sessions like three repetitions of 25-minute climbs in 35 degrees heat. The idea was to build up to doing simulated Tour de France stages, that's 4,000 metres of climbing in a six-hour ride, and doing them back to back.

In all Wiggins aimed for 100,000 metres of climbing to build his threshold and hone his climbing power, and since he was already good at time trials, the effects were clear when he dominated the Critérium du Dauphiné.

However, Wiggins had another weakness: he didn't perform as well on steeper sections of climbs, and there were going to be some steep climbs in the 2012 Tour. To address that, Wiggins went to the gym during the winter of 2011/12 to follow a strength and conditioning programme, doing the kind of work to overload and build muscles, especially in his core, that cycling can't reach to the depth he needed. He also did specific bike training, like high-intensity intervals with varying rest, designed to help him mount powerful anaerobic attacks and recover from them, and cope when others make them, which is crucial.

Wiggins of course won the 2012 Tour de France in style, with Chris Froome in second place, about which there will be more in the next chapter. That year Wiggins also had an amazing run of winning the Paris–Nice, the Tour de Romandie and the Critérium du Dauphiné (for a second time). And he won an Olympic gold medal in the time trial in London.

He is an amazing athlete, but he's been part of an amazing team, first as a member of the national squad, when he was the best endurance track racer of his generation and one of the best of all time, and now with Team Sky.

But the team are amazing too. The British cycling team went from 17th place in the rankings to first in just eight years, and now, after the sniggers and knowing smiles of 2010, Team Sky is the best Grand Tour team in the world with consecutive Tour de France victories in 2012 and 2013. They haven't yet had the same success in the Classics, and they were disappointed when their first serious tilt at them fell short of their high expectations in 2013, but that will be put right in time.

Team Sky have achieved so much by implementing the methods by which British Cycling's performance effort has achieved so much. They've done it by asking a basic question for every challenge in front of them. What does it take to win this? Then they determine the individual demands and plot a course to meet them. Rod Ellingworth describes the next step: "We draw up a list of objectives, then tick them off when they are reached. I did one for the worlds with Cav."

They did the same for the Tour de France, and you can bet that Team Sky will now be working on another list for the Classics.

CHAPTER 10

THE MODFATHER

There are several Bradley Wigginses, but only one real one. The others are public personas, hats he picks up to wear when he likes, although there's probably a bit of each one in the real thing. There's the chippy rock star, the mickey-taker, the man who likes to shock, the entertainer and comedian, and even a grumpy Bradley. But the real Sir Bradley Wiggins is the one only his family and close friends know.

Wiggins was born in Ghent, in Belgium, the son of an Australian father and a British mother. Gary Wiggins was a good track tracer who'd come to Europe to earn fame and fortune in the six-day track races. He was a hell-raiser, though, feared for his fists as much as his speed on the track, and he wasn't in his son's life for long. Bradley Wiggins was brought up by his mother in London and he is fiercely proud of her, as he is of his family now.

He is determined to be nothing like his dad, although Gary must be in there somewhere, lurking.

After seeing his son just a few times in the intervening years, Gary Wiggins died in a bar-room brawl in Australia in 2008. So if you are looking for a father figure in Wiggins's life then Shane Sutton, the Australian-born coach who's worked with him since he was a junior, is a better candidate. "Brad's a stubborn bastard, to be honest," says Sutton. "He listens to people, but nobody influences him. He's a good bloke, though; fun, funny, caring, lovable and a great family man."

Throughout his amazing career on the track Bradley Wiggins also wanted to win big road races, but Sutton never sensed a true commitment to do it. "I've always maintained that Brad had a gift but he never wrapped it very well. I knew he had the ability to be one of the best road racers in the world, a lot of people knew, but he had to go out there and do it, and he never did that," he says.

For his part Wiggins says: "I had started to think I was kidding myself. People are deluded all the time in sport, you hear them saying they will do this and do that, and you know they won't. Taking it further, it's like in *X-Factor*. You see them come on and they think they can sing, they are so sure of it, but they can't. And when the judges tell them, they still can't believe it – you see it in their faces. We all have little self-delusions, and I began to think that what I'd been telling myself for years, that there was no reason why I couldn't be good on the road, in the Classics and maybe even the Tour de France, was my delusion."

But in truth Wiggins was probably held back by the level of doping that was going on in the Grand Tours. At the time when he started out and tried to progress in pro road racing it had reached quite staggering proportions. Then something happened in 2008 to change his view. "After my Cofidis team-mate Christian Moreni got caught in 2007, and the whole Cofidis team got thrown out of the Tour, I began to think to hell with it, to hell with the Tour de France. I had won Olympic Gold on the track in 2004, something that fills me with pride; Beijing was just around the corner. They can keep the Tour, I thought. But someone made a difference in 2008. I was training for Beijing, so I didn't ride it, but while I was away I think the Tour turned a corner regarding doping. What makes me believe it was Christian Vande Velde's fourth place.

"Christian was my inspiration. I knew him, I knew he wouldn't take drugs, and he'd got a top five place in the Tour, when it had got to the point where the public believed that was impossible without doping. So I thought then it would be good to do the 2009 Tour in support of Christian, but to do that I had to climb better, and that meant losing weight. Cycling is physics, it's numbers, that's part of the reason why I like it. You can't bullshit numbers. Climbing is a matter of power over weight. My power was good, but I didn't climb well because I weighed too much."

A project was started with British Cycling help, because Wiggins was part of the Performance Plan as well as being a member of the Garmin pro team. In fact the management levels of the Performance Plan knew that Team Sky would begin in 2010 and they wanted Wiggins to be in it. Wiggins had to lose weight, he had to do more miles in training. It would require higher levels of dedication and determination than he'd ever had to bring to bear before, but Wiggins loves cycling, and that helped.

"Bradley really loves cycling, it's obvious," Sutton confirms. "I've seen it loads of times over the years, but the first time I saw it was in the Munich six-day. I went down to see him after the last session and he came into the cabin laughing and joking with everyone. Munich is tough, and the others looked tired, but Brad had this big smile on his face, then when he saw me he just stuck out his arms out and said, 'Hey, I was born to do this.' He loves it, everything about cycling, he loves the racing and he's the ultimate fan.

"What sort of kid would run home from school in London to watch videos of the Kellogg's criteriums from the eighties and nineties in his lunch break? He used to bring them to training sessions in Manchester to take the piss out of me riding in them. I call him the John Motson of cycling – he knows all the facts. I bet Brad can tell you what socks Greg Lemond was wearing when he beat Fignon on the Champs-Elysées by eight seconds."

Wiggins admits he loves cycling too, although as ever with him there's a slight contradiction. "I won't stop cycling when I stop racing. I love the British amateur club scene; the Sunday runs to cafés and doing an evening ten-mile time trial. I'd even like to carry on racing as an amateur after I stop as a pro, but I couldn't stand getting slower, that would depress me. I don't know why. One of the people I admire most in cycling, Sean Yates, carried on racing for years after he was pro. He got slower but it never seemed to bother Sean, he just liked riding his bike."

According to Sutton, Wiggins's pursuit power output for 4,000 metres was 560 watts, and in a time trial he could ride at 440 to 460 watts. He had the power to be a Tour de France contender, but to put it bluntly at 80 kilograms Wiggins was too heavy. Not that he was anywhere near fat in the everyday use of the word; no track racers are fat. The best way to put it is by saying that where track riders look fit and healthy, Tour de France contenders look fit and emaciated. They have to reduce their body fat down to minuscule levels, because fat holds them back when they climb. Wiggins would also have to lose some of the muscle in his upper body, developed by doing standing starts on the track. In the end it looked like he lost it from his legs as well, which caused some people to question how he did that and kept his power. But how much muscle does it take to put out 400 watts? A kid can do it for seconds. As Chris Boardman points out, "The amount of power you put into a pedal revolution isn't the limiting factor in endurance cycling, it's the length of time you can keep putting out 400 watts or more."

Nigel Mitchell got involved on the nutrition side of the project, and Dr Steve Peters helped Wiggins get into the right frame of mind to see it through, because as Shane Sutton points out, "If you are going to lose weight there are times when you are just going to be bloody hungry. Steve helped him there. It wasn't with big things, you don't get to where Bradley was without having some strong belief systems, but Steve was able to reinforce things for him."

The first thing Wiggins needed was a good winter's training, a road racer's winter training. Fortunately Wiggins is easy to coach, according to Sutton, "so long as you can keep him on his bike." And during the winter of 2008–09 Wiggins kept on his bike. He did all the under-23 academy rides from Manchester, going out into the Peak District for long rides. "The boys thought it was great having him there, and Brad fed off that. He felt committed to them too, and that helped him spend the winter really well," says Sutton.

And the momentum just built from there. Wiggins started the 2009 road season well. He was stronger because of all the extra road training he'd done, and lighter because of his diet. He started getting up there in the races, and that helped him buy into the programme even more.

"I saw a big difference in Brad that spring," Sutton recalls. "One race pinpoints it for me, one race where you could see the mental and physical changes he'd made, and that was Paris–Roubaix. If you look at the pictures of him after that, when he was sat down on the grass in the track centre, all caked in mud and dust. He's already thin there, and he looks like he's been through Hell. But he had – he'd finished 25th in Paris–Roubaix and gone deep to do it. This was a new Bradley Wiggins. The old Brad would have climbed off at one of the feeds. This one fought all the way to Roubaix for the first time. He got stuck in at last."

Wiggins rode the 2009 Giro d'Italia, and he rode well, getting really excited when he dropped Lance Armstrong on a climb. His form was good, and in those days nobody was expecting great performance from him in a race like that – he wasn't the Garmin team leader or anything – so he backed off a bit and used the rest of the Giro as a sort of heavy training camp.

By the start of the 2009 Tour de France Wiggins was a different athlete. From China in 2008 to France in 2009 he'd changed from a world-beating track racer into a contender for Grand Tours. Changing his training had helped; doing long rides and riding more and better road races had made him stronger; but it was losing weight that made him a Tour contender.

"He had the power already," says Sutton. "If you knock out 560 watts over four minutes with your legs going well over 110 rpm, and you can sustain 440 to 460 watts for longer efforts, then if you lose weight you'll ride fast up a mountain."

The man who helped Wiggins lose weight, Nigel Mitchell, explains how they went about it: "We matched Bradley's diet very precisely to his training. Training creates a dietary need, because adaptations in response to training are driven by protein synthesis, so it was a matter of matching the right nutrients in the right load to each training session and not over-swamping anything. Then we included trace nutrients to protect his body, and that is where the advances have been made and where I can't really be specific, but by using these it's possible to go quite low on calorie intake and still build muscle."

A lot of experience and knowledge went into Wiggins's weight loss programme, but there was another factor, one that Mitchell stresses cannot be overestimated: it was the gifted performance machine that Wiggins is. "All top athletes are something special physically. Bradley has a fantastic physiology for an endurance athlete and his body could cope with the process. It made the adaptations, where others would have broken down," he says.

Wiggins went into the 2009 Tour de France privately excited at the prospect of seeing what he could do, but publicly playing this down by saying he might be able to get a stage win or that he was there to support Christian Vande Velde, which he was, in a way. However, it quickly became obvious that Wiggins was the best Garmin rider.

The return of Lance Armstrong and the power struggle going on in the Astana team between him and Alberto Contador was the biggest story of the 2009 race. Mark Cavendish was news too, especially when he won the first two road stages.

Wiggins finished third in the 15-kilometre time trial that opened the Tour, which wasn't so surprising because he's a good time triallist. David Millar nearly pulled off a stupendous win on the stage to Barcelona, but his incredibly brave lone break was caught just 1.3 kilometres from the finish. Then came the first big mountain stage, and Wiggins didn't drop back. He finished in the front group.

The other Pyrenean stage that year wasn't so hard. It had the mountains, but there was 70 kilometres mostly downhill between the top of the last one and the finish in Tarbes. After that Wiggins held it through the middle week, and then came the Alps, starting with a mountain-top finish at Verbier. That was a challenge. Alberto Contador decided to put any question of who led the Astana team to bed and rocketed up the climb to win. Wiggins stuck to his own pace and only lost 1 minute 6 seconds. And at the end of the stage he was more than still there, he was third in the overall classification behind Contador and Armstrong. The game was on.

Wiggins fought like a lion during the biggest Alpine stage, and was still there in sixth overall. He moved up to fourth after the final time trial and had one hurdle left, but it was a big one. The penultimate stage finished on top of Mont Ventoux.

The Ventoux has weather moods and it was windy up there in the 2009 Tour. That may have helped Wiggins, if the headwind restricted attacks until closer to the end, but he was still riding way above the level he had in the past. He'd experienced the back group in Tours past, when they were a training tool for the track. After the 2009 Tour I asked him what it felt like being at the front instead.

"It hurts as much at the back as it does at the front. At the front, though, you have the cameras in your face, the crowd shouting for you and waving flags. You have the feeling of knowing you are at the top of your sport. It's a fantastic feeling. Riding up the Ventoux, knowing at that moment nothing is higher in your sport, it's incredible. The fans are so close, the helicopters are flying above you, the TV is getting every picture, it all helps you. I also kept in mind something Christian Vande Velde told me about riding at the front. He said everybody in that group is a few minutes from letting go. Everybody is at their limit, so just break it down to a few minutes at a time. You hang on for one set of a few minutes, then another, then another and so on. That helped," he said.

It was a big day. The Ventoux is where Tom Simpson died, and Wiggins admires Simpson, you can tell. I can tell, because we've talked about Tom. He knows that Tom and I are related. He spoke about him one day in 2010, just before the Giro d'Italia, reflecting on how Simpson died and how the drugs that he had taken have tended to eclipse what he achieved. "That was another age," said Wiggins. "He wasn't the only one on that mountain using them that day. Tom was probably encouraged by the teams he was in, told it was OK, told that was what the pros did. He wasn't in this team, in Team Sky. If he had been, it would never have happened. He wasn't in this age. Because of that I think it's a shame that the way he died has eroded people's opinion and even knowledge of what he did, because I've raced in the races he won, and his record is amazing. No British rider has done what he did, and he did it virtually on his own. I'd like to see the appreciation of Tom put right."

Wiggins rode up the Ventoux in 2009 with a picture of Simpson stuck to the top tube of his bike. "I wanted to try and draw inspiration from his story, from the courage and spirit that saw him take on the world with no back-up, and I definitely felt something on the Ventoux that day," he says.

He also asked me in 2010 how I thought Simpson would feel in his position, as a British rider about to lead a British team in the Tour de France. I said it was impossible to say, because as he'd pointed out it was a different age. Back then Simpson would have simply thought, I have to win this at any cost, and would have been open to any risk. Now, in Team Sky, he would have been like Wiggins, trained to focus on the process and control the controllables.

In 2010 Wiggins was the same age as Simpson was back then, 29 going on 30, and like Simpson he had two young children.

Between the Giro and the 2010 Tour he sent me an e-mail. "I've just watched the film again [meaning the Ray Pascoe film *Something to Aim At*]. Seeing Tom there playing with his kids, it's very sad," he said.

The 2010 Tour didn't work out for Wiggins. He started fatigued from the Giro, and he hadn't been in the best state of mind after returning from Italy. "I'm my own worst enemy really," he says. "If things aren't going well for me the people around me suffer, and they suffered a lot during those four weeks. Looking back I don't even recognize myself now. I shaved my head, I stopped playing my guitar because Tour contenders don't play the guitar. I didn't touch a drop of wine. My wife loves baking, but I wouldn't eat cake because it 'might' affect the outcome of the Tour. I mean, it's crazy, you don't not win the Tour because you had a glass of wine or ate some cake."

At the end of 2009 there had been a very public tug of war, or what seemed like one, over Wiggins. He still had a year to run on his Garmin team contract, but Team Sky wanted him. An agreement was eventually made between the two, and Wiggins moved to Sky, but he thinks all the questions and doubt directed at him, although he knew what was happening, took its toll. Because of that, as well as his post-Giro tiredness, the newness of being a team leader – Wiggins had never performed that role before – and the problem discovered in tests after the Tour, where his oxygen levels dropped sharply at higher altitudes, he couldn't perform at his best in the 2010 Tour and had to fight hard for 24th place. Somebody remarked that Wiggins's 2010 Tour was his tricky second album. The music lover in Wiggins will have liked that.

He was a lot more relaxed in 2011, and if anything he racked up the diet regime and the hard training some more. He also did a few more races than he did in 2010, saying: "I enjoy racing, so I'm going to race a lot more. I also want to give the Classics a good go. Plus, if you put all your eggs in one basket, like the Tour, and it doesn't work out, your season is a bad one. It makes sense to me to go for more objectives."

He raced on the track over the winter, because he still hadn't lost sight of an ambition he'd held since he first learned the Olympics were coming to Britain. "I had always wanted to win a gold medal there. London is where I grew up, where I'm from. In 2011 I thought my best chance might still be in the team pursuit," he says.

That spring he finished third in Paris–Nice. He was up there in the Critérium International time trial, and he was good in the Tour de Romandie but there played more of a team role and helped Ben Swift win the final stage. Then Wiggins went to Team Sky's altitude training camp in Tenerife, and when he came back he found he'd gone up a level. He won the Critérium du Dauphiné, the third British rider to do so after Brian Robinson and Robert Millar. After that he was masterful in winning the British road race title. He was ready for the Tour de France.

"I thought he could win it in 2011," says Shane Sutton. "When he crashed and broke his collar bone I thought that was it, his chance had gone. Brad had been so dedicated and focused for so long, I didn't know how the crash would affect him. Would he be able to go on like he had been doing for another year?"

The answer was that Wiggins bounced back very quickly. In early September 2011 he led the Vuelta for a day before finishing third overall, while Chris Froome took second place. It was the first Grand Tour podium for Froome, and for Wiggins too at the time, although it would become his second – subsequently he was boosted to third in the 2009 Tour de France when Lance

Armstrong got stripped of the place following the USADA doping enquiry.

A few days later Wiggins took a silver medal in the World Time Trial Championships in Copenhagen, following which he played a crucial part in Mark Cavendish's victory in the 2011 World Road Race Championships.

A few weeks' rest came next then it was November 1, the day Wiggins began preparing for the 2012 Tour de France, which he won. How did he win it? The number-one factor was his commitment to perfect preparation. He followed the previous year's templates but with the adjustments Sky had learned in 2011 regarding altitude training.

The 2012 Tour route suited Wiggins. On his day Wiggins is the best time triallist in the world, as he proved at the London Olympics. Two other contenders for that title are Fabian Cancelarra of Switzerland and a German, Tony Martin, but Wiggins is faster than them. He matches their power, and his solution to the time triallist's number-one enemy, air resistance, is better thought out and has more attention to detail. The 2012 Tour's dice were loaded for a good time triallist, with 96.1 kilometres of riding alone against the watch. Wiggins was second in the short prologue in Liège and won the two long time trials by good margins.

The second thing in Wiggins's favour was that the Tour wasn't that mountainous. This helped, but Wiggins wasn't really tested in the mountains either, and he has become a very good climber. There was some talk when Chris Froome, on being told that he could go for the stage win on La Toussuire, went before it was agreed and that his attack distanced Wiggins. But Sky directeur sportif Sean Yates dismisses the implied problem by saying; "Chris soon knocked it back when I got on the radio to him, and Brad didn't react because he was riding within his limit."

Another reason for saying that Wiggins has improved a lot as a climber is the way he rode some steep climbs that the Tour included for the first time in 2012. Wiggins has struggled on steep climbs before, notably on El Angliru when leading the 2011 Vuelta. The Planche des Belles Filles finish in the Vosges was very steep. Chris Froome won, and one might have expected Wiggins to lose some time there but he only lost a couple of seconds.

The Col du Grand Colombier is said to be the hardest road climb in France. It's 15 kilometres long and is basically two steep bits joined by a flatter section. The steep bits have sections of 14 and 20 per cent in them, but the gradient varies a lot, which is perfect for climbers. Wiggins cruised up it.

The Mur de Péguère is 3.6 kilometres of 18 per cent climbing that starts at the top of another mountain pass called the Col des Caougnous, which is 9.4 kilometres long with an average gradient of 9.4 per cent. Again, Wiggins had no trouble.

The other big factor that helped Wiggins was Team Sky. As an entity in the race the Sky riders were immense. Chris Froome, Ritchie Porte and Michael Rogers were superb in the mountains, with Porte and Rogers setting a blistering but constant pace that suited the time triallist Wiggins, but just burnt up the legs of the specialist climbers. Some criticized the other riders for not attacking, but they couldn't; Sky were riding too fast for them to do it.

Maybe if some climbers had attacked earlier, making Sky chase and use up key team riders like Rogers and Porte – maybe then, with Wiggins more isolated, someone could have had him in trouble. But that would have been a risky strategy, and it could have handed the race to Froome anyway. "I wondered if somebody would try that; they weren't going to win unless they did, so on a nothing ventured nothing gained basis it was worth a go. But they didn't," says Sean Yates.

So the Sky train thundered on like the TGV to Paris. Wiggins says that the best moments of the whole Tour de France for him were: "Crossing the finish line in the second time trial in Chartres, because that's when I knew I'd won; leading Cav out on the Champs-Elysées; and taking the yellow jersey, the first day I put it on."

Of the finish Wiggins says, "The whole thing was overwhelming really, and to be honest I was a bit out of it on the podium. I was so psyched up to lead out Cav. I wanted to do the last two kilometres across the cobbles before the sprint started. I'd been drinking coffee and was pumped. Then it was over and people are pushing you, saying stand there, look at this, go there. It was all a bit of a blur."

His face was a picture when Lesley Garrett sang the national anthem in front of the podium. "Is that who she was?" he said when we spoke about it later. "I didn't know, they just had this big old brass waiting for me and it was like, 'Here you are,' like I'd known her all my life, and I hadn't a clue who it was."

However, he soon regained enough composure to turn the Champs-Elysées into a bit of Britain for a day. The Tour winner is expected to say a few words after all the presentations are made. Wiggins is right, he looked overwhelmed, but not too overwhelmed for irreverent, funny Bradley to take over. When they handed him the microphones and the thousands watching quietened down, he started: "OK, we're going to draw the raffle now." It was brilliant, vintage Wiggo.

A few days later Wiggins rang the bell to open the London Olympic Games. Not many people who've been involved with cycling in this country for any length of time thought they'd ever see that. Until recently there was always the feeling that the sports establishment and the general sports media in the UK looked down their noses at cycling. Not any more they don't.

The first British winner of the Tour de France, and in the 99th edition of the race too, it was incredible. Wiggins kept it together for another ten days and won the gold medal in the Olympic time trial, having worked in vain a few days earlier to help Mark Cavendish fill his Olympic vacuum. Then, finally, it was time to party, although Bradley Wiggins now isn't the Bradley Wiggins who nearly got arrested partying in Beijing, he's much more restrained. Well, he's a bit more restrained.

But not restrained enough to go unnoticed. The British public warmed to Wiggo during 2012 and he won the BBC Sports Personality of the Year award by a landslide, attracting 30 per cent of the vote. He was funny on stage, getting a bit of a double act going with "Susan" Barker. He played guitar with the band at the after-show party. In short, he put personality back into the award.

Since then honours have been bestowed. He's Sir Bradley Wiggins now, but says, "You can still call me Brad, only my wife and kids have to call me sir." Irreverent, yes, but Wiggins is fiercely patriotic and I bet the knighthood means a lot. But what next for Sir Wiggo?

His ambition to win the 2013 Giro d'Italia was thwarted by illness, and any idea of a possible defence of his Tour de France title ruined by a knee injury. But I wonder whether Wiggins has lost the drive a bit, whether the sacrifices and effort and the ups and downs he's endured since the winter of 2008–09 haven't taken some of his sporting desire.

He's led a rarefied life. Eating only when he has to, and only specific doses of food; being away from home at training camps or races for months on end; answering the demands of coaches day after day, then putting it all into practice in the uncertain, no-holds-barred world of top-level pro road racing and delivering day after day in race after race, as he has done over the last three to four years. It takes its toll.

In a conversation in 2010 he said: "I don't see me going beyond 2013. I want to do the London Olympics, which was the long-term plan, to get a gold medal in three Olympics. Then it will be family first. You miss such a lot doing what I do. It's a funny job – you can't kick a ball in the garden with the kids, because it hurts your legs. It's not normal, and I'm really looking forward to being normal."

CHAPTER 11

THE FLOODGATES OPEN

With Team Sky going flat out for the Tour de France, the pressure was on British Cycling performance staff and riders to step up and meet the challenge of at least equalling their achievements in Beijing. Not that mere equalling is ever the BC way.

In many respects Team Sky and BC performance are interchangeable. Sky riders represent Great Britain in the World Championships and Olympic Games, and BC staff provide certain services for Team Sky. But that begs the question: is a lottery-funded national sporting body helping a commercial concern, and is there a conflict of interest?

The question was answered in March 2011 when the accountants Deloitte reported on an investigation into the relationship between the two entities, funded jointly by British Cycling and UK Sport. Commenting on its findings, the chief executive of UK Sport, Liz

Nicholl, said: "The Deloitte review has done exactly what we hoped it would. It has provided us with very good insight at a crucial time and helped to give us assurance about our investment. The fact that the review identified no major risks to the world-class performance programme is good news for everyone involved and our aspirations generally as we look towards London 2012."

So, with that question out of the way, everybody could get on with their work and get the Great Britain cycling team to London in the best possible shape. "About 18 months out it hit us: London was getting closer and it was time to take a long hard look at where we were. Some people got told some home truths, and everybody had to roll up their sleeves and start giving 100 per cent," says Shane Sutton.

One of the most interesting back stories going into the Games concerns the multi-Paralympian Sarah Storey, now Dame Sarah. Formerly a top swimmer, with five gold medals, eight silver and two bronze between 1992 and 2004, she had been forced out of swimming by a series of persistent ear infections and had converted to cycling.

She quickly won two Paralympic cycling gold medals, and then through her characteristic drive in training, and by pushing back the barriers of her disability, she started winning able-bodied national titles and was selected for the English team at the 2010 Delhi Commonwealth Games.

That brought Storey into contention for a place in the able-bodied women's team pursuit squad for the Olympics, which was one of the events that was going into the London Games for the first time, to finally give women Olympic parity in cycling with men. It also meant she was in contention for an able-bodied medal, possibly gold, given that the British women's team were the nailed-on favourites to win.

Talking about her training at the time lifts the curtain on another reason why British Cycling's performance programme is so successful. With so many good riders fighting for a few places, the coaches could say, "You do it our way or no way," but they don't do that. They know better, and understand that individual make-up requires individual training, even if two individuals are going for the same event.

"The team pursuit is essentially a sprint programme," says Storey, "but I don't do well on a sprint programme. I proved that when I was a swimmer. I did better sprint times off an endurance programme than I did when I trained specifically for sprints as a swimmer, so the coaches let me follow an endurance programme then drop into the specific team pursuit training with the rest of the squad."

Storey's disability is with her hand, which is a big problem in any pursuit or shorter event on the track, but by working on her start gate technique with her, and by developing better and better custom-made handlebars, BC helped her improve. Storey did the rest with sheer hard work and application.

"You have to be up to speed within one and a quarter laps, because it's harder to gain time when you are up to speed, so not losing any time in the starts is crucial. When I first did track cycling my 500 metres time was 41 seconds, but now I've got it down to 37, and I did it by improving my starts. I needed to be even quicker for the TP [team pursuit] and when I joined the programme my starts as man one were outside 14 seconds, but you need to do 13.5. I'm down to that now," she says proudly.

Eventually there were five riders contending for the three team pursuit places, and then Storey was part of the team that won the team pursuit at the Cali, Colombia round of the UCI World Cup. But that is where the dream ended. Storey was told she wouldn't get into the Olympic squad of three and one reserve. And that's another thing about BC. Storey winning an Olympic medal would have been an amazing story, but winning a medal isn't enough; if at all possible it has to be gold.

In the end Sarah Storey won four Paralympic gold medals in London, a 100 per cent strike rate in every event she did. That took her tally to six cycling golds and five in swimming. Her total brought her level with Dame Tanni Grey-Thompson and Dave Roberts, and meant that Storey soon joined Grey-Thompson as a Dame Commander of the British Empire.

That ruthless quest for gold at all costs, gold over a good story or even gold over sentimentality, was underlined by the selection of Jason Kenny for the Olympic sprint spot over the reigning champion, Sir Chris Hoy. Not that BC wouldn't have liked Hoy to be able to defend his title. The decision was forced on them by the IOC.

Not content with removing the 1,000 metres time trial event after the Athens Olympics, the IOC took the men's and women's individual pursuits away from London and rolled up the other endurance events into a mish-mash called the omnium. And on top of that they decided that countries would be limited to one competitor per event. They claimed that this was necessary in order to make room for the increase in women's events. It just felt that cycling was being hard done by.

Of course Hoy accepted the decision and the "one country one ride" situation with the same grace he's shown throughout his career. I first met Sir Chris Hoy in the most unusual place you could meet a sprinter, on top of the Alpe d'Huez. He'd just ridden the Etape du Tour, the Tour de France stage that's open for allcomers to ride. It was boiling hot, he'd finished in a very good time, and he'd pushed really hard because he was doing it with a group from BC, including Sir David Brailsford.

"I don't know how far they are behind me," he said when he got his breath back. "I attacked them at the bottom of the Alpe. Well, you have to, don't you?" For all his good grace, Hoy is a fierce competitor in everything he does, even when he's having an argument. "He doesn't argue, he debates, slowly taking apart what you've said," team-mate Victoria Pendleton says.

Before Brailsford sailed serenely across the line some half an hour later, with Shane Sutton acting as his personal domestique, Hoy talked cycling. "At least I've done all my road miles for the year," he said. "Seriously, though, it was nice to do a ride like that, even if I suffered with the mountains and heat. Sprinters don't do much general riding, maybe a bit more at the beginning of a training cycle. We do aerobic conditioning rides maybe a couple of mornings a week, but training for a sprinter mostly means getting in the gym and lifting heavy weights, specific sprint efforts on the track, and skill training like standing starts and bike control. Then there are anaerobic capacity intervals, which are horrible."

Of course Hoy still rode the London Olympics. With the 1,000 metres time trial gone, he transferred his talent for that event to the Keirin, and he rode it in a very similar way, going from a long way out and burning off the opposition. He had used the same tactic to win title after title. Hoy was so fast for so long that even if anyone got in his slipstream they hit a wall of wind if they tried to overtake.

He was pushed closer in London than he had ever been, but Hoy's incredible willpower and stubborn refusal to be beaten showed as never before. He led with two laps to go, riding flat out, but he didn't really have a gap – there were others around him.

Down the back straight on the last lap Maximillian Levy of Germany looked like he was going past, but to beat Hoy he'd have had to get it done in the straight, and he didn't. Hoy had the inside line into the final banking, and Levy was unable to go the long way around him, so his challenge simply melted away. It was Hoy's second gold medal of the London Games after the team sprint with Jason Kenny and Philip Hindes, the sixth one of his Olympic career to add to ten world titles. It was time to retire.

Jason Kenny justified his selection over Hoy in the sprint in the only way he could: he won the gold medal. You'd think he would have felt under pressure, but no. Kenny is a young rider whose cycling career has been spent entirely inside the British Cycling performance system. He knows no other way than to focus on the process and control the controllables. He does his job and has implicit trust that everybody else will do theirs. It's how BC works.

"I just left selection in the team management's hands," he says. "They know all the numbers, they go on what they see in training, on form and on trends. In some respects who is selected is still someone's opinion, but we all want the fastest person or team to go into the event. The riders do, the management do; everybody does. I didn't feel any extra pressure being selected instead of Chris. I was there to do a job, we all were, and you just get your head down and do it.

"You don't feel the atmosphere of a World Championships before your ride, not even an Olympics, not even one in London, you just focus on what you are doing, every step of it. Everybody, the soigneurs, the mechanics, they are all doing the same and you are in this bubble of the team, just too busy to take anything else in," Kenny explains.

It's how to do it. The unemotional bubble that British Cycling performance riders and staff create for themselves and live in while they do their job, which is winning, is the optimum way to practise sport. But it's hard for some people to understand. It's hard when they see things like Sir Chris Hoy refusing to look at a medal ceremony in Beijing when a compatriot was being presented with a gold medal, because he might have got caught up in the emotion of it.

That could release the chimp, which is what Dr Steve Peters calls the emotional side of the human brain. And the chimp can wreak havoc on athletic performance. Chimps have doubts, chimps are irrational, chimps start thinking that the opposition might be better, chimps introduce things they have no control over and start considering them instead of the process. If you let the chimp make decisions, you are in trouble. The bubble, the focus – they all keep the chimp locked up.

Chimps are individuals, though. When Russell Downing raced for Team Sky he went to see Dr Peters for his annual mind MOT at the start of the year. He sat down and Peters asked, "So how's your chimp, Russell?" To which Downing replied, "I took him out over Christmas and got him drunk." "Good, well done. See you next year then," said Peters.

The British Cycling performance bubble is hard to understand if you are outside it, even for some top riders. They don't understand all the elements that come together at the right time so British riders can step up and perform. Even the London Olympic sprint silver medallist and multi-world champion Gregory Bauge didn't seem to understand how Kenny could have beaten him, and in the press conference afterwards asked Kenny, "How did you prepare?" Later on Bauge said that he had prepared in his own way, so he was curious to know how Kenny prepared.

"I just think it was a bit of a surprise to him," says Kenny about the incident. "The worlds are important to us, but this was the Olympics in London, and we turned up with everything we had. Bauge wanted to win and he didn't win. He was caught out, I think. He'll be back at the next worlds, though."

The women's team pursuit squad was another Team GB track cycling unit that should have felt under pressure. The women's team pursuit had been a world championship event since 2008, and Great Britain had won four golds and one silver medal in that time.

The team pursuit is a fast and very precise race. Olympic team pursuit bronze and silver medallist Chris Newton, who is now the BC under-23 coach, says of the men's event, raced over 4,000 metres, "It's like doing four consecutive Tour de France stage sprints, only with no rest in between them. You are in the lead-out four times, then you sprint four times."

The women's team pursuit distance is 3,000 metres and there are three riders, but the principle is the same. It is a series of one-lap full-on sprints done by athletes who can empty themselves in a lap. Then each rider has to hang on for two laps while the others do the same, and the process is repeated again until the end. Throw in millimetre-perfect track skills, muscles that must be able to drink lactic acid, and the stamina to be as fast on the last lap as you were on the first, and you have the team pursuit.

The British girls lived up to the nailed-on favourite tag and won the Olympic gold. Team member Jo Rowsell explains what type of riders make up the perfect pursuit team and why. "You need riders who can be as fast on their last turn as they were their first, and that goes for all the rounds too. At the Olympics there are three rounds over two days, with the semis very close to the final, so you need stamina to get through that and be as fast in the final as you were in qualifying. The ideal team pursuit is to either have two strong riders, who are pursuit/time trial types, and one a little bit faster like me, or have two like me and one really strong one."

Rowsell's speed means she's perfect for the crucial "man one" role, the rider who gets the team to full speed in one and a quarter laps. "That's all you've got, any longer and you can't make it up later. But you've got to be able to absorb the start effort so you don't have to pay for it later too," she says.

Since Sir David Brailsford first started asking questions about the team pursuit in 2000, it has become a far more sophisticated event, and team pursuit speeds have gone through the roof as a result. The British men's and women's teams set new world records to win their gold medals in London. One of the men's team, Steven Burke, explains the choreography that goes into riding 4,000 metres in 3 minutes 51.659 seconds:

"The overall time is faster than 60 kilometres per hour, but when you take the standing start into account we had to ride an average of 66 kph when we were up to speed. It's Ed Clancy's job to get us on the way. Nobody is better in man one. He does one and three-quarters of a lap and we are nearly on 66 kph, but then the next man has to pick it up a bit more. Man three's first turn dictates the pace, he has to get us on schedule, and the schedule we use is to ride one tenth quicker per lap once man three gets us on it.

"The only feedback we get is the coach walking the line. That means he stands with his back to the track, and if he's ahead of the finish line we are ahead of schedule, and if he's behind the finish line we are down. One pace ahead means one tenth up, and so on. One pace behind the line means we are one tenth down. If the coach faces us and points directly at the line it means we are bang on schedule. After man three's first turn we just focus on the coach, responding to what he's telling us about the pace.

"We train at race pace, especially coming up to an event. Before that we might do over-geared longer than race efforts, but closer in it's race pace but shorter than race distances nearly all the time. The race pace efforts are usually done with a flying start, as we tend to practise starts separately. The skills become second nature, because we've been doing them since we were juniors. We change going into the final bend of a lap. It's drilled into us that each turn on the front isn't over until you are on the last wheel. It's easier in the line than on the front, but it's not easy. Being third in the line is the easiest place, easier than last, because in third you have two riders in front of you creating shelter, and the one behind you is in the space where your dirty air flow would be, so there isn't any turbulent air just behind you dragging you back. That's dragging the last man back. None of it's easy, though."

The whole Team GB cycling effort in London was top class: eight gold medals, as well as two silver and two bronze, more than any other cycling nation by far. Laura Trott won two golds: one in the team pursuit with Rowsell and Danni King, and one in the women's omnium. Her boyfriend Jason Kenny won the sprint and team sprint gold. Geraint Thomas took his second successive gold medal in the team pursuit, along with Steven Burke, Ed Clancy and Peter Kennaugh. And Victoria Pendleton ended her career with gold in the Keirin and silver in the sprint.

It hadn't been an easy journey for her. Pendleton is a complicated person who admits she has had issues. And her fight to make the most of her talent, which is huge, exacted a huge toll. "It was a long time before I wanted to look at a bike after London," she says. But she seems happier now, and seemed in her element on *Strictly Come Dancing*. She's certainly leading a more balanced life, because although being a world-class athlete looks like a cool and desirable job, that's because on the outside we don't see the pressure and discipline required within.

Bradley Wiggins's Olympic time trial on roads west of London was imperious, but the road race didn't work out for Mark Cavendish, and the brains of British Cycling might have dropped the ball there. They tried to repeat the tactic that worked so well in Copenhagen for Cavendish, but teams are smaller in the Olympics than the worlds, and there just weren't enough GB riders to counter what was always going to happen. The world's best single-day race riders let Britain control the race until the last time up Box Hill, then they attacked en masse and disappeared up the road.

"The tactic was OK as far as it went, and yes, if the race had ended in a sprint, then Cav would have won," says Barry Hoban. "But the team should have picked a rider like Ben Swift and kept him as a wild card. Swifty could have ridden near the front, not to be part of Britain trying to control the race, but to be there ready to go if what happened did happen. Then he would have had a good chance of a medal, because Swifty is good in a break like that." It's what Hoban would have done, and it might have paid off, because it's a fact that although bikes change, and training and nutrition change, tactics don't change in cycling. Not much anyway. What worked in 1972 would most likely have worked in 2012.

The women fared much better. Their race wasn't controlled, but Emma Pooley's attacks set things up nicely for Lizzie Armitstead to break away with the best women's racer in the world today, and maybe the best of all time, Marianne Vos. Armitstead lost to Vos in a sprint along the soggy Mall, but she's younger and has time to add gold to her London silver.

The success story was continued in 2013. Great Britain fielded a much younger team in the World Track Championships, but still came top of the medal table. Sprinter Becky James stepped right into the centre of the world stage with gold medals in the sprint and the Keirin, and she took bronze in the 500 metres time trial and the team sprint. Plus there was an incredible performance from fellow Welsh girl Elinor Barker, who became a senior world champion in the team pursuit before she had even taken her A-levels.

Barker was already a world junior time trial champion, having won her title in Holland, where Lucy Garner took her second successive road race title. James, Barker and Garner, along with Simon Yates, who won the world points race title in 2013 at the age of 19, and many others, are the future of British cycling, but there's still a lot for the current generation to go for.

Team Sky focused on the single-day Classics in the early part of 2013, but their effort was frustrated by crashes. Sky play a high stakes, all or nothing game and there was criticism. Some said that the controlled training approach they use for Grand Tours won't work in the Classics, where riders have to have their race reflexes as sharp as possible. So the team might change its approach next year. If that happens, Geraint Thomas and Ian Stannard have the ability to win a Classic now, and others have it for the future.

But if Classics are a work in progress for Team Sky, the Grand Tours aren't. After finishing second behind Wiggins in the 2012 Tour de France, Chris Froome took a bronze medal in the Olympic time trial, then tried to win the Vuelta a Espana, but tiredness gradually overtook him and he ended up fourth overall.

Froome was born in Kenya and educated in South Africa. He first became aware of pro cycling and the Tour de France in 2002 – "so quite late in my teens. I started watching it on the TV," he says.

He turned pro at 22 and rode the 2008 Tour de France for the Barloworld team. He impressed Rod Ellingworth, who knew about Froome's British grandparents and asked him if he'd consider using that qualification to become part of the British Cycling system. "I didn't hesitate really," says Froome. "Although I'd raced for Kenya I'd always carried a British passport, and I was brought up in a very

British environment. I know it sounds strange, but I was brought up in a British way. At the same time I have a great passion for Kenya, and for Africa, but I am 100 per cent British."

He signed for Team Sky at the end of 2009, but his progress kept being interrupted by the reccurrence of a tropical disease called Bilharzia. It's a parasitic disease that among other things attacks red blood cells. Froome suffered through 2011 and was said to be in danger of losing his place at Team Sky, but then it cleared up in time for the Vuelta, where second place revealed his potential. The performance certainly made Froome start believing. "It was always a pipe dream to win a Grand Tour, but after the Vuelta in 2011 I realized that winning wasn't a far-off dream."

Bilharzia can come back, and it did in the first part of 2012, but Froome has the disease under control now. "I have a check-up every six months and take the medicine to prevent it coming back. The last check-up was fine, but I will keep on it to ensure it doesn't come back again."

Froome went into the 2013 Tour de France as the undisputed leader of the Sky team, and he delivered an emphatic victory in a totally cool and controlled manner. He didn't look under pressure and when I spoke to him during the Tour of Romandie earlier in 2013, a race Bradley Wiggins had won in his build-up to winning the Tour in 2012, he said he didn't feel under pressure to repeat exactly what Wiggins had done.

"I won Oman and that was unexpected. In my opinion I wasn't flying then. I had a solid winter season and I was very fresh at the start of this season, but I wasn't chasing results and I'm still not. The results I get are an indication of my current form, and I use the races to take away from them what I need to do to get in the best shape for the Tour. It's always good to win, though."

To truly appreciate Froome's 2013 Tour de France victory and what it means to British cycling let's go back to February 2009 and the Lanesborough Hotel in London's Knightsbridge. David Brailsford (not yet knighted) has called a press conference to announce that Rupert Murdoch's Sky corporation will back a professional road cycling team, to deliver a British winner of the Tour de France within five years.

But who with? It was hard to see. Inside ten years maybe, with one of the riders who had been through British Cycling's talent identification and coaching system. But winning within five years required a rider who had Tour-winning potential in 2009. We didn't know that Brailsford already had not one but two candidates in mind, who realised their potential as fabulous winners in 2012 and then again in 2013.

We didn't know about the project that was going on to transform Bradley Wiggins from world-class track to world-class road racer, and we didn't know about a chart Brailsford keeps. The chart displays a racer's potential based on a number of parameters, and Chris Froome was on it, so probably were Ritchie Porte and a number of other riders who are members of Team Sky today.

The chart shows where any rider is in his career, whether he has reached his performance peak or has passed it. Just as importantly the chart also shows where a rider's potential performance peak might be. By consulting it Brailsford can determine a rider's value. At a press conference shortly before Chris Froome wrapped up the 2013 Tour de France, Brailsford said that Froome was the perfect example of a "value added rider".

Born in Nairobi, Kenya, Froome was educated at St John's College in South Africa. After being introduced to cycling through BMX, Froome joined a charity-based cycling club in Kenya called Safari Simbas, run by David Kinjah, which Froome still supports.

The club rode the trails of the Ngong Hills, which rise up to 2,460 metres, and together with his birthplace at 1,800 metres it means Froome has spent a great deal of life riding at altitude.

Where Froome was born is a very important consideration to those who want examine whether he raced clean or not. His birthplace and the time he spent riding at altitude with the Safari Simbas, as well as the time he's spent training with Team Sky at altitude for the 2012 and 2013 Tour de France is strong evidence that Froome isn't doping.

The fact that the runner-up to Froome, Nairo Quintana, is a Colombian born at 10,000 feet and he spent months prior to the Tour de France training in Colombia, is also evidence that cycling could have come out of the EPO and blood doping era. Colombians were challenging to win the Tour during the eighties, but when EPO started being used in the nineties their natural high altitude advantage was taken from them.

This is all good news for the future of British cycling, because as Sir David Brailsford has said, winning unethically would be pointless, and from the devastating way Froome won the 2013 race – dominating in the mountains and strong in the time trials to win by more than four minutes – it seems that he can win more than one Tour de France.

Winning the Tour was more natural for Froome than it was for Sir Bradley Wiggins. Grand Tours are what Froome was made for, whereas Wiggins' potential has a much wider spread. He proved that through a long and glorious track racing career, and Wiggins always has had the ability, and he's still got the time, to add some big single-day races to his Tour win, if he can re-calibrate and rebuild.

Winning the 2012 Tour took it out of Wiggins. With hindsight he stretched what he could do to its limit, and although he could probably do it again – the potential never goes away – it would be a big ask for him mentally as well as physically to win another Grand Tour. However, Wiggins was the first Briton to win, and that will never be forgotten. Wiggins delivered when his country needed him to, and in doing so he opened the door for others.

Froome is far more of a Grand Tour specialist than Wiggins. Even his first cycling mentor, David Kinjah, thought that was the only place where Froome could make his name in cycling. Early in 2013 he told *Cycle Sport* magazine; "Chris is thin and strong, but too long for a real climber. A real sprinter he will never be. But the longer the race, the stronger he gets."

Despite this assessment, it's hard to pick any better climber than him at the moment, but his first European team manager, the Italian Caudio Corti, also thought that long stage races were where Froome could have success. Froome's road race career began with a South African team, Konica-Minolta. From there he went to Barloworld, a much bigger team that took part in the top European races but was registered in South Africa. That's where Corti was manager, and it was with Barloworld that Froome took part in his first Tour de France in 2008, finishing 84th overall. It was also the year Froome was asked by Rod Ellingworth if he wanted to join the British Cycling system, which he did – but he'd actually been on their radar since 2006.

Talking in a 2013 Tour de France press conference, David Brailsford told reporters he'd first seen Froome at the 2006 Commonwealth Games in Melbourne, where he'd been a one man Kenyan cycling team. "He did everything himself, he was the rider and came to the manager's meetings, and he performed really well." Their next meeting was the at the 2008 world road race championships in Saltzburg, at another manager's meeting. "Chris was wet through because he'd ridden to the meeting in the rain. If you're that committed and you're determined enough to do those types of things then translating that into a winning mentality isn't difficult," Brailsford said.

Froome certainly has that mentality. He doesn't waste energy by losing his cool, because it's pointless. Whereas Bradley Wiggins, who is not nearly as tightly buttoned up as Froome, lost his temper at the doping suggestions he heard from the media at the 2012 Tour de France, Froome seems to be able to internalize everything and just politely refused to be goaded.

Even if Froome was having a bad day, you probably wouldn't know and that it a powerful weapon for a Grand Tour racer. There's a lot of poker in these races, the ability to show no emotion is a gift and a great strength. Froome can win more as he seems to eat the pressure of a Grand Tour and use it as fuel.

There certainly wasn't a chink his rivals could exploit in 2013. Froome had a bit of a moment on stage 13 when Alberto Contador's team, Saxo Bank, caused a split in the crosswinds and Froome lost time on the stage. But it wasn't that much. He limited his losses and if he'd had a couple of Sky team-mates a little closer to him exactly when the split happened he might not have lost anything.

It was academic anyway, because Froome won back everything he lost and more next day on Mont Ventoux, where in a beautiful but unplanned moment he made his stage-winning attack exactly where Tom Simpson had collapsed and died in 1967. Nairo Quintana was second, collecting valuable points towards his King of the Mountains title, but Froome had out-climbed him.

Froome then won stage 17, a time trial over two small mountain passes between Embrun and Chorges in the Alps, to put the overall win out of anybody else's reach. The historic double climb of Alpe d'Huez on stage 18 provided some drama when Froome ran out of gas five kilometres from the end. He had to ask his team mate Ritchie Porte to get something to eat from the team car. They were both fined and given a time penalty, but Froome was happy to take his 20 seconds because not eating could have lost him more.

And that gave him a lead that only disaster would have taken from him. The Alpine Marathon on stage 19, and the final mountain stage to the top of Le Semnoz on stage 20, both saw Froome watch and cover and control with Team Sky. Nairo Quintana won at Le Semnoz, and will be a big threat to Froome in the future because he's younger.

I asked Froome before the 2013 Tour how he controls himself, so he doesn't spend energy needlessly, because in the past it has looked as if he really likes to attack. "It's tough, you've got to not think too far ahead and always stay in the day you are on, but you must always remember that anything you spend today you will have to pay for tomorrow. Treating it as 21 single-day races is a good way to stop thinking about how long it is. Then you go into each day with a goal. We try to control everything we can, but of course you cannot control your rivals, so you have to react to what they do as well."

Team Sky didn't look as strong in 2013 as they had in 2012, but it was a different kind of Tour, a much harder one. They tried to fight on two Grand Tour fronts in 2013 too, sending a strong team to the Giro d'Italia to support Bradley Wiggins. But for Wiggins' illness in Italy it could have paid off.

Sky were good though; Ritchie Porte had one bad day in the Pyrenees, but apart from that he was as strong and as loyal to Froome as Froome had been to Bradley Wiggins the year before. Porte is a potential Tour winner too, but for Australia. However, the other 2013 Team Sky standout is home grown, literally.

Peter Kennaugh comes from the Isle of Man and is a product of British Cycling's development system, a system that had already identified him as having the potential to win a Grand Tour one day. The 2013 Tour de France was Kennaugh's first Tour, but he was outstanding while working for Froome and showed real climbing power, underlining his potential to win the Tour de France one day. He is young, too, so has time on his side too.

Mark Cavendish had a frustrating 2013 Tour de France. He won two stages, but Marcel Kittel of Germany won four, which is the number Cavendish would expect to win in a Tour nowadays, so expectant have his admirers become. However, it wasn't so much that Kittel was faster than Cavendish, it was more that his team, Argos-Shimano, were better at leading him out than Cavendish's Omega Pharma-Quick Step team were.

The difference was shown starkly in the final stage that as always ended on the Champs-Elysées. Cavendish was going for his fifth consecutive win in the most prized of sprinters' stages, but his team's lead out ended to early, leaving Cavendish exposed to Kittel, whose team took him to just the right place for him to accelerate away and win.

Cavendish will be back though, and he proved when he won in the crosswinds of the Tour stage that ended in Saint Amand Montrond in 2013 that he could be developing into a more all-round rider. He spotted the breakaway move that Chris Froome missed and worked hard to make it stick before winning, if not easily then very professionally. It was the kind of move that wins single-day classics, so there's no need to think Cavendish's future prospects are diminished. If anything they might have just opened up.

*   *   *   *   *

And so the British cycling story marches on. In track cycling, the country is undisputed world number one, and it's moving towards that on the road. There hasn't been a British mountain bike Olympic medal yet, although there might have been if Liam Killeen had been a bit luckier. Annie Last has the potential to change that.

Mountain bike's winter cousin is another place where British riders haven't been world beaters yet. Louise Robinson is still the only senior cyclo-cross world championship medallist, although there have been two British junior world champions: Stuart Marshall and Roger Hammond. Marshall didn't fulfil his early promise, and Hammond was just too good a road racer to focus solely on cyclo-cross. He had a great road race career, reaching World Tour level. Hammond finished third in the 2004 Paris–Roubaix, and along with Barry Hoban is the highest-placed British rider in that race. Hammond was also second in the 2007 Ghent–Wevelgem, and had other top ten places in the cobbled Classics.

Cyclo-cross isn't an Olympic sport, so it isn't lottery funded in the UK. There was talk of it going into the Winter Olympics once, but it's not an ice and snow sport, so it didn't happen. Until funding begins, a British elite world champion will have to come from a cyclo-cross version of Brian Robinson, someone who lives and races in the world cyclo-cross hot spot of Belgium. And it's happening. Ian Field and Helen Wyman are based in Belgium and have been riding to a high level for a few years. More recently Nikki Harris, a former British Cycling performance rider, has done the same. She finished third overall in the 2012–13 UCI Cyclo-Cross World Cup. A knee injury prevented her taking part in the World Championships, but she has every chance of a medal or even winning in the next few years.

There's been no British BMX medal either, but BMX is different. Olympic medals seem almost inevitable there, because Shanaze Reade has already won three BMX world titles. She's also won two team sprint world championships on the track, where she teamed up with her total opposite, Victoria Pendleton. There was a wonderful exchange before a world title final when Reade turned to Pendleton and asked, "You nervous, Vick?" To which Pendleton replied something like, "Oh God, yes." "Why? It's only pedalling," Reade returned.

She's right, but British cyclists are very good at it. Of course some always were, but there was no system for developing talent, and anyone who wanted to make it had to go it alone, and be really driven. In one case dangerously driven. Now there is a system and, thanks to the volume of recent success, cycling has a high enough profile to inspire young riders to take it up. The past was glorious in parts, but the future looks consistently bright too, and British riders will occupy top spot in all cycling's disciplines for some time to come.

INDEX

INDEX

293

INDEX

PICTURE CREDITS

Plate section 1 photographs, in order of appearance:

All images kindly supplied by Getty Images with the exception of photographs
(7), (11) & (12).

Topical Press Agency (1), Charles Hewitt/Picture Post (2), Poppefoto (3), Getty Roger Viollet
(4), Agence France Presse (5), AFP (6), Offside/L'Equipe (7), AFP (8), Jeff McIntosh (9),
Torsten Blackwood/AFP (10), Offside/L'Equipe (11), Rex Features/Photosport Int (12)

Plate section 2 photographs, in order of appearance:

All images kindly supplied by Getty Images.

Greg Wood/AFP (1), Pascal Pavani/AFP (2), James Squire (3), Bryn Lennon (4 & 5), John
Berry (6), Jerome Prevost/AFP (7), Alex Livesey (8 & 9), Doug Pensinger (10)

Every effort has been made to acknowledge correctly and contact the source and/or copyright
holder of each picture and Carlton Books Limited apologises for any unintentional errors or
omissions that will be corrected in future editions of this book.

ACKNOWLEDGEMENTS

I'd like to thank Mike Breckon for allowing me to quote from Ron Kitching's
autobiography, *A Wheel in Two Worlds*, for which he was the ghostwriter. Thanks to
Robert Garbutt, editor of the IPC Media cycling magazines and Simon Richardson,
deputy editor of *Cycling Weekly* and *Cycle Sport*, and *Cycling Active* editor Luke
Edwards-Evans for their patience while I wrote this book. And thank you to
everybody else who helped with time or guidance.